AFRICAN SE

SCHOLARSHIP FROM TH

AFRICAN INS

Volume 4

FEEDING AFRICAN CITIES

FEEDING AFRICAN CITIES

Studies in Regional Social History

Edited by
JANE GUYER

LONDON AND NEW YORK

Published by
Manchester University Press, Oxford Road, Manchester, M13 9PL, UK

British Library cataloguing in publication data
Feeding African cities: studies in regional
social history. – (International African
Library Series no. 2)
1. Food supply – Africa 2. Cities and
towns – Africa
I. Guyer, Jane I. II. International
African institute III. Series
338.1'9'6 HD9017.A2

ISBN 0 7190 2214 2 *cased*

Typeset in Great Britain
by Northern Phototypesetting Co., Bolton

Printed and bound in Great Britain by
Biddles Ltd, Guildford and King's Lynn

CONTENTS

TABLES AND FIGURES

Tables

Figures

CONTRIBUTORS

Jane I. Guyer was trained in sociology (BA) at the London School of Economics and Political Science, and in social anthropology (PhD) at the University of Rochester, New York. She has done field research on the social organisation of agriculture in Southern Nigeria and Southern Cameroon. Her dissertation was entitled 'The organisational plan of traditional farming: Idere, Western Nigeria.' Publications include a monograph, *Family and Farm in Southern Cameroon* (Boston University, African Studies Center Research Studies No. 15), and articles on local economic history, changing household and kinship organisation in modern Africa, and women's farming.

Michael Watts was educated as a geographer at University College, London and the University of Michigan, Ann Arbor, and currently teaches in Geography and Development Studies at the University of California, Berkeley, USA. He has conducted field research in Nigeria, Senegal, and The Gambia and published on famine and food policy, peasant differentiation, agro-ecology in dryland areas in the Sahel, and small-scale rice production systems. He is currently completing a study of the social history of rice in The Gambia and embarking upon research into petty commodity production and the social organisation of agriculture in California.

Deborah Bryceson graduated from the University of Dar es Salaam with a BA and MA in Geography. She is presently writing a DPhil thesis on Tanzanian food insecurity at St Antony's College, Oxford, and was previously employed at the Institute of Resource Assessment, University of Dar es Salaam, where she was involved in research projects concerned with female employment.

Paul Mosley is Professor of Development Economics and Policy at the University of Manchester. He has been economic advisor to the Kenya Treasury and the UK Overseas Development Administration, and is the author of *The Settler Economies. Studies in the Economic History of Kenya and Southern Rhodesia* (Cambridge University Press, 1983) and *Overseas Aid: Its Defence and Reform* (Harvester Press, 1986). His current research interests are in conditional aid and rural credit.

PREFACE

This volume has taken several years to bring to fruition, for reasons which have to do with the kind of research undertaken on African rural economies. Relatively little primary research is conceived in a collaborative way or oriented towards producing information and interpretations amenable to framed comparison. The cases in this volume are no exception; each author had completed field research before recruitment into the collective project. In no case had urban food supply been the central subject of field or archival research; in fact, the centres of gravity in the authors' total corpus of work span a wide spectrum, from local to national and comparative levels. Realisation of the possibility of reconstructing a history of urban food supply systems emerged from our separate attempts to concretise national processes or to contextualise local processes. Each author's work had already been marked by theoretical stance and primary research interest, and had already been consolidated in published reports. It was therefore a challenge for both the authors and the editor to bring their guiding questions within a certain range of consonance with one another, to make the cases amenable to comparison as well as to present them in all their particularly.

At certain junctures the task seemed too difficult, perhaps premature. The alternative strategy of presenting a single synthetic account, however, was felt to be unacceptable. The limited nature of the available secondary sources on the subject of urban food supply is striking. There is simply not enough information on most areas to begin a reconstruction. Without local archival sources, fieldwork and oral interviews, and reliance on academic studies produced for local distribution only, it would be impossible to have even minimal confidence in the interpretations. Not only that, but such a work would give the impression, by the sheer elegance of argument which the paucity of data allows, that much more can be taken for granted as widely known about African food systems than any of us felt was justified.

Preferring a format which kept us as close as possible to the empirical case material had its costs in time and energy; but it has also brought the enormous benefits of generous support – expressed in the quality of criticism as well as the firmness of commitment – extended to the project by the authors and by others. Colleagues in the USA, in Europe and in Africa have expressed an enthusiasm for the topic itself which often rekindled my own. In the translation of enthusiasm into structure and content the following people have been particularly important. Peter Warwick gave initial support and suggestions, many of which are still reflected in the final organisation of the book. Bibliographical help was given by James Ferguson. An editorial review of my own contributions was done by Marci Hazard-Karplus. Pauline Peters and Sara Berry reviewed earlier versions of the Introduction. Naomi Chazan made trenchant criticisms and constructive suggestions on two drafts of the Epilogue; Richard Joseph offered criticism on the final draft. Over several years Michael Watts made acute observations on various drafts of all my own contributions, and from the inception of the project managed to combine commitment with humour. Members of the Publications Committee of the International African Institute, and particularly Paul Richards, gave important advice at a critical juncture. John Peel's help at various stages of review and publication is gratefully acknowledged. Finally, the authors deserve thanks for remaining committed to an enterprise which experienced several difficult interludes. None of these people, including the contributing authors, is responsible for the use I have made of their suggestions, without which, however, nothing would have been achieved.

The Bunting Institute at Radcliffe College provided the fellowship during which the final revisions of all my own contributions were made.

Jane I Guyer
5 May 1986

1 *Jane I. Guyer*

INTRODUCTION

1. URBAN FOOD SUPPLY: THE PROBLEM AND THE APPROACH

Food supply is a constant routine function in all differentiated societies, taken for granted most of the time by those not directly involved. It is also a public issue which can blaze on to the political agenda with suddenness, urgency, and often ferocity. Academic concern with this most fundamental aspect of the material basis for social life tends to follow the same rhythm. Questions related to subsistence soar across the horizon like Halley's comet, then return to a humdrum position, as just another important component in the dynamics of social and political life. As a result, there have been times of a vast outpouring of literature, such as that described by Bergeron for the French Revolution (1963), or which followed the Great Depression and World War II in this century (Gerschenkron 1943; Lamartine Yates & Warriner 1943). Yet for many cases – even crucially important cases such as the supply of London in the nineteenth century – a single work may stand alone (Dodd 1856). Even more striking is Morgan's finding that the five great companies which have dominated Western grain supplies in war and peace for over a century 'remain shadowy and unknown'; 'it has taken the transformation of the global economy in the 1970s to make them of public interest' (1979:15).

Not surprisingly then, the present food crisis in Africa has aroused a sense of how little is known about the conditions of food supply. Africa's apparently deepening problems have attracted world attention (see, e.g. IBRD 1981; USDA 1981), and have provoked questions about a system which only a few years ago scholars described as innovative and resilient. In 1973 A. G. Hopkins noted the 'success of the (West) African distribution system, which transferred goods and services with unobstrusive efficiency' (1973:244). W. O. Jones wrote: 'If tropical African markets for basic foodstuffs worked less well, we should probably know a great deal more about them. The truth of the matter is that they have done a remarkably good job of their first task, which is the provisioning of cities and towns and of the few large mining developments.' (1972:18).

The positive view of African food markets was informed by a series of studies which showed the vitality of local enterprise (e.g. Bauer 1954), the intricacy of market periodicity (Hill 1966; Hodder & Ukwu 1969), the apparent freedom of prices from the anticipated social constraints of 'traditional' life (Dean 1963), and the sheer extravagance of colour, sound, smell and activity which characterised the African market place. The decade of the 1970s has seen a dramatic shift in perception. The patchwork of knowledge now suggests a different central motif. The peaks of achievement no longer dominate our sense of where the contours lie; they have been replaced by the troughs of shortage, suffering, corruption and declining productivity. Once a continent seemingly immune from the kind of catastrophic famine which affected millions in Asia during the first half of this century, Africa has now become associated with the intractable under-nutrition and malnutrition associated with drought, civil conflict, refugee camps and impoverished labour reserves.

The contrast of image is so striking, and the period of time in which it has developed so short, that one is forced to ask what accounts for it: have the intervening years been marked more by change within Africa and in her relations with the world economy, or have our own perceptions of Africa been wrenched into a new frame by an increase in knowledge, by the contrast with the recent surge in Asian agricultural growth, and by a growing sense of global fragility? Certainly, some scholars writing in the 1950s and 1960s recognised that food supply was not uniformly unproblematic. Even in Ghana, with one of the most commercially sophisticated of indigenous market systems, Poleman described how the post-war period 'witnessed a rash of almost panicky "Grow-More-Food" campaigns and price-fixing schemes to stimulate production' (1961:121). Lawson noted the growing animosity between the independent Government and the redoubtable female traders who ensured the consumer goods market, including the food market, as manifested in the 1965 official Commission of Enquiry into Trade Malpractices (1967). Although she argued in favour of the currently functioning system and against market controls, she also reached the surprising conclusion that in 1959 nutritionally identical diets cost almost twice as much in Accra as in London (1963).

Doubts were expressed about long-term trends in the other most active regional economy, that of Western Nigeria. Güsten reached the sobering conclusion that '(T)he dynamics of development do not by themselves provide an incentive to substantial productivity increase in this (food) sector. In fact, many of the concomitants of development had a distinctly adverse effect on the food producing sector' (1968:92).

The positive Hopkins/Jones view of African food supply is even more at variance with scholarship on French Africa during the colonial period, where Balandier's work on famine in Gabon (1955) combines with Suret-Canale's vision of 'Africa – a dying land' (1971). Dumont's profound reservations about the directions of change under the independence governments (1966) is in stark contrast to the optimism of much Anglophone writing. The single polemically negative work in English from the 1960s is *The African Predicament* by Andreski, whose first chapter is entitled 'Towards starvation' (1968).

In retrospect, these early expressions of doubt seem justified. Within the last few years a certain consensus seems to be emerging that African agriculture is characterised by a particularly detrimental combination of backward techniques and predatory state policy (Hyden 1980; Bates 1981; Eicher 1982; Hart 1982). Hart presents a gloomy picture of 'a sparse population, disease-ridden and poor, farming at low levels of productivity, limited by transport facilities, organised in weak polities, and exposed to the vagaries of climate' (1982:27). Such a base provides unpromising ground for politically inspired stimulation, even if the means and the motivation were there. According to Eicher, both have been lacking; 'agricultural stagnation . . . must also be placed before heads of state and planners who . . . have exhibited a fundamental misunderstanding of incentives, the motivations of their own rural people, and the necessity to overcome technical constraints and restructure agricultural institutions' (1982:168).

Yet in some respects the new *Gestalt* seems just as flawed as the old one, even implicitly to those who have helped to construct it. Certain strengths in indigenous systems have to be incorporated into the vision, otherwise the policy implications are totally bleak; but there is a profound uncertainty about where those strengths should be located. Lofchie's discussion of the policy dilemma is one example of the ambivalence which permeates much of the current work. On the one hand, he sees fundamental problems with African indigenous agricultural practices, which 'have shown themselves to be highly vulnerable . . .' (1980:8). On the other hand, he argues that low supplies are at least partly due to low prices (1980:103). Even within the technical limits, then, price policy seems a priority. Later, however, he expresses misgivings about the probable result of increasing producer prices, namely the intensification of social inequality in the rural areas (1980:309). With some of the same ambiguities of interpretation and policy orientation, the 'low productivity' picture is reiterated in the 1981 World Bank Report (IBRD 1981).

It is not, however, the policy contradictions alone which provoke mistrust of the new image of African food systems. The apparently confident interpretations are often based on, or at least buttressed by, statistics whose sturdiness tends to crumble under close inspection (Berry 1984). For example, the figures on productivity are inadequately explained. Yields are reported in terms of crop per unit area, as if each field were monocropped. It is impossible to tell whether account has been taken of the almost universal African practice of intercropping. Recalculations on the base of calorie equivalents per unit area produce a totally different picture, one more in accordance with Richards's conclusion that 'intercropping is one of the great glories of African science' (1983:27).

Likewise, the interpretation of rising cereal imports is less conclusive than some sources imply. The logical juxtaposition of rapid population growth, declining domestic yields, increasing imports and rising food aid, is not as obvious as it looks. Morrison demonstrates that in middle-income developing countries, including African cases, cereal imports are associated with rising standards of living, not with poverty (1984:18). In low-income African countries, imports have averaged well under twenty per cent of cereal consumption from 1965 to 1977 for most cases, with Senegal, Botswana and Mauritania – for separate reasons – being the only cereal-based food systems going over the twenty per cent mark for import reliance (Morrison 1984:16). Neither is US food aid under PL 480[1] historically associated with areas of need, but rather with 'the access, or potential access, of the United States to markets and raw materials' (Vengroff 1982:43) Since the reasons for increased cereal imports are clearly contingently, and not inevitably, related to absolute levels of need, it is risky to project, as Delgado and Miller do, 'a major transformation in food consumption patterns' (1985:55). We can hardly know, from the figures alone, which 'cause' accounts for the level of cereal imports: the massive failure of a poor and stagnant indigenous agriculture, the equally massive failure and high cost of rural-urban transport within Africa, or consumers' limited diversification of their staple foods due to a rapidly changing, and perhaps even rising, style and standard of living. Probably all three are relevant, depending on the time and place.

The fact that such apparently simple logical connections turn out to require intermediate steps of documentation and interpretation means that strengths and achievements of African production and trade have become very difficult to pinpoint. Neither can the strengths and weaknesses of current systems be unambiguously illuminated by comparison and contrast with large-scale agricultural enterprise within the continent. The clearest success stories of capitalist agriculture, especially in southern Africa, have required decades of state support and protection to supply cheap labour, favourable terms of access to capital and high prices (Wilson 1971; Phimister 1978; Bundy 1979). Almost by definition, the African peasantry has not benefited from high levels of protection and investment; what they might do with it – stagnate in complacency and live on white bread, or vigorously innovate on the basis of ecologically sound and locally appropriate crops and techniques – is hardly predictable.

A similar inconclusiveness pervades the literature on local systems as is evident in national and continent-wide generalisations. Where the data are rich enough to reconstruct the entire food supply chain across geography and history, the familiar shape of a definable 'problem' does not leap into sharp enough relief to inspire confidence in the appropriateness of the models. While food prices may be too low to stimulate the producers, as the World Bank Report (IBRD 1981) presently claims, raising them may make local products even less competitive with imports. Local studies may show, as with rice in parts of West Africa, that African farmers will not work for the returns which characterise Thai peasant economies and which make imported Thai rice an attractive proposition to African urban consumers and their governments (Pearson *et al.* 1981:399). The various links in the food chain may operate at quite different levels of returns to labour and different levels of efficiency. Recent literature on Ghana in the 1970s suggests that production may be declining fairly steeply (USDA 1981:3), while the marketing system is 'remarkably efficient and competitive in the face of numerous obstacles' (Southworth *et al.* 1979:416), and urban wage labourers in Accra are, by 1970, 'considerably worse off than they had been in 1939' (Sandbrook 1977:416). The welfare of urban consumers is not deducible from the technical efficiency of marketing, nor is the intention of urban bias on the part of anxious politicians any reliable evidence that actual income differentials break down neatly across the urban/rural divide.

The inconclusive nature of the emerging view of African food supply is a challenge to research and analysis. One way of approaching the crisis of knowledge and interpretation provoked by the African 'food crisis' is to focus on the single points of agreement in the literature, namely that while the process of food supply is neither well understood nor easily controlled by central policy, it has functioned for most of this century. The question is: how has food supply functioned and in what relationship to the political arena? Can the inevitably incomplete patchwork of the empirical record be made to illuminate the influence on one another of African material and economic life on the one hand, and the blueprints for government social and economic reconstruction on the other?

An approach through case studies in regional social history can go at least part of the way towards addressing these questions. The basis for our approach to food supply systems will be discussed in more detail in the next section. It will suffice to enumerate here, and then discuss briefly the main justifications for pursuing such an approach. First of all, regional social history allows us to explore the domains of social and economic life as related to one another in a system, and thereby to recontextualise dimensions of food supply which have been analytically separated. Particular cities provide conveniently isolable units of analysis, carved out by their own administrative history from larger national structures. They can also legitimately be claimed to represent important sites for focusing on the larger social processes which link local, regional, national and international arenas because the organisations which achieve these articulations are generally urban-based. The historical approach allows us to concentrate on the development of such organisations, on the way in which they function in a shifting social context, and comparatively on any general characteristics which either they, or the dynamics of their engagement with particular political or ecological situations, may possess. Finally, in pragmatic terms, outlining the major contours of a single urban supply system is still a possible, albeit ambitious and demanding, enterprise for the kind of individual scholarship in which most Africanists are engaged. Let me expand on these points as an introduction to the strategy of the collection as a whole and to the choice of specific cases.

While the academic disciplines have made analytical progress by separating the domains of social life – politics, economics, culture and material life – there are junctures at which particular dynamics cannot be studied without a recomposition of the social field. The study of material life in modern Africa seems to be at such a juncture. Food distribution systems are not only market chains which ensure the conveyance of goods and the communication of price information, nor merely a link between the classic dyads of analysis, the producer and the consumer, the peasant and the state. They are also organisations rooted in an articulated social and economic structure. Throughout the continent, they form a bridge between the conditions of production in an African society and ecology and the conditions of exchange and power in a national and international political economy. The study of urban food supply can therefore provide the context for taking a broad systemic approach, in which the mutual implications of organisational form, power bases, entitlement rubrics and material conditions can be traced over time. One can ask not only whether the system 'works' by some objective criteria, but such questions as why some populations excuse the bungling of their leaders while others evade apparently benevolent and enlightened policies, and what makes a particular niche in the market chain the unambiguous scapegoat of an infuriated elite or a starving crowd. One can focus not only on the periods of smooth functioning with their characteristic market 'distortions', but also on the moments of crisis and struggle which form the watersheds of change.

As a unit for systemic analysis, the city offers a restricted terrain which is, nevertheless, a focal point for general social processes in national and international arenas: class formation, the institutionalisation of political elites, and bureaucratisation of social life. Distribution systems offer an insight into the discontinuities, contentions and indeterminacies which global processes generate in local arenas, and the way in which these intersect with an aspect of social life for which regularity, predictability, and accurate synchronisation are at a premium. Distribution systems can be seen, then, as 'organisations of articulation' between local and national forces; they are reducible neither to some primordial African structure nor to a Western administrative blueprint, but to the emergent process of confrontation between the two.

Beyond such shared characteristics, particular urban systems derive their own structures, interests, capabilities, weaknesses and principles of legitimation from the regional context. For most of this century, the staple food market has been a regional organisation. Even in recent years, when international prices and supply sources have become more influential, the distribution of both local and imported foods has still depended on regional transport and trade networks. Individual cities and their political authorities have engaged in their own ways with rural hinterlands, with the exigencies of local ecology, and with the particular configuration of interests represented by producing, consuming, trading and managing populations.

Instead, therefore, of lifting the results of local studies out of context in order to illustrate a general conclusion, we are pursuing the reverse strategy of drawing on as broad an array of sources as possible to recompose geographically and historically specific dynamics. Academic and government studies carried out in a variety of theoretical frameworks, for a variety of purposes, all become relevant as reflections of a particular time, place and set of official concerns. Archives are heavily depended on to document those moments when food supply erupted into public concern, only to subside again and then disappear from the public record, leaving few easily recognisable traces. Field research provides the essential information on local facts, perceptions and responses through which the fragments of official data can be more accurately placed in an interpretative framework.

Recomposition is still a patchwork process; it still, like the construction of the general images discussed earlier, involves filling in the inevitable gaps with hypotheses and interpretations based on the individual scholar's own convictions about the forces at work. Many of the attributes of this collection stem from the self-conscious acceptance of these conditions and limitations. First of all, the choice of cases is only partially reflective of a theoretical ideal. Yaoundé, Kano, Dar es Salaam and Salisbury (Harare) were chosen to illustrate the widest possible range of sub-Saharan African political and ecological conditions. Yaoundé is a new city, a Francophone case, in a rich farming area where root crops and other perishable commodities figure prominently in the staple food base. Kano is an ancient city, located in a drought zone, with a cereal-based food economy and a strong pre-colonial commercial tradition. Dar es Salaam is a port city, in a multi-ethnic political economy, dependent on a poor and drought-susceptible agricultural hinterland. And Salisbury represents a southern African settler economy. Attempts were made to represent other important cases, most notably the Zambian copper belt, the southern Nigerian cities, and the exploding megapolis of Kinshasa. The final cases represented in the book therefore reflect some, but not all, the variety one would have wanted under ideal circumstances; limitations are due to the state of the data base and the research carried out on different urban complexes, and also to the different degrees of temerity with which individual scholars contemplated traversing disciplinary boundaries.

This volume is neither a collection of theoretically unrelated papers on a common topic, nor does it stem from a collectively conceived research project of the sort represented by, for example, Pearson's book on rice in West Africa (1981). Initially, the authors had all completed their research, oriented towards disciplinary issues in geography, anthropology and economic history respectively, before embarking on the re-analysis and, in some cases, further research, required for urban case studies. Writing these studies has involved returning to sources, undertaking new research, and extensively revising the text to bring out comparative themes or contrasting dynamics.

As a common strategy, we have focused on the organisational form of distribution structures, and their shifting links with, on the one hand, the producer population and, on the other, the urban political configuration. Moments of crisis are highlighted because they provide windows onto the issues at stake. Beyond this general orientation, individual authors necessarily draw on their own conceptual framework and knowledge base, and infuse the analysis with their own interpretative argument.

At this juncture in the study of African material and political life there are advantages to such eclecticism. The explicit acknowledgement of gaps and interpretative leaps in the case studies, and the possibilities for comparison provided by juxtaposing different cases and methods, focus attention on specific conceptual, empirical and policy problems rather than on a largely misleading broad sweep of generalisation.

THE SOURCES: CONCEPTUAL AND EMPIRICAL

The enterprise of reconstituting the data on urban food supply systems in a historical framework would be impossible were it not for the work done by earlier scholars. There is, of course, a huge penumbra of relevant literature on African production, colonial history, international markets, urbanisation and so on, but on the specific issue of urban food supply there have been three major traditions of research, generated from three sustained efforts to explore rural production, distribution and urban consumption. They tend to break down along national lines. Although the three endeavours are far from being neatly exclusive, for ease of exposition I will discuss them under national groupings: in the United States, the market analysis associated with the work of W. O. Jones and the Stanford Food Research Institute, and other kinds of formal analysis using a decision-making framework; in France, the ethnographic work of anthropologists and human geographers working from ORSTOM in Paris and with Pierre Vennetier in Bordeaux; and in Britain and the major Anglophone African universities, less organisationally-based studies in an economic sociology mode by scholars such as Rowena Lawson. Taken together, these works provide crucial empirical sources. Conceptually, the contrasts amongst them bring into sharper focus the implications of different approaches. And finally, their common frustrations and limitations indicate the importance of historical and institutional analysis.

A. American themes: decision-making frameworks

Since the 1960s, Stanford economists have been primarily concerned with the efficiency of African markets and the points at which government policy might intervene to improve their performance. The method is centred on price analysis, the margins between producer and consumer, transport costs, storage costs in relation to seasonality of production, and the relationship between domestic and international prices. Jones's major book on staple food marketing documents such contextual sociology as trade networks, government institutions, and the history of market organisations, but the analysis itself is aimed at assessing competition and its effects on prices (1972). The presence of monopoly is derived from the price data, not investigated through sociological methods.

The difficulty lies less in the failure to recognise the importance of history and sociology than in integrating them into the analysis. In reviewing the development of market organisations, Jones implies the importance of national histories: 'Differences observed in the staple food marketing systems . . . derive mostly from differences in the sources and magnitude of commercial demand for foodstuffs and in the political and economic circumstances under which these demands were first manifested' (1972:234). When it comes, however, to reconstructing this history, he suggests a typical evolutionary sequence in competitive dynamics, derived from the logic of costs and interests, which local factors may distort in one direction or another. For example, the introduction of transport methods requiring considerable capital investment may encourage monopolistic collusion, as in the western Nigerian bean trade, or if the market growth is particularly rapid, it may lead to the breakup of collusion, as in the loss of Aro control over trade in Eastern Nigeria (1972:237). The resulting analysis is not so much an integration of institutions and their history, as the use of schematic *ad hoc* sociology to strengthen interpretations based on price analysis.

Emphasis on competitive conditions and price structures has remained the primary orientation in economic studies based at the Stanford Food Research Institute (e.g. Pearson *et al.* 1981) and elsewhere in the USA, but Jones and others have continued to acknowledge the importance of explanatory recourse to cultural, institutional and historical factors. Writing, for example, on small farmers' responsiveness to market conditions, Jones suggests 'faith in (their) efficiency' is not necessarily enough and that policy about the adoption of technical innovations should also aim at 'change in attitudes and aspirations' (1977–8:156, 148) in other words, cultural factors. At the government level, Eicher's list of past policy failures includes 'a fundamental misunderstanding of . . . the necessity to . . . restructure agricultural institutions' (1982:168), in other words, to address local social structures. At the international level, Falcon and Monke conclude that 'Few commodities are so heavily influenced by government policy as the international market for rice' (1979–80:179), in other words, configurations of power are critical to the price-setting process.

The limitations of this approach to culture and politics, as a vaguely defined and imprecisely constructed 'context', are one of the implications of Harriss's broader critique of SFRI studies. She argues that price data themselves are open to different interpretations and are therefore insufficient for policy purposes without additional evidence. Amongst other points, she notes that price stability may reflect competitive conditions, or it may reflect monopolistic market control (1979). She points out that rural prices are treated as if they were producer prices for grain destined for the cities, when they might also reflect rural consumer demand for grain which has been redistributed from urban centres. Her detailed examination of the links between data and interpretation shows that there is no way of deducing one or the other conclusion from the price data alone without corroborating sociological and political data.

While a devastating critique of price analysis, Harriss's article does not offer more specific guidelines on how to approach 'the structural interrelationship between production, exchange and consumption' (1979:215). In fact, none of the market studies quoted provides indications of the kind of concepts and methods required to integrate social and cultural analysis with price analysis. Robert Bates, by contrast, has cut straight into the problem of social context by looking at markets in Africa as political arenas, as 'the setting for the struggle between the peasant and the state' (1981:16). Fragile governments generate situations and pursue policies which ensure alliances. Disequilibrium prices and distorted exchange rates are fields of opportunity for private gain and for reinforcing personal-political obligations (1983:130). He makes a polemic plea for 'an approach (which) *requires* the use of precise and detailed knowledge of cultures, structures and institutional arrangements' (1983:140).

Implicitly, this is also a plea for a historical approach, since cultures, structures and institutions are creations of the past, but Bates's primary concern with policy research veers him away from this position. Less interested in institutional growth and shifting forms of organisation, Bates instead focuses on institutions as the environment for economic decision-making. As a result, organisation, power and struggle tend to be attributed predominantly to the two parties he sees as the major actors in current food policy, the peasant and the state, the private and the public sectors. The sharp focus on this two-party confrontation underplays the social complexity of the peasantry and the private sector, as if all that is not organised in a formal and public fashion is private and disorganised in the sociological sense. This collapses local level, indigenous, and perhaps fugitive forms of organisation into a category analogous to Jones's depiction of Kenyan unofficial marketing as a 'jerry-built system . . . composed of small retailers and wholesalers who have been much harassed by the government' (1972:236). During the 1970s, and in certain countries, the situation might be drawn with broad brush-strokes in such terms, especially when the policy question is whether and how governments can fulfil their modern function of directing the economy. But in terms of social analysis, too much centrality is given to the state and too little to the local power structures and trade networks which actually deliver the goods. The sheer success of the 'private', 'jerry-built' distribution systems in Africa demands that they be taken more seriously, and the fluctuating interest and effectivity of the state in food issues demands that it be taken less seriously. 'Access to state power' may be an important 'means whereby members of a group can coerce themselves' (Bates 1983:91), but it is not the only one, above all for a continent where local loyalties are still very powerful. In a continent where kinship has been shown to have important political and coercive dimensions, 'seeking refuge in . . . the family' is not necessarily 'a private solution' (Bates 1983:130). The very fact that the food market has been 'extremely difficult to control' (Bates 1981:40) means that it must have developed its own forms of organisation. These forms may be elusive, perhaps intentionally so, but they also constitute the more active sectors in many local economies.

The struggles to which Bates alludes have not always featured the same adversaries, precisely because they are not just about choices within a given institutional framework, but about the process of institutionalisation itself. The determination with which small-scale traders and brewers, mostly women, keep returning to markets in which they have been fined, excluded and generally harassed, may be motivated by the pursuit of 'private solutions to the problem of economic welfare' (1983:130), but the endeavour is very important to the emerging form of the food supply system as a whole and the power and price relations within it. By neglecting the dynamics of institutionalisation Bates's own programme is unnecessarily restricted. In other words, bringing in the state or bringing in culture is not enough to discover the dynamics of African food systems; there have to be methods of integrating the study of 'civil society' in a broader sense.

Timmer *et al.*, in their recent book *Food Policy Analysis,* begin to do this when they set the agenda as understanding 'what is driving the system' (1983:ix). They acknowledge the complexities and potential contradictions of integrating consideration of micro-problems with macropolicies, of simultaneously promoting growth and protecting the poor, and of choosing short-run solutions in unstable international market conditions with a keen eye to the long-term implications which 'can eventually be very powerful' (1983:207). A much more detailed social analysis is implied, by class, by region, by position on the market chain, and so on. There remains, however, a wealth of social historical dimensions dealt with only under the crucial – but analytically limited – concept of 'links'. For example, one aspect of the policy dilemma is 'how tightly to link their country's food system to the world commodity markets'; the poor are difficult to reach because of 'their weak link to the food system and the rest of the economy'; interventions must 'find these links that will permit careful targeting of food subsidies to the poor'; research needs to 'specify market linkages that connect one price series to another' (1983:12, 13, 13, 165). How those links have been constructed, what they consist of, how different political regimes have dealt with them in the past, and where the vested interests lie are questions which need to be addressed directly, above all for a continent in which the national markets and economic institutions have been formed rapidly and in a context of political domination and instability.

One problem with formal models and methods is the difficulty of using them to investigate those links. The application of central place theory from regional geography to African distribution systems shows the same promise but comes up against other limitations. Interest in the possibility of using spatial mapping in non-Western market systems as a tool for uncovering social and economic relations, was given enormous impetus by G. W. Skinner's work on China (1964–5;1977), and later by the work of Carol Smith in highland Guatemala (1976). Hodder and Ukwu's studies in southern Nigeria (1969) and Schwimmer's in southern Ghana (1976) explored the encouraging possibilities of applying these methods to Africa. On the basic spatial grid of market places and trade networks might be built an approach to the intersection of economy and polity; power over the market process would locate at particular nodes and thereby be amenable to formal or quantitative analysis.

The difficulty in Africa is that identifiable market places are of very variable importance in the distribution of goods, even today. Most of the continent lacks the centuries of accretion and sedimentation of layer upon layer of economic, social and political functions on a constant territorial base which makes markets elsewhere a key to distribution and a resource to be captured by political elites. As Hodder noted in his well-known Yoruba studies (1962; 1967; 1971), where population density was low and mobility high, permanent market places did not develop. Even where markets were important institutions in the pre-colonial period, such as in the Ashanti area of Ghana, much of the staple food was distributed through other channels. The nobility lived in the capital, Kumasi, and sent clients and slaves out to the farming hinterland to produce food and the other necessities of life. The middle orders of society also had recourse to slave cultivation, while the lower orders operated a circulating labour force within the family, spending their time alternately on the farm and in town (Wilks 1975:93). In systems where such non-market distribution networks cross-cut the spatial division between city and country, the effect of increased urban demand cannot be predicted by a formal market model. Intensification of production may take place in the hinterland without stimulating the development of a market network. Even if markets do develop, the structure may not exhibit the hierarchy of functions predicted in central place theory, as Scarlett Epstein points out for the 'producer-seller markets' of Papua New Guinea (1982:3).

Not only are the local dynamics of market growth unpredictable, but in the twentieth century modern transport has blunted the pressure to which rapid urban growth necessarily subjected its hinterland under pre-industrial conditions. For example, when the population of Kimberley went from almost nothing in 1867 to 50,000 by 1874 after the discovery of diamond deposits (Welsh 1971:172), rather than drawing on its hinterland, it was fed from the American plains as soon as a railroad could be put through to the coast (Wilson 1971:114).

The literature for other places in modern Africa shows a similar lack of correspondence between spatial and social categories with respect to food supply. As much as ten to twenty-five per cent of the urban population may be involved in some sort of agriculture, and urban gardening for provision and profit is very common, even outside the Yoruba case where it is well known that a high proportion of urban residents were farmers by occupation. A study of Bangui showed that in the late 1960s sixty per cent of households supplied themselves with between 10 and 20 kg of food per week from their own plots (Vennetier 1976a:122, 125). On the other hand, not all rural populations are fully self-subsistent. Raynaut's studies in southern Niger show a high proportion of the village population purchasing food (1977).

The existence of urban farmers, rural food purchasers, and supply sources ranging from five to five thousand miles away suggests the limitations of a narrowly spatial approach to the structural relationship between producers and consumers. An eminent advocate of a spatial approach in Africa, geographer Akin Mabogunje, sees it in this way: 'spatial forms represent physical realisations of patterns of social relations' (1980:68), but it is the social relations themselves which are the primary object of study.

In Africa, the relationship between space and society has not been well-captured by the formal models developed for the analysis of integrated market economies or long-standing sedentary peasant societies. Research on food markets that has been carried out in a decision-making or other formal framework indicates the importance of an institutional history of food supply, but does not actually tackle it. There is even some distrust of a historical approach to food supply. For example, the political scientist Henry Bienen, commenting on the study of food shortage in East and Southern Africa, suggests that 'Unless colonial and contemporary histories are well understood, the constraints on policy cannot be made clear', and then adds that there is, nevertheless, a danger in 'conjuring up the past and blaming it for the present' (1983:245). In the neo-classical tradition there is no detailed study of food comparable to Hopkins's general economic history of West Africa (1973).

The absence of such an economic history is due partly to the paucity and shallow time-depth of reliable data on prices and volumes traded. Except in countries and for historical periods where the state managed aspects of food supply, and therefore kept basic administrative documentation, there is simply not enough information to support any but the most general conclusions about the 'performance' of the food sector. The lack of an economic history of food, however, is also a reflection of the limitations of formal models and neo-classical approaches in the face of different, and rapidly changing forms of organisation: shifting modes of self-provisioning in city and country, ethnic control of certain distribution networks, the changing scale of operations in different commodities, and so on.

Precisely this set of topics has been the major thrust of Francophone research into African food supply systems.

B. *Francophone themes: ethnography and human geography*

It is striking how differently the questions are posed in the Francophone literature. Vennetier asks 'how, in towns which have grown very quickly, where the rate of population growth continues to rise, has provisioning been organised?' (1972: Preface). The focus is not on the price/information vectors along market chains from producer to consumer, but on the various forms of social organisation which deliver the goods. The subject is not grain or beans as economic markets, but the 'consumer basket' and how, in terms of logistics, it is filled. A simple descriptive task is assumed to exist of accounting for how the urban consumer's physical needs are met; sources of food, types of transport, fuel, water and housing are all addressed. Vennetier's major edited volume on the provisioning of African cities (1972) and articles published in the journal *Cahiers d'Outre-Mer*, include case studies of the geographical extent of the supply hinterlands to particular cities, the nature and importance of urban gardening, the kind and the frequency of intra-familial transfers of provisions between rural and urban areas, the ethnic organisation of certain trades, and the logistics of supply of different commodities, such as meat, indigenous beer and firewood. An even greater variety of topics is dealt with under the rubric of urban research at ORSTOM by Philippe Haeringer and associates (1983; 1984), from employment patterns to 'popular ways into land holding in African cities' (Haeringer 1984).

Quite different underlying assumptions animate this kind of approach, namely that the institutions of distribution take precedence over market principles as the subject of research. The state is not the site of potentially beneficial policy interventions to make market principles work better, but another institution in the social field, which is potentially, and often actually, at cross-purposes with indigenous organisations. Vennetier writes 'From the beginning of urban growth, the administration has been constantly concerned to control the supply of food and depress prices by organising rural markets, issuing licenses for purchase and transport, opening its own stores etc.' (1972:12).

The difference in perspective is only partly due to the differences between British and French colonial policies, between the vast expanses of the sparsely-populated French territories of the Sahel and central Africa, and the concentrated, urbanised regions of the Gold Coast and Nigeria. It probably has more to do with an entirely different national history in England and in France with respect to staple foods. In French political history there never seems to have been much trust in the hidden hand by which private and public interests were reconciled. The French Government has intervened to control the grain supply to Paris for several centuries and there is a large literature on the political, ideological and physical struggles over food which took place in the public arena. The most outstanding histories of the tensions between operatives in the grain trade and central policy have been written about France in the eighteenth century (Cobb 1970; Kaplan 1984); as Kaplan writes, 'Defined as a principle, the market was elusive. . . . Defined as a place, the market was something the police could invest and control. . . . The police intended the marketplace not to throttle commerce but to domesticate and moralize it' (1984:26). The price of bread in France was controlled from the Revolution to 1978 (*New York Times* 21.12.1980). The same sense of tension between the state, the consumer, the producer and the intermediaries clearly marks French writing on African food.

In subject matter and in assumptions, French scholarship therefore picks up totally different issues than the Stanford market studies, and indeed the two literatures barely refer to one another. The only direct commentary I have found by Vennetier on the Stanford School is a review of Jones's book (1972), which concludes on a note of surprise that the state could ever be considered as an external arbiter, and a tone of cynicism about the effects of past state intervention (1976b: 107).

Ultimately, however, beyond the intrinsic fascination of the data and its enormous resource potential, there is a frustrating lack of focus. The fundamental questions one is left with, in reviewing this literature for conceptual and analytical methods and insights, are: How are the research priorities defined? Which issues are most important, and why? Vennetier's summary conclusions are a useful antidote to an excessive and misleading simplification of the social field into 'public' and 'private', but they do not go far enough in redefining the central issues. In his interpretative review he does identify critical processes. He sees the provisioning of cities as being 'the most active element' in economic and political dynamics in Africa, in a situation where price controls have been imposed on almost all export crops, and in this, his view converges with Hart's position that 'the burgeoning cities constitute a glorious opportunity for dynamic exchange between town and countryside' (1982:153). Unlike Hart, he expects the fulfilment of the 'glorious opportunity' to be a conflictual process; 'the resistance of the traditional milieu is a stronger brake than urban domination' (1976a:173–4). In the end, however, the conclusions remain descriptive; he finds that 'between the countryside and the town . . . the variety of operations is extraordinarily wide' (1972:487).

What is missing is a focus on such dynamics in the work itself: in the topics chosen, in the analytical methods, and in the perspective. The state is only mentioned; it is not analysed in relation to food supply. It is a 'spanner in the works' rather than a 'magic wand', but plays no more part in the social process than in the neo-classical tradition. Organisation by itself gives no sense of political clout or vulnerability, nor of the implicit bargaining through which prices are constructed. The means by which the African farmers, traders and consumers so graphically depicted have influenced policy and prices through their various forms of organisation remain little explored. The collapse of food supply to Accra in the late 1970s, as traders reoriented their sales to Togo and the Ivory Coast, provides incontravertible evidence that indigenous operators have developed responses to 'urban bias' policies which go far beyond passive resistance or withdrawal from the market, and which affect conditions in the entire regional food economy.

Again, a direction is indicated but not taken. One is made aware of the social and political processes through which urban and rural are linked, but not presented with strategies for exploring, for example, 'the historical roots of urban bias . . . the reasons for its relative strength in some societies and weakness in others . . .' (Byres 1979:217), nor for understanding parastatals in the 'wide array of structural, group, institutional and individual phenomena that span market and polity' (Wilson 1984.22).

C. British themes: economic sociology

There is a somewhat older and different tradition of work on urban food supply in the British colonies, geared to an ongoing Civil Service function of monitoring urban real incomes. Unlike the French research, which concentrates centrally on consumption and deals far less systematically with incomes, the British experience with wage unrest at home and with the construction of consumer subsidies during and after World War II, encouraged keen attention to the determinants of the urban standard of living (Warren 1966; Cooper 1982).

Of all the research carried out in Africa in the 1950s and 1960s which linked prices and market institutions to real incomes, the work of Rowena Lawson on Ghana stands out as the most comprehensive. Her early papers focused on the cost of living (1963) and the difficulty of applying Engel's Law to a population supplying much of its own food and living under 'demand conditions in a dynamic economy' (1962:43). The possibility that households in the lower-income classes consumed higher proportions of home-produced food was invoked to explain the fact that cash expenditure patterns on food by class ran counter to predictions. Hence Lawson could indicate that social class and local social structures could intersect in quite specific and varying ways. From this initial focus on the standard of living and its social determinants, she went on to analyse both production (1972) and distribution (1967; 1971) of foodstuffs as well as consumption, but always with a focus on the income implications – for the producer, the trader and the final consumer.

By the early 1960s, Ghana's powerful indigenous market system had provoked a polarised set of academic and political stances. On the one hand was Bauer's earlier work (1954), showing the efficiency of the high level of competition and entrepreneurship, and on the other was the official mistrust of wealthy operators who appeared to be hoarding and profiteering. In response to the enquiry into 'Trade Malpractices', Lawson's review of domestic marketing made a more subtle argument, that the indigenous traders were the only people who could 'collect vast quantities of local foodstuffs from far and remote areas and . . . redistribute them in small quantities to 7 million consumers' (1967:204), but that very few were getting rich in the process; 'Nearly all traders operate at low levels of turnover (under conditions of) low level of technology and low opportunities for the employment of uneducated women' (1971:386).

Wages, real incomes, and, by implication, class, are the central lodestones of Lawson's work, as they are in the more mundane government function of collecting standard-of-living data. If consumers were devoting forty per cent of their cash income in both rural and urban areas to food (Lawson 1962:45), or fifty-eight per cent of their domestic outlay in the urban areas (Poleman 1961:143), what did this mean about prices and welfare levels? In his analysis of incomes in Ghana during the 1960s, Knight pays consistent attention to the relative impoverishment of particular groups within both the urban and the rural context, 'the unskilled wage-earners and the cocoa farmers' (1972:213); that is, like Lawson, his focus is on class or occupational category rather than the urban-rural divide itself. In this framework one can pose questions about the class implications of economic processes and bring poverty into the picture in ways which are less possible with the other two approaches.

Through its emphasis on dynamics and change in academic analysis, and through the monitoring of cost-of-living indices over time in administrative practice, the incomes orientation in the study of food supply is implicitly engaged with history. It is concerned with how acceptable, or at least livable, income levels have been established in different areas, under different political conditions. Unlike the policy orientation of American work, which tends to be phrased in terms of interventions to achieve efficiency, British policy work tends to focus on monitoring to ensure economic welfare and hence political stability. The historical dimension is not fully developed, largely because the time-frame is not long enough, but the direction is pre-figured. By extending such analysis over longer periods of time and integrating state policies, one might more fully illuminate the patterns of differentiation which are becoming the entrenched structures of African social and economic life.

D. *The possibilities in social history*

Only those bodies of work which are explicitly about urban food supply have been discussed. Surprisingly, very little work on this issue has been generated in the historical literature, regardless of theoretical persuasion. Van Onselen has incorporated analysis of food and liquor supply into his histories of the mines of Southern Rhodesia (1976a) and the Rand (1976b). But food supply is missing again from his further historical studies of the Rand (1980, 1982), as Turrell remarks in his review, supposing that 'thin evidence dictated this great gap in these volumes' (1984:89).

The daunting problems of 'thin evidence' will be raised again in the following section, but one can point to well-known works on the history of food supply in modernising Europe which might serve as a guide: for example, E. P. Thompson's work on the Assize of Bread (1971), Slicher van Bath's summary of European agricultural history (1963) and Kaplan's analysis of the politics of the grain trade in France (1984). Studies such as these demonstrate the importance of building up from the local level. This is where much of the data is, where the political and organisational systems can be defined, and where one can pursue the broader theoretical issue of the articulation of regional, national and international structures and forces. They also demonstrate the need to bring together the three dimensions which have tended to be separated in Africanist work: market prices, the social and political organisation of production and trade, and the class implications of incomes. If such an integrated approach is needed for the history of Europe, where market growth was endogenous, it must be central to the study of Africa, where colonial rule confronted different economic structures and engendered social and economic forms which remain a challenge to Western analytical methods. It is a step towards coping with what Lonsdale considers 'perhaps the most enduring weakness of African studies, . . . that we have not yet devised means of analysing societies doubly divided by both community and class' (1981: 150). Such larger theoretical issues are necessarily implicit rather than extensively explored, but they do cast the shadow of their presence over the present enterprise, from the initial focus to the pragmatics of managing the data.

DATA AND INTERPRETATION

The thinness of the data base on urban food supply mentioned by Turrell is one problem in the reconstruction of a social history. Certain kinds of analysis are simply ruled out for many cases, such as calculations on the basis of a continuous time-series for producer and consumer prices, or traders' profit margins. Entire periods, or sectors of the market, or even crucial organisations and events may leave only a hint in the record, or, besides oral testimony, no trace at all. But meagre data itself is less of a problem than it may initially seem. Sources are available in a variety of places, enough to support an exploration and interpretation of the broad outlines of change. The greatest difficulty is in placing and interpreting the sources.

The most obvious fact is that records are generally official, and that the documentation therefore reflects the responsibility assumed by the state, itself one of the objects of study. Long silences in the official record, sometimes lasting several years, cannot be taken as evidence that the market system was functioning with soundless efficiency from all participants' points of view, as Watts's chapter on Kano shows. Where government was loath to accept any responsibility, one of the tactics was not to know, or to document properly, what was going on. Silences on particular sectors or operatives may likewise reflect their relationship to the state, rather than indicating either that they did not exist at all, or that they were unproblematic to others within the system. Many operatives in the food trade have kept no records at all. In some cases kinship and clientage forged the basis for business trust; in others, activities may have been technically illegal; in yet others, the oral tradition was used to avoid inviting official intervention. Enigmatic silence can surround even those official organisations whose existence and mandate are public knowledge. Some parastatals are inaccessible, either because, as Jones found in Sierra Leone with respect to the Rice Corporation, their records are not available to the public (1972:168), or because, as I found in Cameroon with respect to the Provident Society, the detailed records of actual transactions no longer exist. The silences in the official record have to be contextualised carefully from other sources before they can be assumed with some confidence to indicate a particular state of affairs.

The same scepticism has to be exercised about the sources which do exist. The reasons and the means for keeping any records at all should themselves be part of the study. Urban supply systems in the twentieth century emerged from a confrontation of administrative, economic and cultural rubrics. Parties to any economic transaction, to any organisational process, to any crisis of physical supply or threat to entitlement, undoubtedly had different interpretations of the event, judgments about the interests it served, and projections of the unfolding implications. Statements have to be decoded. What does it mean when officials claim the food supply is 'unpredictable'? That there were actual interruptions in supply, or that the producers and/or traders tended to withdraw from the market as a bargaining tactic? Behind a statement ostensibly about technical capacity and efficiency may lie an assumption about just prices or a fear of organised resistance.

Differing testimonies and opinions are not always available in the record. Thanks only to a market study done in 1956 is there accessible knowledge of the vendors' boycott of the Lusaka market: that it started over a disagreement about the just rate for fees for market stalls and that it was 'one hundred per cent effective and peaceful' from 1 March to 30 November with the customers' sympathy (Nyirenda 1957:59). From a study made in Yaoundé after the market boycott of 1972, one can deduce that the 'traditional' market women were objecting to the enforcement of a maximum retail price because of the inroads it made into their incomes as businesswomen, while the modern administration was operating with a kind of 'citizen's obligation' model, whereby food supply to the capital was considered a patriotic duty (Diarra 1974). Surely far more confrontational bargaining of this sort was resorted to than we can document.

Our focus in this volume on periods of crisis therefore has a pragmatic as well as a theoretical justification; periods of crisis provide a much greater possibility of seeing the different interests at moments when they are most starkly defined than do the less noisy 'working misunderstandings' during periods of relative calm. The former then provides guidelines to the latter.

The central problem remains to reconstruct how the supply system functioned, at whose expense, to whose benefit, with what level and type of state control, and with what long-term implications. We have to approach such questions as how and why the Hausa peasantry were able to sustain seasonal and periodic deprivation, apparently without major political confrontation; why the producing population in the Yaoundé hinterland chafed under the requisition system run by the chiefs, even though there was little material deprivation involved; and in what form the 'parallel market' has developed differently in the more managed economies of Tanzania and Zimbabwe.

The fact that many of such questions about entitlement, responsibility, political struggle and the material interests of various parties cannot be answered at the moment does not reduce the importance of raising them. It is essential to locate the gaps in data and criteria for interpretation, gaps massively symbolised by what one might call the 'Kinshasa problem'; for Africa's largest city outside South Africa, with one of the fastest population growth rates on the continent, there appears to be no plausible interpretation of how it is fed. Imported cereals cannot be the whole answer. Food imports rose fairly slowly in the 1970s (Economic Intelligence Unit 1981, III), and even in the 1980s, a ninety-four-country world study reported Zaire with the lowest cereal share in total calorie consumption, at sixteen per cent, in the entire sample (quoted in Morrison 1984:20). The literature on Kinshasa is shot through with incredulity, at the sheer implausibility of people's survival under such conditions, including a decline of about two-thirds in the real value of salaries over the years between 1970 and 1977 (Pain 1979:218). McGaffey reports an open letter to Mobutu by thirteen parliamentarians in December 1980, noting that 'not even the Secretary of State . . . can feed a family of six on his monthly salary at current food prices' (1983:354). According to Pain, the number of women working in the informal sector has increased dramatically, to the point where there is estimated to be one seller for every twenty inhabitants (1979:238). Market prices are fixed, but actual prices bear little relationship to the official level; they are subjected to the attempt of every person along the chain to take a maximum cut (Pain 1979:268). In the process, a whole set of avenues to income and forms of organisation has sprung up whose amenability to government control, through policy, in the name of public interest or in accordance with an economic plan, is strictly limited. The 'market' owes less to the latter than to private interest, operating at the interstices of, perhaps parasitic on, the institutions of a repressive state (McGaffey 1983).

Kinshasa may not be understandable under present circumstances, but it is the extreme case which underlines the importance of focusing on the development of those organisations which, in all their variety and interdependence, have articulated the relationship between state and peasant, world and local markets, urban employment and real incomes.

2. AN OUTLINE HISTORY OF AFRICAN URBAN FOOD SUPPLY

Largely a regional affair, African urban food supply can nevertheless be placed within an overall context, shaped by the common forces to which it has been subjected and to which it responds. Most of Africa's major cities are creations of colonial rule. Their administrative blueprints were derived from the colonial powers' experience in other parts of the world and with their own metropolitan agricultural and consumer populations. By virtue of that fact, these blueprints tended to cluster into a finite set of alternatives. Local dynamics, propelled by their own ecological and social forces, intersected (as it were) diagonally with shifts in administrative policy, which were shaped by metropolitan dynamics and thereby common to all colonies of a particular European power. The means by which sectors of the economy were promoted or protected in relation to metropolitan and world markets shifted in characteristic ways across the colonial world. In the last two decades since independence, the commonalities from one African region to another are due less to policy integration than to market integration; African food supply is increasingly affected by conditions in the world grain and energy markets. All local and national economies in Africa are subject to such similar exigencies as the cost of transport and competition from imported rice and wheat. Without implying that cumulative articulation with the world political economy has homogenised the African 'problem' into a single 'issue', it is appropriate to place the case studies into a broader context.

From the perspective of external forces, three major watersheds characterise African urban history: the imposition of colonial state structures in the late nineteenth century, the years around World War II when colonial modes of economic control shifted, and a five-year period around 1970 when instabilities in grain prices, exchange rates, terms of trade for African exports and energy costs of all intersected with, and in part provoked, internal political instabilities. The four sections of Part 2 address each period in turn, paying particular attention to the conditions under which policies were formulated, and the consequences to which they gave rise.

PRE-COLONIAL FOOD SUPPLY

The critical issue in the study of pre-colonial food supply is not to characterise entire economic structures or to construct typologies, but rather to explore whether, where and under what conditions particular categories of a population became permanent consumers. An institutionalised home market can only develop when people become 'professional' consumers, whether by dispossession, at the bottom of the social scale, by occupational specialisation at a higher rung of the ladder, or by virtue of wealth and leisure at the top. For the present purposes, a focus on specialist consumers provides a more strategic entry point than starting, as is usually the case, with the conditions of production; it is impossible to understand the structure of supply and demand with a polarised concept of subsistence versus market orientation.

From this vantage point, social history and archaeology show that the particularity of pre-colonial Africa by comparison with the rest of the Ancient World is not that it lacked craft specialists, elites, traders, or cities. What it did lack was a politically and numerically significant category of permanent food dependents. Although recent research has revealed a food trade of much greater scope than a self-subsistence model of African economies implies (Roberts 1980a, b; Lovejoy 1980), the food market was a shifting target. Very few populations fulfilled optimum conditions for generating market demand, namely that they were permanent food dependents, spatially concentrated, and lacking alternative relations, such as kinship or clientship, through which food supply could be assured. In pre-colonial Africa, not only goods, but people, could be redistributed over the landscape. Population mobility and the social relations which structured it meant that food and people could be brought together in a variety of ways. Although for convenience one can start from the question of how cities were fed, the real question is how permanent consumers were fed, wherever they happened to be located spatially or socially.

By pre-industrial standards African cities were not particularly small. The Yoruba cities and Benin had populations estimated at 15,000–20,000 (Hopkins 1973:19). Timbuktu and Djenne ranged from 15,000–80,000 in the fifteenth and sixteenth centures (Hopkins 1973:19), and Koumbi Saleh may have been as large as 30,000 in the tenth century (Levtzion 1980:24). Such figures are all the more relevant when compared to the populations of other pre-industrial cities in the world. Before 1500 Cologne was the largest city in Europe, with a population of 20,000, and Western European settlements referred to as towns had less than 2,000 inhabitants (Braudel 1973:20, 375). Only a few cities exceeded 100,000: Istanbul, at 400,000 in the sixteenth century (Braudel 1973:21); Ancient Rome, at one million in the first century BC (Rickman 1980:9–10); and certain Chinese cities, at about one million in the twelfth century (Elvin 1978:79).

African cities were not, therefore, concentrated exclusively at the small end of the population scale; but African urban demography was characterised by more striking seasonal and annual fluctuations than other cases. Wilks suggests that the permanent inhabitants of Kumasi in 1817 numbered about 12,000, whereas during the festival season the population rose as high as 100,000 (1975:94). Kano was estimated at 30,000 in the mid-nineteenth century, but doubled at the height of the trading season (Hopkins 1973:19). At the end of the nineteenth century, the East African port city of Bagamoyo was augmented by 30,000–40,000 porters during the peak trading season (Iliffe 1979:45), although its 'regular' population may have been as low, at 10,000, as that of the comparable port of Mombasa in the 1840s (Cooper 1977:104).

By contrast with many other urban populations, African city dwellers of all social strata had residential bases in the countryside and lived only intermittently in the urban centres. The proportion of the population whose provisioning then fell into the routine political economy of urban distribution may have been quite small. As many as half or more of the peak population consisted of temporary passers-through who stimulated a vital retail trade in prepared food and drew on a variety of social relations as sources of support, thereby leaving a relatively small political and economic space in which an institutionalised wholesale market with professional traders might have developed. From the viewpoint of either traders or political authorities, transient populations represent a different kind of opportunity or vested interest to that of a permanently dependent consumer population.

To a large extent, the categories which did constitute centres of demand – the elites, the armies, the specialist producers – were provisioned without the development of independent intermediaries. Mobility and authority bridged the spatial and social gap between producer and consumer. The wealthy of indigenous Africa were directly supported, in kind, by slave cultivators, clients and requisitions from the subordinate population. Non-market provisioning in staple foods was characteristic, whether the elite were urban residents, as in parts of West Africa, or lived in mobile royal villages, as in parts of central Africa. The Ashanti elite drew on their political followers and slave labour to do most of the agricultural work (Wilks 1975:93). The Hausa nobility and office-holders held rural domains worked by slave labour, both for provisions and for the production of cotton as a commercial proposition (Lovejoy 1978). Further west in the savanna, Samori is said to have had, at the peak of his power in the late nineteeth century, 'tens of thousands' of farm slaves, settled in agricultural villages to cultivate rice (Person 1968:837–8). Vansina presents a similar picture of slave villages in the hinterland of the capital for the kingdoms of central Africa (1978); and further east, among Lozi, Bemba and other peoples now of Zambia, royalty was supported by requisitions (Richards 1940). In Southern Africa, labour to support the aristocracies was provided through cattle clientage. Almost everywhere, taxes were paid in consumption items such as grain, cattle, bush-meat, roofing thatch and so on, as well as in the local medium of exchange. In the larger polities, the incorporation of different peoples and production systems allowed specialisation in the forms of taxation, so that very varied goods passed through the links of servitude and clientage towards the centres of power.

There is an obvious political rationality to direct provisioning for elites. Dependence on professionals for the basic provisions of life implies vulnerability; it introduces the danger of monopoly control, the power to hold the city to ransom. This dilemma was evident throughout the Middle Ages in Europe as indicated, for example, by Miskimin: 'Towns everywhere, despite all efforts to guarantee food supplies and to control the agricultural districts surrounding them, led a precarious existence' (1969:79). This dilemma finds its counterpart in Africa only in the case of the great desert centres in the Western Sudan, where grain supplies were necessarily distant, and transported along exposed caravan trails and stretches of river. For these cities, Johnson mentions the exact situation which pertained in medieval Europe: Timbuktu was 'at the mercy of whoever controlled the stretch of river between the town and its food supplies' (1974:180). Even here, however, some of the food supply was 'met by the grain grown by slaves of Timbuktu residents established on land in the northern delta (of the Niger)' (Johnson 1976:490).

The Sahel is the single major region of Africa where an internal grain trade, run by professional merchants, has a long history, continuing into the present. Research on how the trade functioned is relatively recent, on the degree of specialisation, financial arrangements, relations with producers and consumers and the control of labour. Like professional trading populations in other parts of the world, these networks appear to have relied heavily on ethnic, familial and religious relations (see, e.g., Roberts 1980 a & b).

For the rest of the continent, elites and their immediate dependents do not appear to have surrendered their fate in the same way. By controlling political relations they ensured food for their own support, for feasting and for redistribution, without putting themselves in a weak position *vis-à-vis* an intermediary group with free status and, therefore, in principle with a choice not to comply.

Aside from the desert cities in the centuries preceding colonial rule, the largest populations requiring a predictable staple food supply were the armies. Relatively little has been written about the logistics of military campaigns, through every army 'marches on its stomach', as Napoleon is quoted to have said. Support by subject communities along the line of march is one probable source. The Mfecane wars in Southern Africa involved cattle raiding and plunder, a method of provisioning which most armies have used at one time or another. Shaka allowed his troops to eat meat during campaigns, though their diets were restricted during peacetime (Guy 1980). Samori's army supplies were provided by a less opportunistic system. The constituent groups of free peasants were made to work as organised military suppliers. The basic unit of Manding political life was the *kafu*, consisting of several villages attached to a maximal lineage of founders and leaders. A *kafu* had its own political hierarchy, its own market, and collective responsibility in the context of Samori's state. In case of war, each *kafu* was levied a certain number of soldiers to serve in the army along with the food supplies to support them. In this way, Samori avoided centralised responsibility for feeding the army; each political unit supported its own people (Person 1968:878). For short campaigns this may have worked very efficiently and most warfare in pre-colonial Africa was seasonal. During inadvertently long campaigns, it is probable that like everywhere else in the world, armies became the enemy of friend and foe alike. A series of papers on West African warfare documents the destruction which unsupplied armies wreaked (ASA 1981). Greater knowledge of exactly how military campaigns were planned in relation to systems of provisioning would provide a window into food supply logic in the differentiated states of pre-colonial Africa.

The political domination of food supply must also be kept in mind with respect to interpreting the 'self-subsistence' of local communities. In times of seasonal or cyclical shortage, the elite could radically affect which sector of the population suffered. In the pastoral economies, the elites could draw in their resources loaned out in better times along the links of clientage. This had the effect of diffusing the shortage or even famine to the outlying areas and the lower social strata (Baier 1980; Peters 1983). Such populations would have constituted centres of demand for market services if such had existed and if village people had been able to generate 'purchasing power'. As it was, they were self-subsistent by default.

It is a mistake, therefore, to assume that lack of evidence for long-distance trade proves that food was not moved over long distances, or that communities fared well in their self-subsistence. Problems with the high cost of transport (Hopkins 1973; Goody 1971) are less technical than they are political. As their annual requisition, people drove livestock and headloaded grain, shea butter, kola, oil, cloth and artisanal products to Samori's capital from all over the empire (Person 1968:876). Neither is the absence, or low level, of food trade evidence that local communities were self-subsistent at an adequate level under all circumstances. Demand and supply were mediated largely by political structures, rather than by professional traders responding to price incentives.

When one looks, then, at the organisation of distribution in the stratified societies of precolonial Africa, 'trade' in foodstuffs takes a relatively small place alongside the other institutional frameworks. There were, of course, many local trading systems for particular food items. The internal trade in dried fish in West Africa may have been extensive, and the ports of Mombasa and Malindi were net grain exporters to the Arabian peninsula by sea

(Cooper 1977:85–86). In spite of such vital trade networks for particular commodities, and in specific regions, there is little evidence however, with the possible exception of the great cities of the Sahel, that the relationship which becomes critical to urban life in the twentieth century – the relationship between consumers' incomes and the price of food – was forged primarily in the cities. On the other hand, the wage-price relationship cannot be seen as an arbitrary colonial imposition, with no foundations or articulations at all with African institutions and African pre-colonial history. Wages and prices had to be integrated with the conditions of production in African rural economies.

It seems more plausible that another, rapidly expanding, consumer population laid the foundations of the wage-price relationship in the mid-nineteenth century, namely the porters carrying rubber, palm products and ivory to the coast for export. There were enormous numbers of them, as the figures quoted earlier for the East African ports show. At their point of destination, porters may have been fed from slave plantations run by the traders, as Cooper describes for the East African coast (1977). But whether slave or free, they could neither grow nor carry their own food supplies along the journey. Unlike the retainers and clients of earlier periods, porterage crews had no authority behind them to ensure free support from village populations. They had to be fed along the line of march, through some kind of commercial transaction. Records suggest that a basis for wage levels and food prices was already in place by the time colonial governments became major employers of porters in the late nineteeth century. The earliest claims for wage labour are made by Daaku, who dates wage payment and food purchase in cowries in Ashanti in the seventeeth century, existing alongside slavery (1971:169). In East Africa, Iliffe describes the nineteenth-century trading caravan as an internally differentiated organisation, with guards, personal servants, cooks, guides, porters, slaves and sometimes wives as well, each with their own mode of livelihood and remuneration (1979:169). Iliffe's quotation of porters' wages is particularly significant because it suggests that the rate paid in 1874 'became the standard rate among European employers thereafter' . . . (T)hey earned the same thirty years later' (1979:45). This means that wage rates were already customary and presumably bore some relationship to the cost of living. From the viewpoint of colonial administrators and European employers, the wage-price relationship had to be, not created *ex nihilo,* but shaped in order to bring it into consonance with standards of profitability set in accordance with the larger colonial enterprise. This relationship was forged within indigenous economies, but for an occupation in which the older principles governing food supply could not be invoked; it was a logistical impossibility for workers to be self-subsistent, and politically impossible that they draw on the bonds of clientship. This would imply that the development of urban employment and food supply institutions neither evolved directly out of pre-colonial urban institutions, nor originated purely from colonial domination. It involved, rather, the extrapolation of the wage-price link forged on the bush paths between the interior and the coast, to an urban context, a more complex consumption bundle, and a more tightly calculated and controlled economic and administrative enterprise.

ADMINISTRATORS AND WAGE WORKERS FROM THE 1880s TO THE 1940s

In many areas of Africa colonial state power was limited, either because vast regions could hardly be dominated effectively by a small, vulnerable Civil Service with a high turnover rate, or because the colonial rulers depended on indigenous rulers. With respect to the small wage-employed population, however, it was considerably more powerful, above all because the state was itself a major employer. Only in the mining and settler-farmer economies was colonial rule marked by a quantum leap in the consumer population; elsewhere, while the number of wage workers was relatively lower, the early colonial period was still a critical phase for urban food supply because, even on a limited scale, the wage-price relationship was institutionalised.

The cities themselves grew relatively little before World War II. According to Vennetier, in 1920 only two to three per cent of the African population lived in towns, and forty per cent of these were Nigerians whose populations had lived in towns for over a hundred years (1976a:31). The main growth areas were the port cities which expanded to handle the import-export trade, and the mines of central and southern Africa. Other administrative capitals were often small and, like Nairobi, were located in pleasant climates for European residence, rather than integrated with economic centres. Where old cities became administrative or commercial centres they remained important, but great pre-colonial cities such as Timbuktu were totally bypassed. In 1940 only six African cities outside South Africa had populations over 100,000: Ibadan, Kano and Addis Ababa were pre-colonial cities which took on new administrative functions; and Lagos, Dakar and Accra were ports (Vennetier 1976a:32). The largest city in Africa was the mining centre of Johannesburg, with a population of 500,000.

The two new consumer populations whose needs had to be kept under government surveillance were colonial Civil Servants and wage employees. The cost of living for these two categories clearly influenced the viability of the entire colonial enterprise. From an administrative perspective, the civilian and military cadres had to be supplied, without the political embarassment of sacrificing autonomy to the growers and suppliers of their rations, and without the economic inconvenience implied in relinquishing price control of a commodity whose stability was essential to wage projections in the national budget. Since commodity prices and currency values fluctuated widely on world markets throughout the first half of the twentieth century, there was a premium on maintaining some measure of control and predictability in domestic wages and consumer prices.

From the perspective of European private enterprise, profits and competitive advantage depended on keeping wages and the cost of living low. What was meant by 'low' was heavily influenced by the cost of labour in the tropical Asian colonies where similar goods could be produced: palm products, sugar and rubber. The low price of rice from Burma and Thailand permitted low wages: for example, a Malayan labourer earned 120 dollars a year in 1918, of which eleven–twelve per cent was sufficient for a year's supply of rice (Kratoska 1982:287). The comparable proportion for Southern Rhodesian miners was nineteen per cent (van Onselen 1976a:47). In Africa, neither a free peasantry nor settler-farmers would produce staples for such low returns. The cost of living and the cost of labour were high relative to South-East Asia, resulting in a corresponding pressure on wages. The expense of African labour – the continual complaint of private enterprise – tended to limit operations to those sectors with a clear comparative advantage (e.g. diamonds, copper and gold), and to places where the state could protect markets or subsidise the factors of production.

For private enterprise control of wages, prices and food supply was a profitability issue, whereas for governments it was also part of the larger concern with controlling local societies. Measures imposed reflected both purposes, although the results did not necessarily satisfy both to the same degree. One control measure which had negative implications for the local food trade was the Government's attempts to monopolise currency. Indigenous currencies were first given a standardised exchange rate against the colonial currency, and then eliminated altogether from official transactions. Food purchases at the retail level were generally made with the smallest pieces of currency; in West Africa cowries mediated much of the market exchange in food (Arnold 1957). In regions where food was purchased in small amounts, one day at a time, the Western currencies were in denominations too large to be practical. When copper coinage was introduced into the Gold Coast in 1909, cowries were valued at 100 a penny, whereas small purchases could go as low as five cowries. It was a challenge with no simple solution to control currency and simultaneously maintain low food prices.

One solution pursued by employers throughout Africa was the negotiation of bulk food purchases to provide workers with food in kind. Food supply paid in kind to subordinates draws on military models of food distribution, rather than market models or the experience of colonial powers with their own working-class populations. Cost-of-living considerations were thereby removed from the agenda of relations between employers and workers, to be replaced by struggles about the quality of the provisions.

The provision of food in kind has been best explored for the mines of Southern Africa (van Onselen 1976a), but the explicit separation of food provision from wages in cash occurred elsewhere. In Cameroon, workers' pay was either supplemented with provisions or an amount was deducted from the cash wage to reimburse the employer for the cost of food supplied (Guyer 1978). Governments implemented guidelines to regulate workers' rations, as did the League of Nations with respect to the mandated territories. These measures achieved two things: they gave some protection to workers' minimum standards of health, while also giving producers a guaranteed market. For example, the imposition of minimum legal requirements for mineworkers' meat rations in Southern Rhodesia in 1908 (van Onselen 1976a) also provided the struggling settler cattle industry with an expanded home market (Phimister 1978). Bulk purchases of food encouraged large-scale producers and wholesale trade, as well as avoiding currency problems and meeting regulated dietary standards for workers' rations.

While this set of conditions was quite general throughout Africa, regions varied in the institutions which emerged to meet the demand for a cheap and predictable food supply to concentrated populations of wage workers. There were four major alternatives pursued during the pre-war period: reliance on expanded production and trade in the indigenous system; requisitions from the local population; the creation of settler agriculture; and imports. These measures can be seen as a repertoire. Most governments tried more than one, or resorted to each intermittently and situationally, but by the end of the pre-war period certain regional patterns were established. Food provision in West Africa was almost entirely in the indigenous sector, except for high levels of Asian rice imports in Senegal and the Gambia. In Southern and East Africa, settlers had been given such favourable conditions that indigenous production and trade were clearly disadvantaged. In many parts of central Africa a requisition economy persisted until 1945, and was reimposed in many other places, including East Africa, under wartime conditions (Spencer 1980). By the end of this period, imports had declined, particularly in South Africa, where they had played an important role during the mineral boom.

Each policy thrust arose out of different circumstances, facilitated the development of different kinds of organisation in the food system, and created different political configurations, even though all of them 'solved' the problem of cheapness and predictability.

(a) West Africa and indigenous markets

The dominance of the indigenous sector in West Africa is largely due to the way in which it was built on pre-colonial institutions. Food supply was left outside the sphere of state control to a degree unparalleled elsewhere. Meillassoux's position that the 'social division of labour . . . if it exists, is based on the after-effects of slavery' (1971:79) is misleadingly terse, but inequalities were sustained, in a legitimised form. Indigenous marketing was the activity of a wealthy elite, of particular religious or ethnic categories, or of women. These traders drew on expertise, networks and financial resources developed for trade at earlier historical periods. Clients, junior kinsmen, apprentices and wives supplied the inexpensive labour within the moral framework of family, religion and allegiance. Each category had its own range of commodities and activities, corresponding to its capacity for capital mobilisation, geographical mobility and access to clientele. Food may have been only one of such commodities; a guiding question for historical research on the 'free markets' of West Africa is the way in which, and degree to which, the food trade has been grafted on to other activities as part of a broader commercial 'portfolio'.

The wealthy merchants of Northern Nigeria were confirmed in their pre-eminent position by Lugard's policy of indirect rule. When cocoa and coffee production expanded in the coastal forest belt, trade networks for meat and beans were extended southwards, manned by clients and mediated by religious brotherhoods (Cohen 1969; Hill 1970; Baier 1980). As Watts's chapter points out, it was not so much that merchant networks functioned effectively, but that intervening in them had political implications and possibly incurred high costs for the colonial authorities. It seems likely, in fact, that the authorities had only a hazy idea of how food supply functioned at all.

In the southern coastal region of West Africa the vitality of indigenous food production and trade has other sources. The growth of urban demand built on pre-existing cities and markets which were capable of expansion. Basic technical capacities and social networks had already been developed, all based on the specialisation of the female labour-force in processing and trade (see, e.g., Robertson 1975–6). Women expanded their operations. More women went into trade, operations were enlarged, hinterlands extended, and occupations differentiated. Using the example of Afikpo market in Eastern Nigeria, Jones has suggested that rapid market growth was 'probably typical' of the indigenous economy's responsiveness to growing demand (1972:41). Looked at in comparison with other African cases, however, it seems more likely that the rapid growth in small-scale trade in West Africa depended on the position of women in domestic and colonial economies. West African women could assert the right to mobility and a certain measure of financial independence, but the scope of occupations open to them has always been, and has remained, limited. The cheapness and predictability of food supplies was probably based on women's ability to devote labour to processing and trade, and their willingness to work for low returns.

Accurate figures on relative returns to labour are lacking for the first half of the century, but subsequent studies are unambiguous. In Nigeria in the 1950s, women's work might earn as little as one-fourth the returns to labour as men's farming and trading (see Guyer 1980). In Accra in 1969, eighty-three per cent of the traders were female and the retail trade was so competitive that urban prices for food were below retail prices in rural centres (Reusse & Lawson 1969). Lawson concluded that the low cost of marketing services was largely a function of limited alternative opportunities for the employment of 'unskilled' female labour. Other local studies concur (e.g. Handwerker 1974), as does Mintz in his review of female labour in small-scale trade (1971). The differentials may not have been as wide during the earlier decades of the century, but without a doubt the efficiency of food supply throughout the colonial and post-colonial periods has relied heavily on the kind of female enterprise described in the recent ethnographic literature (see Marshall 1964; Trager 1980; Dumor 1982; Robertson 1983).

(b) Requisitions

Food requisition was a method resorted to by most colonial governments at one time or another, even where it did not constitute the primary means of supplying the urban population and the wage labour force. For example, cattle were requisitioned from the Kenyan peasantry for army supplies during World War II (Spencer 1980:509). But in parts of the French, Belgian and Portuguese empires, particularly in the low-density areas of central Africa, requisitioning was a regular practice. The lack of an indigenous market system which could be expanded, the limited means of transport, and the non-existence of commercial farming left the government and private enterprise with two alternatives: to deal with the indigenous chiefs and headmen who controlled agricultural surpluses, or to impose an administrative system based on forced labour. As the Yaoundé case shows, bargaining with headmen proved unpredictable and frustrating whereas requisitions required only a framework of strategic incentives and sanctions. It was generally the administrative chiefs who managed provisioning under a requisition regime. They were ordered to supply given kinds and quantities of food on a regular schedule to cities, work-sites, porterage crews and administrative headquarters. The food was rarely paid for, and if it was, the proceeds went directly to the chief. Prices were entirely arbitrary, where they existed at all, so little purchasing power diffused into the ordinary population. It was sometimes accompanied, however, by innovative farming by the chief. New crops were introduced, such as rice, which had good storage properties and low transport costs.

As a means to developing a market sector, requisitions were retrogressive. By virtue of filling in for the absence of a vital food trade, they prevented its development. Requisitions departed totally from the competitive market model, and could prepare the way for market development only in indirect ways. Markets did not evolve directly from requisitions. As one simple index, the geography of hinterlands in central Africa during the colonial period was quite different from the West African case. In the latter, networks and centres for different goods overlapped, rather than duplicating one another over the same geographical grid (Jones 1972:24; Hill 1966; Hodder & Ukwu 1969; Schwimmer 1976). In a requisition system the hinterlands of cities are administrative boundaries; they do not, in principle, overlap or compete with one another. Even today, in regions once subjected to requisitions administrators may respond negatively to the development of a free market which allows producers in their own hinterlands to sell to others instead.

In the long run, requisitions were precarious, because they rested on the political fortunes of the indigenous chiefs, but they did set up an expectation of cheap supplies, delivered on a regular schedule, as a right of the urban wage and salary earner. The food trade was considered not just another gainful activity, but a civic duty, and this perception persisted long after the requisition system itself had been abandoned.

(c) Large-scale farming and settler agriculture

The most radical state intervention in African food supply systems was the creation of large-scale settler farms and wholesale marketing in Eastern and Southern Africa. In the late nineteenth century part of the expanding food demand was met from indigenous farms. In Western Kenya, Lugard noted 'the enormous quantities of flour brought in for sale' (Ogutu 1979:217). Similar responses to demand are documented for South Africa (Bundy 1979) and for Rhodesia (Palmer & Parsons 1977). Even after the great rinderpest epidemic of the 1890s, African agriculture remained one of the major supply sources for the mines and urban centres.

Settler agriculture was created by a whole set of discriminatory and protective policies implemented by governments, mainly after 1910. In view of the numerous arguments that such policies resulted in inefficiencies (Wilson 1971; Jones 1972), and of the observations that on occasions they generated 'levels of profit beyond the dreams of avarice' (Spencer 1980:507), it seems very unlikely that settler agriculture produced the least expensive food supply possible. But it did establish an organisation which state and private interests could predict and manipulate. Producers were part of the explicit political bargaining process, rather than outside it. In Kenya, for example, settler farmers were powerful enough within the political arena to limit Asian involvement in wholesale staple trade.

The staple food economy of the settler colonies was an integrated aspect of the politics and economics of expanding capitalism, and not simply a subordinated and articulated stratum of the colonial enterprise. Unlike the case in West Africa, farming interests were represented in the national political arena. The crops increasingly grown, maize in particular, were the ones which had benefited from developments in Western farming technology and could be sold for industrial uses on the world market, or even locally to whisky distillers. The old staples of millet and sorghum were partially displaced. Such integration was reflected in patterns of price fluctuation and in business fortunes. Prices were more vulnerable to fluctuations in the international market than in other areas. During the depression of 1929–32, some South African farmers went out of business, whereas evidence suggests that in other African economies domestic food prices responded very little to international prices. In Cameroon, the cash price of exports dropped to one-third or one-fourth of the 1929 rate, but food prices hardly changed at all (Guyer 1978). Wages also remained more or less constant; Iliffe's figures for wages show the same stability up until 1935 (1979:45) as found in the Cameroon reports.

(d) Imports

Since Africa came under colonial rule when the politics and technology of international trade were highly developed, resort to food imports was an available option from the beginning. Elites imported specialised products. In 1922 Cameroon imported meat, milk, wheat flour, rice and sugar (League of Nations 1921–38). Regular resort to imports on a large scale to feed a substantial proportion of the African population was limited to Senegal and the Gambia. By the eve of World War I there was an established pattern of specialisation in peanut production by the rural population, with rice imported from Indo-China to feed the cities. During the inter-war period, rice imports tended to fluctuate with peanut exports; when the market for edible oils collapsed during the 1930s and shipping was suspended during World War II, rice imports were also curtailed. But after each crisis, the pattern of rice imports re-emerged (Craven & Tuluy 1981), whereas in most other countries imports were themselves a response to crisis in the more accessible and economic local supply channels. Imports constituted an interim measure, to tide over a shortage. As Figure 2 (p. 42) shows, Africa as a whole only became a net grain importer after about 1970.

By the end of the 1930s the urban and employee populations were still small, but price relationships had been set up or confirmed, and so had the vested interests which met the needs of urban life and the requirements of government. Food had been brought into the commodity economy, although in markedly different ways in different parts of the continent. One of the key elements of government control in many areas, however, was the control of population mobility. Rural populations in most countries were not free to relocate into the cities as they pleased. Restrictions on urban migration in accordance with the employment situation gave governments a powerful means of keeping the nature, extent and social complexity of the food question within bounds. Their inability or unwillingness to perpetuate such measures after World War II released new dynamics, particularly characterised by the growth of the informal sector of the labour market.

URBAN GROWTH AND THE INFORMAL SECTOR, 1945–70

Not until the time of World War II did urban growth gain momentum in Africa. No simple list of factors can account for it, but certainly the abolition of direct controls on population movement in French Africa, the increase in investment funds made available through the state, and the shift in African political activity from rural protest to urban-based associations, combined to produce powerful incentives for urban migration. In Southern Africa population movement was strictly controlled until independence, so the watershed is somewhat later, while in South Africa an early surge of urban growth has been heavily, and increasingly, controlled since 1948. But whether in French Africa in the late 1940s or in Zambia in 1964, shifts in migration control had the same implications for the consumer population: 'the structure of urban employment shifted strongly towards the informal sector' (Fry 1979:49).

Employment figures are difficult to assess because statistics on both the total population and the employed evade strict categorisation. With so many people retaining a home in the rural areas, African urban populations fluctuate in size and composition. Some employment surveys fail to enumerate the occupations of women, or they define the formal sector to exclude indigenous small businesses, or they can deal only with the number of people actively seeking work by being registered at employment bureaux. But to give some indicative figures, Mombasa in 1969 had barely one-third of its adult population in enumerated employment (ILO 1972:51); Dakar in 1965 had only ten per cent of its adult population in industry or the Civil Service (Grandmaison 1969:138); and Lusaka, with its history of population control, had a high of sixty per cent in the formal sector and domestic service in 1969 (Fry 1979:59).

Figure 1 illustrates the growth patterns of major African cities from 1900 to 1972, and Table 1 gives national urbanisation rates for 1970 to 1980.

The informal sector presented a new element for the administrative authorities' management of food supply because none of its activities – production, incomes, consumer demand nor consumer prices – could be easily manipulated with the old methods. Indeed, one opportunity for making a living was in the food sector itself, if not in entrepreneurial trading

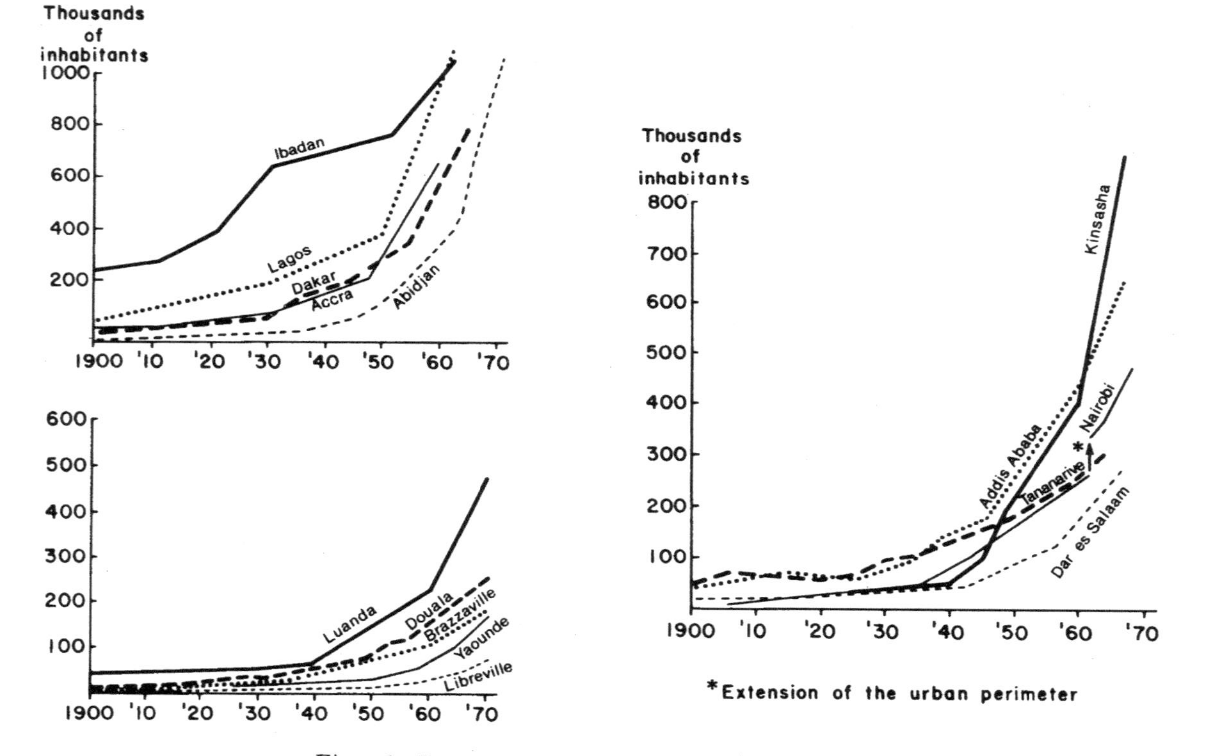

Figure 1 Demographic growth of African cities, 1900–72
Source Vennetier 1976.

Table 1 *Urbanisation in selected African countries 1970–80*

Country	*Population in urban areas, 1980 (%)*	*Urban population growth rate, p.a.*
Sahel		
Mali	20	5·5
Niger	13	6·8
Senegal	25	3·3
West Africa		
Cameroon	35	7·5
Ghana	36	5·2
Ivory Coast	38	8·2
Nigeria	20	4·9
Sierra Leone	25	5·6
East Africa		
Kenya	14	6·8
Tanzania	12	8·3
Uganda	12	7·0
Central Africa		
Angola	21	5·8
Congo	37	3·2
Gabon	32	—
Zaire	34	7·2
Southern Africa		
Botswana	12	—
Malawi	9	6·2
Zambia	38	5·4
Zimbabwe	23	6·4

Source USDA 1981:11.

at the wholesale level, then in small-scale retailing and processing. For a certain, perhaps large, section of the urban population, real incomes were conditioned at both the income/employment and consumer price points by the opportunities and constraints of the market in basic provisions. People were living *from* incomes generated in the food system, and living *with* the food prices which resulted. From the Government viewpoint, the dynamics of supply and demand, price relationships and consumer preferences became an urgent subject for research. Facing politically threatening situations in many colonial urban centres (Joseph 1974; Furedi 1977), and more liberal political ideologies at home, post-war governments began to explore indirect interventions rather than direct controls over labour and commodity markets.

The methods of market intervention introduced in British West Africa and in the French colonies included market surveillance, expansion of agricultural research, road development, extension of co-operatives, and the institution of marketing boards. All these measures were routine features of an agricultural and marketing policy in Europe, aimed at institutionalising the food market and making it accessible to state policy without the state taking responsibility for the entire food supply function. In Africa, this was a new challenge. Under early colonial conditions the market system had either been essentially autonomous from the state, as in British West Africa, or entirely incorporated into it. There was now the far more complex issue of developing the linking institutions, of encouraging or undermining current structures, or of replacing them entirely with new ones patterned after rubrics developed under other colonial or metropolitan conditions.

By the early 1970s the responsibility of government for the food supply of the population at large, not just the administrative and wage labour forces, was forcefully claimed. For example, Jones wrote in 1972 that 'Adequacy of food supplies is an appropriate concern of government, and action to ensure a regular flow of foodstuffs at reasonable prices is generally accepted as a proper government function' (1972:1). Similarly, the ILO report on employment and incomes in Kenya states that 'reasonable stability in the prices of essential foodstuffs is a necessary ingredient for an effective wages policy' (1972:269). The question was how such stability could be maintained, both in the technical sense of bringing supply and demand into a viable and predictable interrelationship, and in the class-interest sense of achieving this within a framework of vested interests which also ensured political stability and preserved established economic ties to world markets.

The record of government success in managing food crises in the immediate post-war period is not well-documented, but it does not appear to be stellar. During the severe drought in Nyasaland in 1949, employers had to send workers back to the villages for food, and the Government hierarchy was relatively ignorant and ineffective in predicting and managing either indigenous methods of coping with famine or supplementary food distribution (Vaughan 1982). Governments were acting with no great experience in an African context, and with an acute sense of potential unrest waiting to be fanned by food shortages or high prices.

Early studies of the urban cost of living were not encouraging. Major studies of incomes in the informal sector were not made until the 1960s and 1970s, though it was generally assumed that life was yet more precarious and income more intermittent than in formal employment. The results of studies done on wage employees are striking, especially when compared with the pre-war pattern of payment in kind, rationing, and a twenty to twenty-five per cent allowance for food in a bachelor's wage. In 1950, Kenyan wage labourers in Nairobi were devoting seventy-two per cent of their total expenses to food (Kenya 1951:12); in Accra in 1953, the proportion was fifty-three per cent (Gold Coast 1957:11); in a Durban shanty town in 1958 it was 55·3 per cent (Maasdorp & Humphreys 1975:37). If the gainfully employed, many of whom were not supporting their families from these wages, were living at such levels, then a serious question was raised as to how the rest were managing.

Growing nationalism in Africa and liberal philosophies in Europe meant that direct control measures were implausible, except in Southern Africa and the Portuguese colonies. The main government policies of the 1950s were aimed at intervention in, and influence over, domestic marketing, rather than at changing the conditions of production or consumer prices. Major investments were put into improving the transport infrastructure. Many of the staple food marketing boards were instituted during this era. In French Africa rural co-operatives were developed, and in the hinterlands of larger cities they were mandated to serve a similar purpose, to 'rationalise' – in other words, make predictable from the authorities' point of view – the supply of food to consumers.

Like their counterparts in Europe and the empire, these commercial organisations were created, mandated, and financially backed by the administration, but were independent bureaucratic and legal structures. The possibility of targeting funding for parastatal organisations from public and private grants and loans put them in a politically powerful position, regardless of their technical success. In Cameroon, for example, the investment resources controlled by the Provident Societies, and deriving largely from FIDES, were five times as high as the budget for the regular agricultural services of the administration (UN 1955:104). The ways in which the political and economic resources represented by parastatals were captured by different elements in African and expatriate society is a crucial issue, only now being approached in all its regional variety and complexity of implications for economic functioning (Wilson 1984).

Research was carried out throughout independent Africa in the 1960s, focusing on the commercial network. Almost the entire academic literature on African markets, in all disciplines, dates from the late 1950s, with Bohannan and Dalton's seminal edited volume appearing in 1962. Academic interest parallels the policy concerns. The money flowing into the Provident Societies in Cameroon in the 1950s was overwhelmingly devoted to developing transport rather than production, reflecting both the current philosophy of commercial development and, possibly, the kinds of expatriate business interests thereby satisfied. An evaluation published at the time of their demise in 1962 showed that transport accounted for 'seven times the grants to agriculture, three times the assistance to stock-raising and ten times the aid to forestry' (Barboteu *et al.* 1962:101–2).

The results of policy-oriented research, however, did not find very striking opportunities for improvement in the commercial sector. At the risk of oversimplifying Jones's conclusions about staple food marketing, it seems that market imperfections were either minimal or so dominant as to be politically unassailable. In Southern Nigeria and other vital indigenous market systems, the impression of market-place congestion had planted the expectation that the aggregated margins of so many intermediaries must add up to the considerable proportion of the final price. In fact, the market chain turned out to be surprisingly short, at three to four intermediaries, and the returns to retailers were lower than the agricultural wage rate (Jones 1972:90, 118). The farmer's share of the retail price was as high as sixty-six per cent, half as much again as the comparable proportion for American farmers (Jones 1972:193). If incomes and trading margins were within an acceptable range, then the possibility of increasing efficiency lay in improvement of interregional communication to enlarge and integrate supply hinterlands, and the provision of physical plant such as storage facilities and market places. Jones reiterated this conclusion in 1984.

In countries where food supply was managed by state marketing boards, Jones and his colleagues identified policies which were detrimental either to the maintenance of low urban prices or to the provision of adequate incentives to rural producers, but they could not necessarily target politically acceptable changes. Sierra Leone had depressed rice prices by importing from Asia, thus favouring the urban population and the importers, while Kenya had inflated maize prices by monopoly control, thus favouring the large farmers. In both cases, the policies and their administrative bureaucracies were deeply entrenched.

On the other hand, the food supply situation was cause enough for alarm that the patient and piecemeal approach to 'economic evolution' – 'As tropical African economies mature it is expected that . . .' (Jones 1984:133)) – seemed untenable. For Ghana, the best-documented economy of the early 1960s, Knight showed that the value of the minimum wage fell by thirty per cent between 1952 and 1967, while the income of food farmers rose (1972). In the face of declining urban real incomes, political unrest or outright civil war, and increasing international market instabilities, other avenues of control were explored.

One cannot leave the post-war period without commenting on the importance of political independence in urban development. In my own view, a quantitative but not a structural change emerged between 1945 – or its analogues in different countries as direct control over labour mobility was released – and 1970. Capital cities took a new leap in size, by virtue of the Africanisation of the Civil Service, the expansion of education, and the extension of the administrative infrastructure. But the dilemmas of coping with urban migration and employment patterns in the context of an urban-based political opposition are characteristic throughout, as is the dominant form of intervention, through the state assuming, in various organisational forms, responsibilities in marketing. The most recent decade, one whose implications are hardly lived out, is characterised by the unpredictability of government revenues in a period when African production seems to be, at best, growing only in proportion to population growth, while world grain surpluscs arc growing by lcaps and bounds.

MARKETS AND INTERVENTIONS IN THE 1970s

The complexity of political and economic pressures within African food economies in the 1970s is too great to summarise briefly, but it is a period during which food supply has become defined as a comprehensive, national-level issue. It is no longer considered a problem restricted to a narrowly-defined section of the national labour force, nor the cities alone. Although the political rhetoric about food supply may present stark and seemingly simple solutions, actual interventions depend on a more comprehensive approach than *laissez-faire,* the heavy hand of forced labour or restricted mobility, or targeting of one sector of the food chain. At the very least, governments have integrated controlled recourse to international sources to complement local food economies, and have extended their involvement in the conditions of production beyond the earlier concentration on marketing, to include credit provision and production projects.

Outside the settler economies, and except for the particular case of the *paysannat* policy in the Belgian Congo, there had been relatively little effort to supply credit and technical packages to food producers. Through such broad-based programmes as 'Operation Feed Yourself' in Ghana and 'Operation Feed the Nation' in Nigeria, food production became a potential investment sector, competing with others – at both the individual and national levels – for available funds. Many of the agricultural investment banks were established during the late 1960s and early 1970s. It then became clear that the returns to investment in food production were low and the risks high. Seeing high failure rates in relation to technical aims (see, e.g., Shepherd 1981), commercial bankers have often steered clear of private agricultural enterprise. As a Nigerian bank credit manager put it: 'agriculture being one of the few risky, less profitable and uncertain areas, banks being profit oriented were less inclined to it' (quoted in Wallace 1981:256).

Through state policies on currency exchange rates and import licences, domestic food systems have been brought into explicit and calculable conditions of competition with foreign production. Imports picked up momentum in the 1970s, under conditions of at least nominal state control of prices and state mediation of access to trade licences (see Figure 2). The amounts of imports, and the reasons for their rapid growth, are controversial, but two fairly sound conclusions can be drawn from the statistics: that imports of cereal grains are rising, but that they are rising much faster in the relatively richer countries (see Delgado & Miller 1985:58; Morrison 1984).

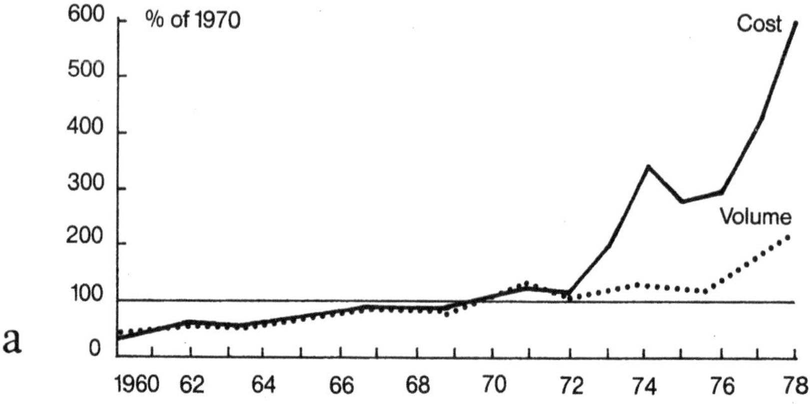

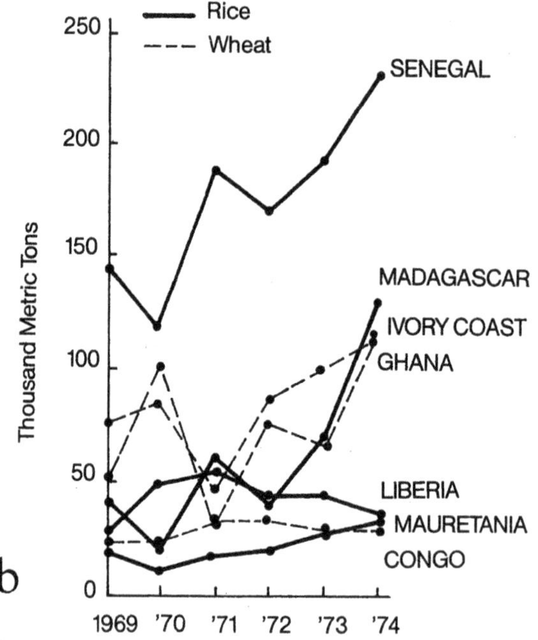

Figure 2a Sub-Saharan Africa, indices of grain imports, volume and cost
Source USDA 1981:5

Figure 2b Selected major food imports by countries of tropical Africa, 1969–74
Source Morgan 1977.

In spite of such increases, indigenous staples still dominate the diet. Delgado and Miller's figures on per capita consumption of various cereals for Nigeria in the years between 1976 and 1980 show only 8·5 kg of wheat per capita per year, while millet and sorghum taken together as the two major though by no means exclusive – local sources of staple food were consumed at rates of 60·3 kg per capita per year. That is, people consumed more than seven times as much millet and sorghum together as wheat. Rice consumption is yet lower than wheat consumption (1985:57). Small amounts of rice and wheat are grown within Nigeria, so the proportion of imported grains in the national diet is actually lower than the consumption figures by staple would imply. Even though there are high proportional rises in imported grains from year to year, it may be quite misleading to project this directly as a progressive trend; the limits of staple food diversification and substitution are not well understood.

The social and economic importance of imports is less, however, in their quantities as a proportion of the diet, or in the indication which rates of change may afford of a 'food crisis', than in their strategic significance as a site of control and accumulation in an otherwise frustratingly recalcitrant food economy. According to the USDA report on African food, there is hardly a single country in which the price of the world market grains (maize, rice and wheat) is not, in principle, officially fixed (1981). By controlling external sources, a small number of well-placed intermediaries can mediate short-run domestic shortages and make profits to their own advantage, at one and the same time. The opportunity for public interests and private gain to intersect – at least potentially, although often not in the actual event – lodges in few institutional *loci* in African food systems: in small-scale production and trade of local goods, where people have no other choice for making ends meet than to work for low margins, in large numbers, on a regular basis; and at levels where operators can count on the rewards of oligopolistic control with which to develop professionalism, permanent social networks and capital intensive enterprises (otherwise amenable to description as ethnic or class collusion). In the sociological middle ground generally envisaged under market models, where full-time, professional producers and traders make a competitive living from food, alternative and supplementary occupations are more rewarding. Indeed, the ways in which operators at all levels shift their resources in and out of the food system and graft food on to other economic activities remains one of the great underexplored issues. Making food production and trade an attractive proposition remains as difficult in Africa today (see Berry 1984) as it was in late nineteenth-century Britain, where a realist observed that 'of all roads to wealth, agriculture is the slowest' (Graham 1892:203).

The long-term implications of food imports may nevertheless be serious. Imports are made possible by large and increasing world grain surpluses.

Market competition leading to lower and lower prices undercuts advantages of locally produced food, above all when the high cost of oil raises the marketing costs between hinterlands and cities. As the USDA report notes, 'in many cases it is easier to import rice and wheat than to transport maize and cassava from the rural areas to the cities' (1981:174). Pearson *et al.*'s study of rice production in five West African countries (1981) concludes that local rice is at a significant comparative disadvantage in relation to Asian rice. Historically, this opens a new stage in the century-old competitive relationship between the Asian and African tropics. The competition has become increasingly unequal as Asian agricultural production expands; Thai rice is imported into Africa, Thailand has recently captured a lucrative international market for processed cassava, a crop well suited to and widely grown in Africa (Nelson 1983), and multinational 'agribusinesses' such as Unilever can relocate African projects to Asia (Dinham & Hines 1984:23). Africa's defensive position is now further complicated by an aggressive search for markets on the part of grain producers in temperate zones.

It is important to keep the international and domestic political context in mind when stepping back to ask why the current situation is primarily seen as a food crisis, rather than a more general consumer crisis. Of course, the riveting images of famine are persuasive, along with graphs of declining production and rising imports and such widely-reported troubles as the urban riots over the price of rice in Monrovia. But food is singled out, in disproportion to its contribution to an increasing gap between incomes and the cost of living. When one examines recent urban budget studies and cost of living indices, it is evident that the cost of housing has been rising steadily throughout the post-war period, but receives far less attention than the food component of urban expenditure. In the 1950 Nairobi study, half the respondents were housed by their employers, and many others were staying with friends or relatives and therefore not paying rent (Kenya 1951:12). In the Accra study of 1953, two-thirds of the respondents were paying rent, which together with fuel and light added up to 10·1 per cent of their expenditure (Gold Coast 1957:11). Inhabitants of a Durban shanty town were paying five per cent in rent in the 1950s (Maasdorp & Humphreys 1975:37).

The proportion of income devoted to rent in the 1970s is considerably higher. In Kenya in 1980, the cost-of-living index was calculated with and without housing, because rent was rising faster than other costs; for the low-income category, the price of food had contributed less than any other major item to the increased cost of living since 1975. Rent was more than double its 1975 level, whereas food was only sixty per cent higher (Kenya 1980:282). For the Durban sample, restudied in 1964, there had been a decrease in the proportion of income devoted to food, not due to rising incomes but to the increased costs of 'unavoidable items such as rent, transport, fuel and light' (Maasdorp & Humphreys 1975:105). Ayeni identifies overcrowding and 'rocketing rents' as one of the greatest problems facing the inhabitants of Lagos (1981:134). For potential owner-occupiers, fees to cover the official requirements for house-building in Tanzania can be as expensive as two months' salary for a working man (Stren 1982:81). It is not totally unwarranted to speculate that the focus on food in the urban consumer crisis is prompted by the political feasibility, and indeed advantage, to the elite of intervening here, rather than in real estate, which represents one of the most profitable forms of private investment.

The overwhelming evidence of a triumvirate of dominant conditions in present-day African food economies – low production at the farm level, high levels of management by the state, and pressing conditions in the international economic context – must not, however, eclipse the continuing, and perhaps increasing importance of all those forms of organisation which continue to funnel food from rural areas to cities. In terms of actually feeding the cities, as distinct from generating a commotion about it, the non-state sector is still critical. Were it not for the complexity of local production patterns and transactions of the kind described by Vennetier, the current crises over imports and balance of payments would surely have more far-reaching effects on levels of welfare. Parallel markets, unauthorised sales across international borders, small-scale production and experimentation, self-provisioning in the urban and peri-urban areas, legal and illegal entrepreneurship and hunting and gathering in the urban jungle are the local processes which support the food market and at the same time undermine any possibility of complete control over it.

The dilemma of the informal sector continues. If, for example, significant proportions of the urban poor are employed in food provision of one kind or another, then 'rationalising' the supply to them as consumers undermines their access to income as producers. This is particularly critical for women, whose pursuit of a personal income appears again and again in the literature as a factor in market efficiency (Lawson 1967) or as a casualty of market control (Robertson 1983). The profound antagonism, crossing over into violence (see Robertson 1983), with which some authorities have approached women's trade is at variance with the fact that many cities, from Accra to Bangui (see Adam 1980) and Lusaka (Muntemba 1982), depend to a significant degree on goods produced, processed and/or traded by women.

Only recently has the scale and resilience of the indigenous sector begun to be documented again. Large-scale operations are being discovered, which draw on significant capital and work through clientage networks in the idiom of personal dependency and long term relationships inherited from the past but applied to a new situation and new kinds of personnel. In some cases the continuity with the past is direct; for example, 'Muslim clerics, to this day, are disproportionately responsible for furnishing the traders and brokers to many Sahelian market systems' (Cullen & Waldstein 1982). In others, the social and cultural origins of market organisation are obscure, syncretic and innovative. Magendo in Uganda (Kasfir 1983) and the equivalent extra-legal practices in Zaire (McGaffey 1983) are what keep commodities moving – around and between regulations, under the table and across borders, that is, at the interstices of the formal structures. Whatever their organisational base, operations in the 'informal sector' are not necessarily small-scale, disorganised and potentially or actually beyond control; they are beginning to be lucrative and to benefit, perhaps in indirect ways, from state structures. Smuggling, for example, is big business. But so, also, is the entirely legal international trade in millet beer which Saul estimates transports the perishable raw materials for the production of 700 million litres a year, produced from 240,000 tons of red sorghum grown especially for the purpose, from rural Burkina Faso to Abidjan on the coast. Individual traders may purchase the daily output of up to one hundred women producers (Saul 1981; Pallier 1972), in an industry which neither the restrictions of Islam nor the competition of European breweries has driven out of business. Like the Hausa cattle trade described by Cohen (1969), the Hausa grain trade described by Clough and Williams (n.d.), the Yoruba women's networks in the staple food trade described by Trager (1980), and other modern, mid-scale, highly effective enterprises, the millet beer industry is embedded in indigenous social organisation at all stages of production, processing, transport, trade and consumption.

Transport is another sector intrinsically important to food supply, in which substantial businesses have developed. Barbara Lewis has shown that the transporters' union in the Ivory Coast is a powerful force in local politics, based on Dioula trade networks which have criss-crossed West African commercial geography for several hundred years (1971). One of the most striking recent research studies shows how businessmen from a particular Igbo town gained control of a significant proportion of the entire Nigerian transport and automobile spare-parts industry, and even regained substantial dominance after the Biafran War (Silverstein 1983). Again, the idioms of local social structure are a resource in the organisation, maintenance of discipline, and long-distance management of market information.

In other areas, the indigenous rulers are still important managers of resources and communications. It was reported, for example, that the Sultan of Njamena, the capital of Chad, 'had the right to regulate the river traffic (on the Shari between Chad and Cameroon)', and to take taxes on the crossing (*New York Times* 3 May 1983). The collapse of central administrative structures in some countries is almost bound to enhance the relative importance of all those other local leaders who can claim legitimacy to govern. The African countryside is not necessarily disorganised; it is simply that new forms of organisation may be appearing, using indigenous templates rather than the Western ones encapsulated in the classic dyad of political thought about agrarian society, the peasant and the state.

This is not to say that individuation and fragmentation are not occurring. The indigenous beer trade in places other than Burkina Faso resembles the individual survival tactics of the very poor more than it does an incipient business (e.g. Nelson 1979; Colson & Scudder 1975). Although Zairois described by McGaffey are becoming 'rich amidst devastation' (1983), others are engaged in occupations like the food trade, pursued with 'a savage individualism born of penury' (Pain 1979:268).

In summary, the food trade is one aspect in the construction of a new African civil society whose contours are poorly perceived through the lenses of our current models. The social and material process is not entirely dominated by the ethnic factor assumed in the past by anthropologists, the state domination assumed by political scientists, the evolution of a recognisable market system by neo-classical economists, nor the class formation assumed by Marxists. Concentration on particular local arenas where all these processes meet is one step towards understanding the organisation of this society. Understanding the influence which former organisational rubrics and material conditions exert throughout a particular region's pre-colonial, colonial and post-colonial histories, is an agenda with which the case studies engage but which is, ultimately, a far broader social scientific problem.

NOTE

[1] Public Law 480 was signed into law by President Eisenhower (10 July 1954) as the Agricultural Trade Development and Assistance Act. It provided for the sale of surplus US farm commodities to 'friendly nations' on favourable terms, and for the gift of such commodities for famine relief. In 1966 it became known as the 'Food For Peace Program'.

REFERENCES

Adam, Michel. 1980, 'Manioc, rente foncière et situation des femmes dans les environs de Brazzaville (Répubique Populaire du Congo),' *Cahiers d'Etudes Africaines*, 20, (1–2): 5–48.

Andreski, Stanislav. 1968. *The African Predicament*, London: Joseph.

Arnold, Rosemary. 1957. 'Separation of trade and market: the great market of Whydah', in K. Polanyi, C. Arensburg & H. Pearson (eds.), *Trade and Markets in the Early Empires*, pp. 177–87. Glencoe, Illinois: The Free Press.

African Studies Association. 1981. Session on *Warfare and Material Life in West Africa*.

Ayeni, Bola. 1981. 'Lagos', in M. Pacione (ed.), *Problems and Planning in Third World Cities*, pp. 127–55. New York: St. Martin's Press,.

Baier, Stephen. 1980. *An Economic History of Central Niger*. Oxford: Clarendon Press.

Balandier, Georges. 1955. *Sociologie Actuelle de l'Afrique Noire. Dynamiques des*

Changements Sociaux en Afrique Centrale. Paris: Presses Universitaires de France.
Barboteu, Gerard, Urbain Poisson, & Pierre Vignal. 1962. *Etudes des Structures Rurales*. Cameroon: Ministère de la Coopération.
Bascom, W. R. 1955. 'Urbanisation among the Yoruba', *American Journal of Sociology*, 60: 46–54.
Bates, Robert H. 1981. *Markets and States in Tropical Africa. The Political Basis of Agriculture Policies*. Berkeley: University of California Press.
—— 1983. *Studies in the Political Economy of Rural Africa*. Cambridge University Press.
Bauer, P. T. 1954. *West African Trade*. Cambridge University Press.
Bergeron, Louis. 1963. 'Approvisionnement et consommation à Paris sous le Premier Empire', Fédération des Sociétés Historiques et Archéologiques de Paris et de l'Ile de France, *Paris et l'Ile de France:* 14: 197–232.
Berry, Sara S. 1984. 'The food crisis and agrarian change in Africa', *African Studies Review*, 27, 2: 59–112.
Bienen, Henry. 1983. 'The impact of colonialism on modern economic patterns of distribution', in R. Rotberg (ed.) *Imperialism, Colonialism and Hunger: East and Central Africa*, pp. 225–49. Lexington, Ma: Lexington Books.
Bohannan, Paul & George Dalton. 1962. *Markets in Africa*. Evanston: Northwestern University Press.
Braudel, Fernand. 1973. *Capitalism and Material Life, 1400–1800*. New York: Harper & Row.
Bundy, Colin. 1979. *The Rise and Fall of the South African Peasantry*. Berkeley: University of California Press.
Byres, T. J. 1979. 'Of neo-populist pipe dreams: Daedalus in the Third World and the myth of the urban bias', *Journal of Peasant Studies*, 6, (2): 210–44.
Clough, Paul & Gavin Williams, n.d. 'Marketing with and without Marketing Boards: Cocoa, Cotton and Grain Marketing in Nigeria'. Unpublished ms.
Cobb, A. C. 1970. *The Police and the People. French Popular Protest 1789–1820*. Oxford: Clarendon Press.
Cohen, Abner. 1969. *Custom and Politics in Urban Africa. A Study of Hausa Migrants in Yoruba Towns*. Berkeley: University of California Press.
Colson, Elizabeth & Thayer Scudder. 1975. 'New economic relationships between the Gwembe Valley and the line of rail', in D. Parkin (ed.), *Town and Country in Central and Eastern Africa*, pp. 190–210. Oxford University Press for the International African Institute.
Cooper, Frederick. 1977. *Plantation Slavery on the East Coast of Africa*. Yale University Press.
—— 1982. 'Urban Disorder and the Transformation of Work. The Docks of Mombasa 1934–55'. Unpublished ms.
Craven, Kathryn & A. Hasan Tuluy. 1981. 'Rice policy in Senegal', in Scott R. Peason *et al. Rice in West Africa*, pp. 229–62. Stanford University Press.
Cullen, M. & A. Waldstein. 1982. 'Analysis of the food marketing system in Niger: possible A.I.D. interventions'. Washington DC: USAID.
Daaku, Kwame Y. 1971. 'Trade and training patterns of the Akan in the seventeenth and eighteenth centuries', in Claude Meillassoux (ed.), *The Development of Indigenous Trade and Markets in West Africa*, pp. 168–81. Oxford University Press for the International African Institute.
Dean, Edwin R. 1963. 'Social determinants of price in several African markets', *Economic Development and Cultural Change*, 11, (3): 239–56.
Delgado, Christopher L. & Cornelia P. J. Miller. 1985. 'Changing food patterns in West Africa: implications for policy research', *Food Policy*, 10, (1): 55–62.

Diarra, Fatoumata A. 1974. *Commercialisation des Produits Vivriers de la Lékié par les Bayam-Sellam*. Yaoundé: UN & Ministry of Planning.
Dinham, Barbara & Colin Hines. 1984. *Agribusiness in Africa*. Trenton: Africa World Press.
Dodd, George. 1856. '*The Food of London. A sketch of the chief varieties, sources of supply, probable quantities, modes of arrival, processes of manufacture, suspected adulteration and machinery of distribution of the food for a community of two millions and a half*. London: Longman, Brown, Green & Longman.
Dumont, Louis. 1966. *False Start in Africa*. London: André Deutsch.
Dumor, Ernest. 1982. 'Commodity queens and the distributive trade in Ghana: a sociohistorical analysis', *African Urban Studies*, 12: 27–45.
Economic Intelligence Unit. 1981. *A Study on the African Economies: their structure and outlook in the 1980s*.
Eicher, Carl. 1982. 'Facing up to Africa's food crisis', *Foreign Affairs*, 61, (1): 151–74.
Elvin, Mark. 1978. 'Chinese cities since the Sung Dynasty', in Philip Abrams & E. A. Wrigley (eds.), *Towns in Societies. Essays in Economic History and Historical Sociology*, pp. 79–89. Cambridge University Press.
Epstein, T. Scarlett. 1982. *Urban Food Marketing and Third World Rural Development. The Structure of Producer-Seller Markets*. London: Croom Helm.
Falcon, Walter P. & Eric A. Monke. 1979–80. 'International trade in rice', *Food Research Institute Studies*, 17 (3): 279–306.
Fry, James. 1979. *Employment and Income Distribution in the African Economy*. London: Croom Helm.
Furedi, Frank. 1977. 'The African crowd in Nairobi: popular movements and elite politics', in Janet Abu-Lughod & Richard Hay Jr. (eds.), *Third World Urbanisation*, pp. 225–40. Chicago: Maaroufa Press Inc.
Gerschenkron, Alexander. 1943. *Bread and Democracy in Germany*. Berkeley: University of California Press.
Gold Coast. 1957. *Accra Survey of Household Budgets, February 1953*. Office of the Government Statistician.
Goody, Jack. 1971. *Technology, Tradition and the State in Africa*. Cambridge University Press for the International African Institute.
Graham, P. Anderson. 1892. *The Rural Exodus. The Problem of the Village and the Town*. London: Methuen.
Grandmaison, Colette Le Cour. 1969, 'Activités économiques des femmes Dakaroises', *Africa*, 39: 138–51.
Güsten, Rolf. 1968. *Studies in the Staple Food Economy of Western Nigeria*. New York: Humanities Press.
Guy, Jeff. 1980. 'Ecological factors in the rise of Shaka and the Zulu kingdom', in Shula Marks & Anthony Atmore (eds.), *Economy and Society in Pre-Industrial South Africa* (pp. 102–19). London: Longman.
Guyer, Jane I. 1978. 'The food economy and French colonial rule in Central Cameroon', *Journal of African History*, 19, (4): 577–97.
—— 1980. 'Food, cocoa and the division of labor by sex in two West African societies', *Comparative Studies in Society and History*, 22, (3): 355–73.
Haeringer, Philippe (ed.). 1983. *Abidjan au Coin de la Rue. Eléments de la vie citadine dans la métropole ivoirienne*. Paris: ORSTOM.
—— 1984, *De Caracas à Kinshasa. Bonnes feuilles de la recherche urbaine à ORSTOM (1978–1983)*. Paris: ORSTOM.
Handwerker, Penn W. 1974. 'Changing household organization in the origins of market places in Liberia', *Economic Development and Cultural Change*, 22, (2):

229–48.

Harriss, Barbara. 1979. 'There is a method in my madness, or is it vice versa?', *Food Research Institute Studies*, 17, (2): 197–218.

Hart, Keith. 1982. *The Political Economy of West African Agriculture*. Cambridge University Press.

Hill, Polly. 1966. 'Notes on traditional market authority and market periodicity in West Africa', *Journal of African History*, 7: 295–311.

—— 1970. *Studies in Rural Capitalism in West Africa*. Cambridge University Press.

Hodder, B. W. 1962. 'The Yoruba rural market', in Paul Bohannan & George Dalton (eds.), *Markets in Africa*, pp. 103–17. Evanston: Northwestern University Press.

—— 1967. 'The markets of Ibadan', in P. C. Lloyd, A. L. Mabogunje, & B. Awe (eds.), *The City of Ibadan*, pp. 173–90. Cambridge University Press.

—— 1971. 'Periodic and daily markets in West Africa', in Claude Meillassoux (ed.), *The Development of Indigenous Trade and Markets in West Africa*, pp. 347–58. Oxford University Press for the International African Institute.

—— and U. I. Ukwu. 1969. *Markets in West Africa. Studies of Markets and Trade among the Yoruba and Ibo*. Ibadan University Press.

Hopkins, A. G. 1973. *An Economic History of West Africa*. New York: Columbia University Press.

Hyden, Goran. 1980. *Beyond Ujamaa in Tanzania. Underdevelopment and an Uncaptured Peasantry*. Berkeley: University of California Press.

Iliffe, John. 1979. *A Modern History of Tanganyika*. Cambridge University Press.

International Bank for Reconstruction and Development. 1981. *Accelerated Development in Sub-Saharan Africa. An Agenda for Action*. Washington, DC.

International Labour Office. 1972. *Employment, Incomes and Equality. A Strategy for Increasing Productive Employment in Kenya*. Geneva.

Johnson, Marion. 1974. 'Cotton imperialism in West Africa', *African Affairs*, 73: 178–87.

—— 1976. 'The economic foundations of an Islamic theocracy – the case of Macina', *Journal of African History*, 17, (4): 481–95.

Jones, W. O. 1972. *Marketing Staple Food Crops in Tropical Africa*. Ithaca: Cornell University Press.

—— 1976. 'Some economic dimensions of agricultural marketing research, in C. A. Smith (ed.), *Regional Analysis*, Vol. I, pp. 303–26. New York: Academic Press.

—— 1977–8. 'Turnips, the Seventh Day Adventist principal and management bias, *Food Research Institute Studies*, 16, (3): 141–57.

—— 1984. 'Economic tasks of food marketing boards in tropical Africa', *Food Research Institute Studies*, 19, (2): 113–38.

Joseph, Richard A. 1974. 'Settlers, strikers and *sans travail*: the Douala riots of September 1945', *Journal of African History*, 15(4): 669–87.

Kaplan, Steven Laurence. 1984. *Provisioning Paris. Merchants and Millers in the Grain and Flour Trade during the Eighteenth Century*. Ithaca: Cornell University Press.

Kasfir, Nelson. 1983. 'State, *magendo* and class formation in Uganda', *Journal of Commonwealth and Comparative Politics*, 21, (3): 84–103.

Kenya. 1980. Statistical Abstract.

Kenya Colony and Protectorate. 1951. 'The pattern of income, expenditure and consumption of African labourers in Nairobi, October–November 1950'. East African Statistical Department.

Knight, J. B. 1972. 'Rural-urban income comparisons and migration in Ghana', *Bulletin, Oxford University Institute of Economics and Statistics*, 34, (2): 199–228.

Kratoska, Paul H. 1982. 'Rice cultivation and the ethnic division of labour in British Malaya', *Comparative Studies in Society and History*, 24, (2): 280–314.
Lamartine Yates, P. & D. Warriner. 1943. *Food and Farming in Post-War Europe*. Oxford University Press.
Lawson, Rowena. 1962. 'Engels's Law and its application to Ghana', *Economic Bulletin, Economic Society of Ghana*, 6, (4); 34–46.
—— 1963. 'A human needs diet. The Western pattern in Ghana', *The Economic Bulletin of Ghana*. 7, (1): 35–6.
—— 1967. 'The distributive system in Ghana. A review article', *Journal of Development Studies*, 3, (3): 195–205.
—— 1971. 'The supply response of retail trading services to urban population growth in Ghana', in Claude Meillassoux (ed.), *The Development of Indigenous Trade and Markets in West Africa*, pp. 377–98. Oxford University Press.
—— 1972. *The Changing Economy of the Lower Volta 1954–1967: A Study in the Dynamics of Rural Economic Growth*. London: Oxford University Press.
League of Nations. 1921–38. Annual Reports to the Permanent Mandate Commission by the Government of Cameroun.
Levtzion, Nehemiah. 1980. *Ancient Ghana and Mali*. New York: Africana.
Lewis, Barbara Caroline. 1971. 'The Transporters Association of the Ivory Coast: Ethnicity, Specialization and National Integration'. Northwestern University, unpublished PhD thesis.
Lofchie, Michael. 1980. 'Introduction', in R. Bates & M. Lofchie (eds.), *Agricultural Development in Africa. Issues of Public Policy*, pp. 2–8. New York: Praeger.
Lonsdale, John. 1981. 'States and social processes in Africa: a historical survey', *African Studies Review*, 24, (2/3): 139–225.
Lovejoy, Paul. 1978. 'Plantations in the economy of Sokoto Caliphate', *Journal of African History*, 19, (3): 341–68.
—— 1980. 'Kola in the history of West Africa', *Cahiers d'Etudes Africaines*, 20, (1–2): 97–134.
McGaffey, Janet. 1983. 'How to survive and become rich amidst devastation: the second economy in Zaire', *African Affairs*, 82: 351–66.
Maasdorp, Gavin & A. S. Humphreys. 1975. *From Shantytown to Township. An Economic Study of Poverty and Rehousing in a South African City*. Cape Town: Juta & Co. Ltd.
Mabogunje, Akin L. 1980. *The Development Process. A Spatial Perspective*. London: Hutchinson University Library.
Marshall, Gloria. 1964. 'Women, Trade and the Yoruba Family'. Columbia University, unpublished PhD thesis.
Meillassoux, Claude. 1971. 'Introduction', in C. Meillassoux (ed.), *The Development of Indigenous Trade and Markets in West Africa*, pp. 49–86. Oxford University Press for the International African Institute.
Mintz, Sidney. 1971. 'Men, women and trade', *Comparative Studies in Society and History*, 13, (3): 247–69.
Miskimin, Harry A. 1969. *The Economy of Early Renaissance Europe 1300–1460*. Englewood Cliffs: Prentice Hall.
Morgan, Dan. 1979. *Merchants of Grain*. Harmondsworth: Penguin Books.
Morgan, W. B. 1977. 'Food supply and staple food imports of tropical Africa', *African Affairs*, 76: 167–76.
Morrison, Thomas K. 1984. 'Cereal imports by developing countries. Trends and determinants', *Food Policy*, 9, (1): 13–26.
Muntemba, Maud Shimwaayi. 1982. 'Women and agricultural change in the railway region of Zambia: dispossession and counter-strategies', in Edna G. Bay (ed.),

Women and Work in Africa, pp. 83–104. Boulder, Colorado: Westview Press.
Nelson, Gerald C. 1983. 'Time for tapioca, 1970 to 1980: European demand and world supply of dried cassava', *Food Research Institute Studies*, 19, (1): 25–49.
Nelson, Nici. 1979. 'Women must help each other', in Patricia Caplan & Janet M. Bujra (eds.), *Women United, Women Divided*, pp. 77–98. Bloomington: Indiana University Press.
Nyirenda, A. A. 1957. 'African market vendors in Lusaka, with a note on the recent boycott', *Rhodes-Livingstone Journal*, 22: 31–57.
Ogutu, M. A. 1979. 'Agriculture and the development of markets in the Western Province of Kenya 1930–1960', *Hadith*, 7: 216–42.
van Onselen, Charles. 1976a. *Chibaro. African Mine Labour in Southern Rhodesia 1900–1933*. London: Pluto Press.
—— 1976b. 'Randlords and rotgut 1886–1903; an essay on the role of alcohol in the development of European imperialism and South African capitalism', *History Workshop*, 2: 23–89.
Pain, Marc. 1979. 'Kinshasa. Ecologie et Organisation Urbaines.' Université de Toulouse, unpublished Thèse de Doctorat ès Lettres.
Pallier, Ginette. 1972. 'Les dolotières de Ouagadougou (Haute Volta)', in P. Vennetier (ed.), *La Croissance Urbaine dans les pays Tropicaux: dix etudes sur l'approvisionment des villes*, Pp. 119–39. Travaux et Documents de Géographie Tropicale, No. 7, Paris: CNRS.
Palmer, Robin & Neil Parsons. 1977. *The Roots of Rural Poverty in Central and Southern Africa*. London: Heinemann.
Pearson, Scott R., J. Dirck Stryker, Charles P. Humphreys *et al.* 1981. *Rice in West Africa. Policy and Economics*. Stanford University Press.
Person, Yves. 1968. *Samori. Une Revolution Dyula*. Dakar: Institut Fondamental d'Afrique Noire.
Peters, Pauline E. 1983. 'Cattlemen, Boreholes and Syndicates in the Kgatleng District of Botswana: An Anthropological History of the Transformation of a Commons'. Boston University, unpublished PhD thesis.
Phimister, Ian. 1978. 'Meat and monopolies: beef cattle in Southern Rhodesia, 1890–1938', *Journal of African History*, 19, (3): 391–414.
Poleman, Thomas T. 1961. 'The food economies of urban Middle Africa. The case of Ghana', *Food Research Institute Studies*, 2, (2): 120–74.
Raynaut, Claude. 1977. 'Aspects socio-économiques de la préparation et de la circulation de la nourriture dans un village Hausa (Niger)', *Cahiers d'Etudes Africaines*, 17: 569–97.
Reusse, Eberhard & Rowena M. Lawson. 1969. 'The effect of economic development on metropolitan food marketing – a case study of food retail trade in Accra, *East African Journal of Rural Development*, 2, (1): 35–55.
Richards, Audrey. 1940. 'The political system of the Bemba tribe – North-Eastern Rhodesia', in Meyer Fortes & E. E. Evans-Pritchard (eds.), *African Political Systems*, pp. 83–120. Oxford University Press for the International African Institute (reprint 1987, KPI).
Richards, Paul. 1983. 'Ecological change and the politics of African land use', *African Studies Review*, 26, (2): 1–72.
Rickman, G. E. 1980. *The Corn Supply of Ancient Rome*. Oxford University Press.
Roberts, Richard. 1980a. 'The emergence of a grain market in Bamako, 1883–1908', *Canadian Journal of African Studies*, 14, (1): 37–54.
—— 1980b. 'Long-distance trade and production: Sinsani in the nineteenth century', *Journal of African History*, 21, (2): 169–88.
Robertson, Claire. 1975–6. 'Ga women and change in marketing conditions in the

Accra area', *Rural Africana*, 29: 157–72.

—— 1983. 'The death of Makola and other tragedies', *Canadian Journal of African Studies*, 17: 469–95.

Sandbrook, Richard. 1977. 'The political potential of African urban workers', *Canadian Journal of African Studies*, 11, (3): 411–33.

Saul, Mahir. 1981. 'Beer, sorghum and women: production for the market in Upper Volta, *Africa*, 51, (3): 746–64.

Schwimmer, Brian. 1976. 'Periodic markets and urban development in Southern Ghana', in C. A. Smith (ed.), *Regional Analysis*, Vol. I, pp. 123–45. New York: Academic Press.

Shepherd, Andrew. 1981. 'Agrarian change in Northern Ghana: public investment, capitalist farming and famine', in G. Williams, J. Heyer & P. Roberts (eds.), *Rural Development in Tropical Africa*, pp. 168–92. New York: St. Martin's Press.

Silverstein, Stella. 1983. 'Socio-Cultural Organization and Locational Strategies of Transportation Entrepreneurs: An Ethno-Economic History of the Nnewi Igbo of Nigeria'. Department of Anthropology, Boston University, unpublished PhD thesis.

Skinner, G. William (ed.) 1964–5. 'Marketing and social structure in rural China, parts I–III, *Journal of Asian Studies* XXIV, (1): 3–43; (2): 195–228; (3): 363–99.

—— 1977. *The City in Late Imperial China*. Stanford University Press.

Slicher van Bath, Bernard Hendrick. 1963. *The Agrarian History of Western Europe, 500–1850*. London: Arnold.

Smith, C. A. (ed.). 1976. *Regional Analysis*, New York: Academic Press.

Southworth, V. Roy, W. O. Jones & Scott Pearson. 1979. 'Food crop marketing in Atebubu District, Ghana', *Food Research Institute Studies*, 17, (2): 157–95.

Spencer, Ian. 1980. 'Settler dominance, agricultural production and the Second World War in Kenya', *Journal of African History*, 21, (4): 497–514.

Stren, Richard E. 1982. 'Underdevelopment, urban squatting and the state bureaucracy: a case study of Tanzania', *Canadian Journal of African Studies*, 16, (1): 67–91.

Suret-Canale, Jean. 1971. *French Colonialism in Tropical Africa, 1900–1945*. London: C. Hurst.

Thompson, E. P. 1971. 'The moral economy of the English crowd in the eighteenth century', *Past and Present*, 50: 76–136.

Timmer, C. Peter, W. P. Falcon & S. R. Pearson. 1983. *Food Policy Analysis*. Baltimore: The Johns Hopkins Press.

Trager, Lillian. 1980. 'Customers and creditors: variations in economic personalism in a Nigerian marketing system'. *Ethnology*, 20, (2): 133–46.

Turrell, R. V. 1984. Review of van Onselen, *Studies in the Social and Economic History of the Witswatersrand*, *Africa*, 54, (1): 87–9.

United States Department of Agriculture. 1981. *Food Problems and Prospects in Sub-Saharan Africa. The Decade of the 1980s*. Washington, DC.

Vansina, Jan. 1978. *The Children of Woot*. Madison: University of Wisconsin Press.

Vaughan, Megan. 1982. 'Poverty and Famine: 1949 in Nyasaland'. Chancellor College, Malawi, unpublished paper.

Vengroff, Richard. 1982. 'Food and dependency: P.L.480 Aid to Black Africa', *Journal of Modern African Studies*, 20, (1): 27–43.

Vennetier, Pierre. 1972. 'Réflexions sur l'approvisionnement des villes en Afrique noire et à Madagascar', in P. Vennetier (ed.), *La Croissance Urbaine dans les Pays Tropicaux. Dix Etudes sur l'Approvisionnement des Villes*, pp. 1–13. Travaux et Documents de Géographie Tropicale No. 7. Paris: CNRS.

—— 1976a. *Les Villes d'Afrique Tropicale*. Paris: Masson.

—— 1976b. Review of W. O. Jones, *Marketing Staple Food Crops in Tropical Africa*, *Les Cahiers d'Outre-Mer*, 113: 107.
Wallace, Tina. 1981. 'The challenge of food: Nigeria's approach to agriculture 1975–80', *Canadian Journal of African Studies*, 15, (2): 239–58.
Warren, W. M. 1966. 'Urban real wages and the Nigerian trade union movement', *Economic Development and Cultural Change*, 15, (1): 21–35.
Welsh, David. 1971. 'The growth of towns', in M. Wilson & L. Thompson (eds.), *The Oxford History of South Africa*, Vol. II, pp. 172–244. Oxford University Press.
Wilks, Ivor. 1975. *Asante in the Nineteenth Century*. Cambridge University Press.
Wilson, Ernest J. III. 1984. 'Contested terrain: a comparative and theoretical reassessment of state-owned enterprise in Africa', *Journal of Commonwealth and Comparative Politics*, 22, (1): 4–27.
Wilson, Francis. 1971. 'Farming 1866–1966', in M. Wilson & L. Thompson (eds.), *The Oxford History of South Africa*, Vol. II, pp. 104–71. Oxford University Press.

Newspaper
New York Times.

2 Michael Watts

BRITTLE TRADE: A POLITICAL ECONOMY OF FOOD SUPPLY IN KANO

INTRODUCTION

. . . as Lenin said, 'History has got much more imagination than we have.' By that, I mean the imagination of the human kind and the 'objective subject' . . . who makes his/her history not like a single-minded subject but like a huge body of millions of subjects engaged in struggles, with their victories and their defeats.

Alain Lipietz

A great deal has, of course, been written on pre-colonial mercantile systems in West Africa and more generally about the commodities that entered these regional and international circuits of trade. But it is paradoxical that comparatively little attention has been paid to the rather prosaic question of how the ancient, cosmopolitan cities of the Central Sudan were actually fed, and how the food supply systems were organised.[1] By almost all the usual canons of city life, the splendid Sudano-Sahelian cities of Kano, Gao, and Timbuktu unquestionably warranted the label 'urban': they stood as nodes or central places in systems of exchange, they were complex and socially heterogeneous agglomerations and, above all, were symbolic – what Paul Wheatley (1972) calls 'cosmo-magical' – constructions, classically labyrinthine as befitted the ancient Muslim pattern of cities and city-states. In spite of the size of the city populations consisting of myriads of petty commodity producers, merchant-traders, bureaucrats, a praetorian guard, clerics, seasonal migrants, and so on, it is often assumed that large urban configurations were readily sustained by peasant food producers in the immediate hinterland. Effective long-distance movement of bulky staple foods was constrained by the means of transportation and cities were therefore fed either by urbanites who also farmed (not infrequently within the city walls), as Max Weber noted long ago, or by the surpluses extracted from local rural producers. The latter implies a strong, extractive state apparatus and a sufficiently intensive agrarian base (for instance, an

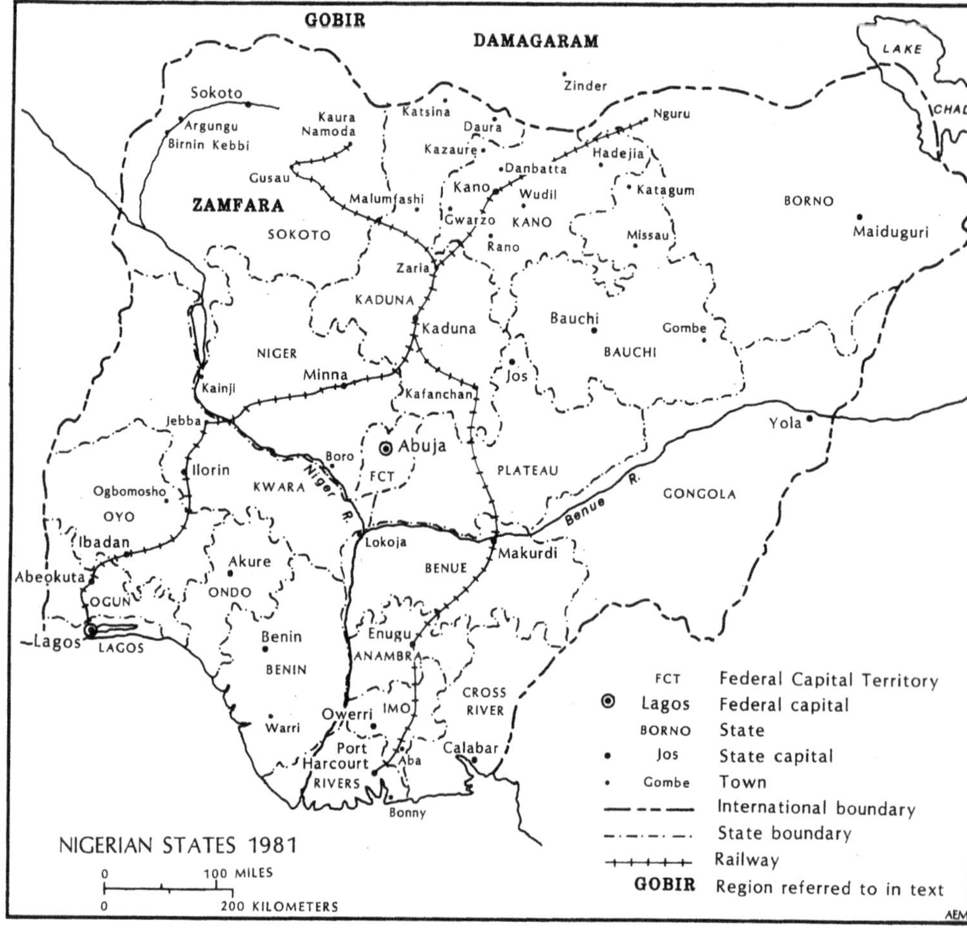

Figure 3 Current state boundaries, Nigeria

intensive, heavily-manured, permanent system of rain-fed cereal cultivation in the case of the West African savannas) to support cities of perhaps 50,000–60,000 people. In this view, the grain trade and food supply are taken to be relatively unproblematic.

Whatever the veracity of this purportedly local self-sufficiency, the colonial period clearly necessitated important changes quite specifically in the trade in staples for wage-workers (wage foods), the peasant farming and cropping systems and the magnitude of urban food markets. In northern Nigeria, for example, the spectacular genesis of the groundnut trade (and later of cotton) transformed Kano into a sprawling mercantile city, demographically fuelled by immigrant bureaucrats, clerks and traders from the South who occupied the Sabon Gari township outside the old city walls, by the armies of seasonal migrants in search of dry-season wage-labouring and, not least, by the demands imposed by a growing Native Administration (NA) bureaucracy and its attendant institutions. Furthermore, the regional food economy was restructured by the significant inroads made by export commodity production into the cycle of peasant reproduction (in Kano, Katsina and Zaria for example), by the gradual emergence of commercial foodstuff-producing areas in the North (Borno, Southern Katsina) and also further south in the Middle Belt (Bida, Minna and Bauchi) to supply both the cities, and the considerable demand for wage foods generated by over 50,000 seasonal workers in the Plateau tin mines.

Once again, however, analyses of colonial food systems tend to claim if not local sufficiency, then at least effortless self-reliance and a remarkably smooth performance of the entire trade network (see Jones 1980). The cogs of this food system were lubricated by peasant producers (as opposed to plantations or state farms) and by private mercantile channels, notably indigenous merchants' capital and European firms (as opposed to statutory monopolies such as the Marketing Boards). It is true that on occasion the colonial state did intercede *directly* in food policy, notably through wartime requisitioning, market rigging and a fledgling famine relief policy, but for the most part new food demands were met by myriads of farmers and traders. This peasant-based and purportedly competitive and efficient food supply system has, of course, been canonised by Myint (1971) who suggested in his vent-for-surplus theory that the colonial expansion of agrarian commodity production was achieved without a significant increase in population, without a corresponding decline in either land or labour time devoted to foodstuffs (i.e. self-sufficiency) and without a technological revolution. It is in this way that one can understand W. O. Jones's deduction – that I shall subsequently show to be quite erroneous – that 'Nigeria has known famine only once in this century [during the Civil War] . . . which demonstrates that private marketing systems can be relied on to feed the population' (1980:340). Some Marxist-inspired theoreticians also arrive at rather similar conclusions; Warren (1980:130), for example, believes that the development of colonial capitalism was a 'progressive force' (transportation, public health) which marked the disappearance of famine altogether after the 1920s, while Bryceson (1981), on the basis of her Tanganyikan study, posits that a major function of the colonial state was the 'regularization of the productive base on pre-capitalist modes of production' (p. 91), largely by famine relief and amplified food security.

In this chapter, I shall question all of these lines of thought, in an examination of the manner in which Kano city in northern Nigeria has been

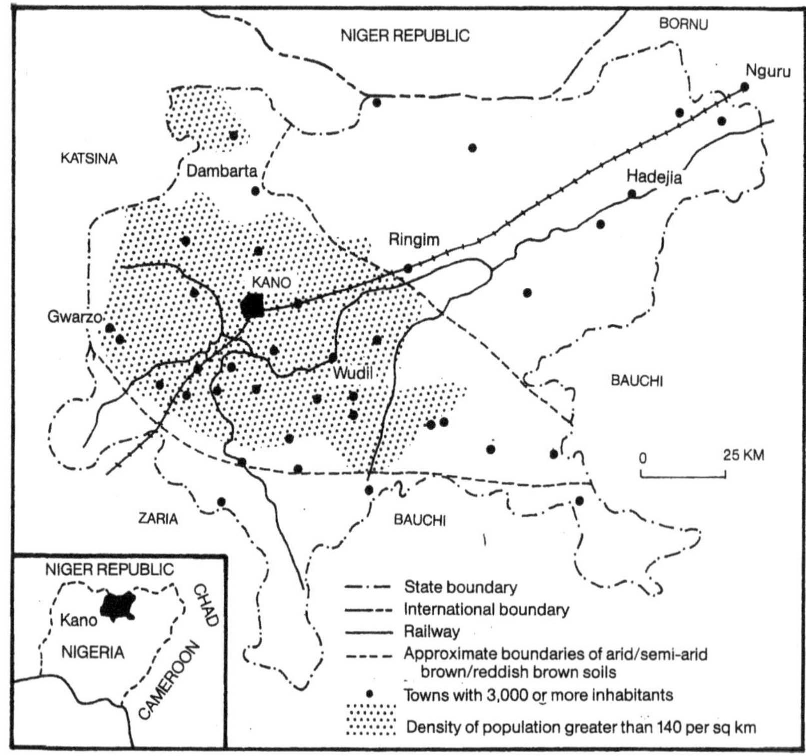

Figure 4 Kano close-settled zone
Source Mortimore 1970.

provisioned from the mid-nineteenth century to the present. Rather, I want to argue that in the nineteenth century many of the peri-urban districts of Kano city – the heavily-populated and intensively cultivated close-settled zone (see Figure 4) – were not self-sufficient in foodstuffs and were certainly incapable of provisioning thousands of city dwellers. Food entered regional trade networks partly supplied by large-scale estates in peripheral 'commercialised' food-producing areas and partly by specialised grain traders (*Yan Kwarami*). On occasion this city food system disintegrated altogether but, as I shall endeavour to show, these crises (famines) also occurred in the colonial period. Expanded commodity production after 1903 did not imply a smoothly functioning colonial food economy for Kano city; indeed, it was in many respects quite brittle. So brittle in fact that the colonial state was constantly preoccupied by what one political officer called the 'annual lottery' of the food harvest; in short, by the inability to regulate and control local grain merchants, and by their evident inability to secure stable peasant production or to provide sufficient famine relief in the event of a crisis. On several occasions, *contra* Jones (1980), Kano city faced famine conditions – though hardship was often much more severe in the countryside – and periodic scarcities. Cooper's (1983) comment that capital's assault on Africa produced a 'guerrilla army' that cluttered up the city and undisciplined 'troops' (farmers) who 'failed to produce enough food to feed the city' (p. 18), is an apposite encapsulation of Kano's colonial experience. An explanation of the history of food supply in Kano resides not, as Hill (1982) suggests, in a 'withdrawal' from the countryside due to the collapse of estate agriculture after conquest and the absence of lucrative crops to attract merchants (p. 225). On the contrary, an explanation must be sought not in retreat but in advance; in the dynamic character of household production, in the partial commoditisation of the rural economy, in the social organisation of trade, and in the critical, but contradictory, role of the colonial state. In other words, explanation lies in the changing idioms of rural accumulation and commoditisation, not in supposedly inert, stagnant and neglected dry grain modes of production (Hill 1982).

In the first part of this chapter I attempt to situate the provisioning of Kano within the social relations of the Sokoto Caliphate.[2] An identification of the politico-economic terrain of the nineteenth century informs both our understanding of why the Kano close-settled zone was a deficit grain producer and the specific forms and functions of grain circulation. I give particular attention to the pattern and organisation of grain trade and production, the role of the Caliphal state in relation to food security and the provision of Kano city, and finally the technical limits of the food system itself. In the second part, I examine the impact of the colonial state on the regional food economy. While the imperial mission upgraded the communications infrastructure, improving the efficacy of large-scale grain movement, the colonial state also negotiated the contradiction of simultaneously wishing to expand peasant supplies of export commodities (for political, strategic and fiscal purposes) and also to increase foodstuff production for rapidly growing urban populations, the minefields and the military. Throughout the colonial period these contradictory impositions placed on household producers were never effectively resolved; the colonial state did not develop either a regularised food supply system (which remained largely in the hands of local, Levantine and European merchants' capital) or an effective famine relief programme. On at least four occasions between 1903 and 1980 the Kano city food supply system – and indeed the large segments of the regional food economy – collapsed and the *birni*[3] was confronted with famine conditions. In part three, I briefly detail the Kano city food system following independence, but concentrate principally on what is arguably a new phase in 'feeding Kano', following close upon the heels of Nigeria's oil boom and the sluggish performance of the agricultural sector. The onset of a deepening and diversification of industrial import substitution (what Lipietz (1984) calls 'peripheral Fordism') has seen a parallel change of taste among Kano workers and Civil Servants, new forms of politicisation of food supply associated with the expanded role of a *rentier* state in Nigeria's oil-fuelled transformation, and the growth in significance of international trade in the provision of staple foods. Nonetheless, in attempting to make concrete descriptions of these processes, one is still confronted by ignorance of so fundamental a subject as how the most important city in the entire West African savannas was actually sustained. This includes, for example, the contribution of the millions(?) of freed slaves — who presumably became a food and export crop-producing peasantry – to the food trade. While a critical issue, almost nothing is known of this process and its impact (Lovejoy 1984).

1. FEEDING KANO IN THE NINETEENTH CENTURY

It has been suggested by Murray Last (1978:3) that there was a sense in which the political and intellectual history of northern Nigeria in the nineteenth century was an extended exercise in the implementation and reform of Usman dan Fodio's original blueprint for social, political and constitutional development in the new emirate system. The practical political consequences of this grandiose social design was the birth of a huge Muslim community, the Sokoto Caliphate, covering some 150,000 square miles, which welded together the thirty emirates. The central figure of the new emirate system was the Sultan (*amir al-muminin*), located at Sokoto, with authority over the entire Muslim community as supreme ruler. The Caliph was juridically and ideologically bound to the Sharia and the Sunnah, though in practice this was mediated through a complex process of advice and consent from the Islamic intelligentsia. Within the political community of the Caliphate, the constituent units or cells were non-sovereign emirates subject to the discretionary powers of the Sultan who devolved power to his representatives, the emirs, who had direct jurisdiction over their territorial domains. The emir was an official of the Caliph, therefore, vested with specific powers – most notably the performance of religious duties, tax collection and material improvement – whose appointment or dismissal was the sole prerogative of the Caliph. The execution of emirate functions was undertaken by a large bureaucracy of office-holders who used their functionary positions as personal prebends.

Polly Hill (1977:1–3) has described the major responsibility of the organs of central government as the regulation and supervision of the 'fief-holders', the *sarakunan kasa* or *hakimai*, all of whom were attached to particular lineages and who operated through their own agents in the lower echelons of the settlement hierarchy. As Weber's description of patrimonial bureaucracy suggests, the affairs of the state were grounded in the authority of the emir; consequently, dynastic change necessitated a turnover in the emirate personnel who occupied client niches within the bureaucratic edifice. High-level emirate government was composed of urban-based offices, each vested with unique rank, prestige, tradition, rights and authority (*iko*); territorial administration was effected through prebendal land allocations from which taxes, labour and military forces were levied; and each emirate capital, irrespective of the extent of bureaucratic decentralisation, contained a palace, or court, a treasury, a prison, markets, mosques, a prayer-ground and state compounds. The echelons of senior officers were sustained by state endowments and by a prebendal distribution of fiefs.

The growing significance of Kano in the Caliphal political economy is not to be explained solely in terms of the city's relation to the textile, kola, livestock or elite goods trade. The Kano close-settled zone was above all a regional economy of prodigious output, due not only to favourable ecological and demographic conditions but also to technical conditions of production, patterns of technological innovation, institutional linkages, and in the active role of the state in encouraging production and slave importation (Shea 1981). The famous Kano textile industry – which Barth (1965) estimated to be worth in excess of 300 million cowries in the 1850s – dramatically illustrates the degree of full-time commodity specialisation; there was a complex social division of labour with large-scale, merchant-dominated textile production employing wage, slave, client and domestic labour, technical innovation (for instance, the development of deep *laso*-lined pits), and an interventionist state utilising fiscal and tax incentives to promote cloth dyeing and weaving. These conditions were not limited to Kano city but were region-wide, and a good deal of craft production and long-distance trade (*fatauci*) was rurally based, well beyond the city walls (Hill 1977; Shea 1975, 1981).

For all these reasons, a dynamic Kano economy encouraged considerable labour mobility, and a good deal of voluntary and involuntary immigration into the city occurred throughout the later nineteenth century. Opportunities for craft production, trade, clientage, scholastic study and refuge made Kano the centrepoint of a centripetal vortex of human movement which seemingly intensified as the nineteenth century wore on. When Clapperton visited Kano in the 1820s he estimated the population of the city to be 30,000–40,000; in the 1850s Barth posited a figure of 30,000; but seasonal in-migration of dry-season migrants (*masu cin rani*) and traders might well bring the *birni* to at least double that figure (Hill 1977; Watts 1983). Indeed,

Staudinger (1889), who visited Kano at the height of the trading season in 1885, posited 60,000–80,000 souls resident within the city walls, and six years later Monteil passed through 100 km of continuous cultivated farmland as he approached the *birni* (Frishman 1977). In sum, Kano Emirate, a territory of some 13,000 square miles, supported three to four million individuals, free and slave, within its boundaries by the last quarter of the nineteenth century (Hill 1977:19). It is quite probable that almost two million lived in the close-settled zone (i.e., within thirty miles of the city walls), largely in dispersed homesteads. In some districts population densities were doubtless in excess of 300 per square mile and presumably had been for some considerable time (Mortimore 1967, 1970).

How, then, was this huge metropolis – the capital of perhaps the wealthiest, and certainly the most populous, emirate in the Sokoto Caliphate – sustained and provisioned with staple foodstuffs during the nineteenth century? The contours of the city food system are defined, I believe, by four fundamental conditions which structure the particular historical dynamics of supply. First, the Sokoto Caliphate was overwhelmingly agrarian in character. If Hill's (1977:18) demographic speculation of ten million at the turn of the century is at all plausible, then at least eighty per cent of this total who resided in the countryside were engaged very largely in agricultural occupations. In the savannas of the Central Sudan wealth lay in 'the production of an agricultural surplus and proximity to the desert, with its strong demand for grain, other foodstuffs and manufactured articles' (Baier 1980:21). Moreover, the basic unit of production was the household, typically extended in form (*gandu*) embracing kin, client, slave and very occasionally wage labour. Though Kano Emirate is characteristically seen as a 'high density' slave system (Lovejoy 1978a) in which servile farm labour was employed quite regularly on the farms of both large and small producers, the bedrock of the rural economy was free peasant production based on household labour.

Secondly, the agrarian basis of society was unequivocally intensive, permanent and, to use the vocabulary of an early traveller in Kano, E. D. Morel, 'scientific'. Most especially in the close-settled zones such as Kano, long-term upland swiddening of millet, sorgums, and cowpeas[4] had been replaced by permanent cultivation in which soil fertility was maintained through complex patterns of intercropping, rotation, manuring and weeding. One only need reflect casually on the travel diaries of Barth, Richardson, Clapperton and Imam Imoru to appreciate not only the sophistication and assiduity of Hausa rain-fed cereal agriculture but also the existence of 'export-oriented' rice production zones in the Rima and Hadejia Valleys. Although agrarian technologies were quite simple, systems of labour scheduling, moisture control, manuring and both species and varietal interplanting were dynamic and highly developed enough to reduce the risks of failure in the face of climatic variability (Richards 1983; Watts 1983).

Thirdly, one can assume that for Kano, as Max Weber posited for all pre-industrial cities, 'the urbanite of old was also a farmer'. In the nineteenth century, a high proportion of city dwellers – though not the majority – had some access to land. According to Frishman (1977), even in the 1830s when the area within the city walls was roughly 5,400 acres, only 1,824 acres were actually inhabited. Doubtless there was some agricultural production within the *birni* walls and a good deal more within four to five miles of the city gates. Most of the significant fiefholders – and most notably the Emir – held large plantations (*gandaye*) near to the city or in their districts that provided subsistence for their huge patrimonial households. As I shall detail, some urban-based merchants and clerics produced huge quantities of grain using slave labour on estates dotted throughout the northern Emirate, far beyond the territorial confines of Kano.

And finally, the claims of agrarian intensity, high productivity (per unit of land), and home production by city residents, should not imply local food self-sufficiency. Indeed, within some of the closely-settled central districts – and perhaps over the entire emirate – where the development of a rurally-based export-oriented dyed cloth industry was predicated on the emergence of full-time specialists, grain self-sufficiency was highly tenuous, if not altogether impossible. Even though year-round artisans could secure part of their familial subsistence through slave production (M. G. Smith 1954:19), grain demand outstripped local supply. The following commentaries by two turn-of-the-century colonial officers in Kano are especially instructive:

> In spite of the fact that there is little land not under cultivation, the district is not self feeding, even in a good year. . . . This can be traced to two causes. First, that few of the people are pure farmers, nearly all having some subsidiary trade, and secondly deterioration of the soil. (Mr Webster, NAK SNP7 4055/1912)

> I do not think that people have ever realized how much corn is imported from the north. I had always looked upon Kano as self supporting in this respect, but I find such is not the case. Not only are we now in Kano getting corn from the north but even from the Gwari Country of W. Zaria. (Mr Palmer, NAK SNP7/1907)

All this strongly suggests that feeding Kano in the nineteenth century was, above all, a regional enterprise, that the conventional assumptions of household, community or local self-sufficiency may be specious in spite of high agricultural productivity, and that the demands of the state and of urban non-producers must be situated in terms of a vital grain trade and large-scale estate production.[5]

These pre-conditions paint a rather different picture of the rural-urban political economy in the Sokoto Caliphate than that presented by Hill (1976:6) in her account of the *birni* as an administrative apex 'with no properly articulated market-places in the countryside' (1976:6). She believes further that the Kanawa were a people lacking hierarchical systems of chieftaincy and village administration and is accordingly puzzled by the question. 'How was the socio-political structure (of Kano) maintained in the absence of both an . . . institutionalized hierarchy of authority and of segmentary lineage systems' (1977:16). Under the Tolstoyan load of rural autonomy which Hill imposes, the role of the state apparatus itself, and its reproductive demands, disappear altogether. For Hill, there was a radical separation of town and country, only bridged by a few influential individuals who 'straddled the gap between the two worlds' (1982:230). The matrix of rural vitality – self-sufficiency, trade, craft production – was independent of a centralised state without 'bureaucratic articulation' (1982:230); in short, the state had little or no power, function or interest in either the rural areas or in food supply (1982:229).

But it is clear that the state did intervene *directly* in the rural economy and it is precisely extra-economic surplus extraction – that is, tax-rents on peasants by the state as a politically-based exaction for the right to cultivate – which gives the Caliphate its particular political-economic form. Last (1983) and Usman (1981) show clearly how attempts at rural integration by the state commenced in the early seventeenth century with settlement, labour mobilisation and construction, and that rural administration and tax collection had progressed considerably by the mid-nineteenth century. Even if we grant (to a degree) that the formal properties of authority were attenuated in some areas and the administrative structure was perhaps top-heavy, the existence of systematic rural–urban linkages can be readily detected in two widespread institutional forms. First the cleric (*ulema*)–merchant networks and the Islamic brotherhoods described by Tahir (1975) which I discuss in detail later; and secondly, the so-called *chaffa* or *chappa* system[6] in which the local non-resident *chappa* patron had fief over families, not land, and whose nominal power transcended that of village heads. The ties were not necessarily by location, occupation or some other classification but were 'partly based on historical connection and custom and for the rest on inclination' (NAK Sokprof 85/1906). While most pre-capitalist states tend to be insecurely anchored in their territories, these political and quasi-political ties suggest something much more than a 'weak sub-structure' and indeed I shall concentrate on the social organisation of town and country linkages, namely the ties of patronage, allegiance and clientelism, which were integral elements of Kano's food supply system.

There are four dimensions of the Kano food system I propose to pursue systematically here. The state appropriation of grain through a canonical Muslim tax (*zakkat*); large-scale grain production on servile or client-based merchant – cleric estates; the regional grain trade; and internal circulation, what I shall refer to as an urban 'moral economy.'

1 *State grain appropriation*

The major source of emirate income was derived from a baroque arrangement of taxes levied on agriculture, manufacture, trade and personal properties and collected through vassals and subordinate officials. A number of taxes were subsumed within the general category of *kharaj* or *kurdin kasa* (literally 'land money'), the latter being a legacy of the pre-*jihad* period, and co-opted after 1804 as a legitimate Islamic impost. The surpluses appropriated by the state assumed three forms: (a) labour rent, largely drawn as *corvées* for public works and on demand for the farms and estates of the officeholders; (b) rent in kind, most particularly the grain tithes and (c) monetary rents levied on some special crops and craft goods.

The principal tax/rent of the late nineteenth century was *zakkat*,[7] a ten per cent canonical grain levy obligatory for all adult Muslims which, being paid in kind, supplied the *sarakuna* with their means of subsistence through extra-market channels. It was the opinion of Resident Newby of Kano Province that *zakkat* was, by the late nineteenth century at least, 'the biggest channel for extortion and robbery' (NAK SNP 111/1908). It was doubtless never uniformly collected and usually in haphazard instalments and, according to Newby, at least one-third was 'lost' in transit. Nevertheless, *zakkat* did constitute one quarter by value of all state revenues and, in an emirate of perhaps one million potential contributors, constituted a huge urban food conduit: 'the ruling classes[es] and . . . the emir [of Kano] and his huge following practically subsist on the zakka, the whole emirate forming a sort of granary from which they drew supplies' (Resident Cargill, cited in Paden 1973:1010). The manifest purpose of *zakkat* was, of course, to sustain granaries for the upkeep of the poor and destitute (Abubakar 1975) but M. G. Smith's remarks suggest that such functions were decidedly secondary: 'From the stores, the ruler made annual distributions to his officials, in amounts which varied with rank. As Secretary, the Magaji Bakebbi recorded the ruler's donations and reserves, the latter being kept as security against famine or loss through war' (1967:112–13.).

Zakkat certainly constituted one state function, namely famine relief through urban-based granaries, public works employment and grain relief. Throughout the Caliphate these sorts of central responsibilities were firmly embedded in notions of adequate government, and Usman dan Fodio's treatise on government laid considerable emphasis on the particular administrative functions of material improvement, charity and relief. The *zakkat* grain tithe, as irregular and variable as it may be have been, at least ensured the possibility of grain accumulation during the bountiful years.[8] The accumulation of foodstuffs was not simply an instance of state benevolence, or an unambiguous concern for peasant welfare. The urbanites clearly benefited from the security which large granaries conferred, especially in an epoch when military seige was far from infrequent. Equally, the *zakkat* sustained the enormous palace household of the Emir, the dry-season state projects and *corvée* labour employed on public works. A proportion of the *zakkat* was deliberately held in some of the district capitals and brought into Kano city when required. For the commoners, the central granaries under the jurisdiction of the *sarkin Hatsi* constituted the last desperate gasp in the hierarchy of indigenous famine assistance. If all else failed, as peasant wisdom had it, 'the Emir [of Kano] never ran short of food'.

2 *Merchants' capital and estate production of grain*

Kano-based merchant capital had secured a prominent place in the political and economic architecture of the Emirate, particularly as agricultural investment and commodity production grew in the course of the century. Tahir's (1975) work on early merchant–*ulema* networks reconstructed what he termed 'primitive corporations – usually with a pronounced scholastic influence – that seem reminiscent of pre-Restoration Japanese firms. Enormous commercial edifices, they were built upon complex patterns of kinship, clientage, slave labour and religious affiliation. These wealthy merchants stood at the apex of diversified commercial organisations that integrated the production of crafts and food – especially cloth and grain – with credit services, patronage, and protection. In Kano Emirate, as in many other African societies, the merchant and the scholar tended to be closely linked, if not one and the same person. Tahir's (1975:275) reconstruction of Tulu Baba's mercantile empire, based in Kano city during the 1830s, one of the few available case studies, consisted of fifteen slave-run grain estates in four emirates, one factor agent in Gwanja, and three cloth 'corporations' in Kano. Two of the largest and most influential groundnut and grain merchants in the colonial period – Dantata and Uba Ringim – were part of households associated with client and slave-based estate production of grain in Kano, Zaria and Bida Emirates during the late nineteenth century. The social overlap of large-scale merchants (*attajirai*) and Muslim clerics produced vast, ramifying social networks; they were predicated on ties of primary clientage and trust (*amana*) and the patron (*maigida*) stood as the fountain-head of a vast manufacturing-agricultural-commercial enterprise which locked town and country together in a mutually supportive embrace. In this fashion, Kano-based merchants not only sustained their huge patrimonial households, often in excess of 100 persons, but also channelled grain into the city market to be sold by grain retailers (*ma' auna*) ultimately to be purchased by consumers and the women who dominated the flourishing cooked-food trade.

The aristocracy and office-holding classes also engaged in estate production drawing upon *corvée*, client and slave labour. Questions remain, however, as regards the extent to which grain from these sources was complementary to, or competitive with *zakkat,* and in particular how merchants exercised influence with state officials. Certainly by the nineteenth century nobility and merchants were linked through marriage and military finance, and estate food production was probably a critical mechanism by which commercial, political and domestic enterprises were held together.

3 *Regional grain trade* (*Yan Kwarami*)
A third level transcends local spheres of influence to embrace inter-ethnic trade and linkage between essentially urban grain-catchment areas, such as the *azalay* trade. Baier and Lovejoy (1977), for example, have shown how the Sudanic savannas and the Sahel were closely intertwined and how these symbolic relations were thrown into sharp relief during the periods of food shortages:

> During hard times, nobles, their families, and retinues depended on the hospitality of dependents on estates in the savanna, including many Agalawa villages as well as servile villages and farms close to Tuareg grazing camps. Nobles remained at the southern end of their network until the weather improved and the herds began to grow again, so that these southern communities in effect acted as a safety valve in times of scarcity. (1977:404)

Patterns of social structure, most particularly the gradations of servility among Touareg lineages, contributed to the general pattern of cultural plasticity and symbiosis among adjacent ecological niches. However, this model of Touareg and servile diaspora communities and associated patterns of trade and movement actually presents a sort of parasitism, for it was the southerly emirates which provided the haven to which the Sahelian populations retreated during periods of hardship.

This simple retreat-expansion model calibrated with the drought cycle actually oversimplifies a rather complex two-way interdependency. Under closer scrutiny, the emirates and the northern cities, like Kano in particular, were to a large extent dependent upon grain production in the southern Sahelian regions of Adar, Damagaram and Damerghou. H. R. Palmer, for example, while the Resident of Kano, noted that at the turn of the century much of Hausaland proper was not a huge granary as the colonial Administration hypothesised:

> But in this connection when I was touring in the northern part of the Province I met a great number of caravans going to fetch or returning with guinea corn from French territory. I learn that they have to resort to outside sources for their supply of guinea corn at this time of year. I mention this matter as it is the impression that Katsina Province is the granary of the Protectorate. (NAK Katprof 1789:1904)

Thus while the horizon of the Touareg communities was towards the southern refuges in the savannas, Kano urbanites regularly looked north to meet grain deficits.

These critical food circuits were the domain of a particular class of traders, *yan kwarami*, frequently drawn from specific ethnic communities, especially *buzu* (servile Touareg) and Maguzawa. A Sokoto District Assessment, for example, commented upon the continual trade to Gobir in the North, farmers returning 'loaded with grain' (NAK SNP 10 379/1913:10). Where the trade was localised and small-scale, single donkey-based *dan kwarami* purchased grain directly from the household producers. In other cases there was a permanent need to import grain over much greater distances. The buoyancy of the grain market was reflected in the tendency among Kano merchants to devote slave-based *gandu* production to millet and sorghum cultivation. In nineteenth-century Zamfara, wealthy merchants were invariably those with a close connection with either grain production or distribution. Kaura Namoda near Gusau in fact emerged as an important locus of the regional cereal trade, and local grain merchants (*yan sakai*) built a reputation for their enormous wealth.

Although the precise character and organisation of nineteenth-century trading remains cloudy, there were particular ethnic circuits. *Buzu* traders certainly dominated the foodstuffs network in the Sokoto area, bringing millet from the Adar and returning with cotton (NAK SNP 10 102p/1915). Kebbi traders from Argungu and Birnin Kebbi took rice to the more arid northern reaches of Sokoto, and the famous long-distance trade in cereals from Zamfara and Southern Katsina was especially associated with non-Muslim Hausa (Maguzawa) who had a reputation for farming excellence. Many of these traders bought directly from the farmer and supplied rural deficit areas as well as urban markets, although it is unclear how and in what ways they interacted with large Kano-based merchants.

The general impression, at any rate, is that grain was not a marginal commodity in Kano's distributive circuits. Indeed Shea (1975) established that in the peri-urban districts around Kano city in the nineteenth century some peasants became rich by bringing grain from Missau and Katagum to the east, while large quantities of grain were brought to the city by 'people from Katsina and by Maguzawa (non-Muslim Hausa) of the more rural areas'. (Ibid: 67). In view of the erratic nature of rainfall and the fear of poor harvest, the pre-colonial grain trade had obvious practical virtue.

Clearly, the efficacy of the grain trade was ultimately framed by the nature of pre-colonial transportation. Its technical character – dependent largely on camels and donkeys – prevented the rapid transmission of large quantities of staple foodstuffs. Kano food demand, nonetheless, drew upon a catchment area from Zamfara or Damagaram, a round trip of three to four weeks. In light of the limits imposed by the technology and by volatile prices and low purchasing power, the role of state apparatus and emirate elites assumed a signal importance.

4 *The urban moral economy*

Though kinship provided the fundamental setting for the most important social relationships in Hausaland, a great number of individuals participated in client networks. M. G. Smith, in describing nineteenth-century Zaria (Zazzau), suggested that ties of political patronage and clientage constituted the very fabric of Hausa society beyond the family:

> Clientage is thus coterminous with Hausa society and is accordingly almost as complex, this complexity expresses the multifunctional character of the institution. In some situations clientage is candidly political and its focus is office; or it may be directly economic, balancing work and reward. In other situations its functions are covert . . (1960:260)

All forms of clientage (*barantaka*), however, demanded similar standards of performance, namely the 'premise of a voluntary, dissoluble consociation entered upon to the mutual benefit of the contracting parties' (Low 1972:19). The ties of loyalty (*cafka*) intrinsic to dynastic politics and patrimonial state systems – particularly between the Sultan and emirs, between emir and courtiers, or between merchants and his clients – afforded protection, reductions in the tax burden and, in many cases, the provision of food, clothes and marriage expenses. Effectively-controlled clients (*barori*) were instrumental in the functioning of large merchant networks, as they were for political support.

In practice, *barantaka* was far more complex than simple dyadic unions; it intertwined large sections of the Kano urban community in huge social networks. In a society in which office-holding was an object of intense political competition between persons eligible by birth for appointment, clients were attracted in proportion to the local estimate of their prospects (M. G. Smith, 1960:12). Of course, we cannot assume that the terms of exchange, or the maintenance of dependency and resource distribution among patrons and clients was exogenously given. Competition among clients (and especially between clients and kin) was intense and the pattern of reciprocity which emerged reflected relative bargaining power as much as the binding power of local ethical standards. While clientage provided a vehicle for subsistence security it also contributed to the reproduction of inequality. Yet because it provided an opportunity to demonstrate trust, integrity and courage it was a relationship of moral equality. In Hausa society where notions of honour and shame (*kunya*) had, and continue to have enormous normative significance, the demands of patron–client relations were morally and culturally sanctioned. These webs of urban patronage were structurally akin to the delicate balances and polarities between plebeians and patricians in eighteenth-century England, what Edward Thompson (1978b) calls the 'moral economy'. In Kano, the poor imposed upon the rich some of the duties and functions of the paternalism by which they were supported. There is no need to idealise the moral economy, because as Raymond Williams points out, 'there was very little that was moral about it' (1973:37), but it did provide the means by which grain circulated among urban residents.

The Koranic school and Islamic networks in nineteenth-century Kano provide a vivid illustration of the urban moral economy. The *ulema* were, of course, directly supported by the emirs, office-holders, state functionaries and wealthy merchants, but many urban *talakawa* and rural folk were incorporated into these webs of Islamic learning. This participation was in fact part of a tradition taking the form of seasonal migration (*cin rani*) of youths to study with respected *mallamai*. The dry-season departure of aspirant scholars relieved pressures on household granaries, and the tradition of the peripatetic *mallam* offered a positive economic inducement, not simply in an ideological sense of deepening the adoption or practice of Islam, or achieving upward mobility as a scribe in the patrimonial bureacracy, but also in that it assisted household reproduction. Koranic students who resided in Kano often engaged in casual wage labour but the ethics and status-norms of Kano society also demanded that students receive alms, which was in fact a form of redistribution of wealth from the more affluent urban dwellers to the sons of rural dwellers under the norms of Islamic charity (Lubeck 1986).

THE LIMITS OF KANO'S FOOD SYSTEM

In all probability the food production system of Kano city was not highly commoditised. Staple foodstuffs were certainly drawn into the *birni* from far afield because many of the peri-urban districts were in deficit due to a highly developed craft economy, but the role of the market was limited despite the occupational division of labour. The market-dependent consumers were wage labourers, urban poor, full-time craft producers and low-level state functionaries and clients. Urbanites with small farm holdings also purchased grain and the supplies were exhausted. But much of Kano's food circuits were sustained through home production – city dwellers who were also farmers – and the huge patrimonial household network of the nobility, the aristocracy and the merchants based on estate production.

However, in a society in which transportation was technically limited and agricultural returns to labour comparatively low, Kano's food system was necessarily vulnerable to crises of 'the old type' (Brenner 1976). Drought in particular was an integral part of the ebb and flow of the Central Sudan and in the event of a particularly severe upland harvest failure, the urban food system might collapse entirely. Imam Imoru's nineteenth-century commentary points to the fact that harvest variability was transmitted directly to the Kano food market:

> When a *taiki* of cereal is sold in Kano [ca. 1890) for 2,500 or 3,000 cowries, it means food is abundant. When it is being sold for 4,000 or 5,000, there is neither hunger, nor is there an abundance of food. When it is sold for 6,000 or 7,000, hunger is approaching, and when it is sold for 10,000 cowries, there is real hunger.
> When we were children in Kano [ca. 1840] and it was sold for 10,000 cowries, there was serious hunger . . . [some people] have seen a *taiki* being sold for 40,000 cowries in birnin Kano. (Ferguson 1973:325)

Many of the early European commercial agents and explorers passed judgement on these price rises in Kano since they too suffered from the grain scarcities and high costs. Many of the city folk turned to wage labour to sustain themselves as prices rocketed. But as grain became ever more scarce, payment for casual labour was converted from kind to cowries. Oral histories revealed that a distinguishing feature of the great famines (*babban yunwa*) was the total absence of grain in the market place, rather than inadequate entitlements. As I shall document, the paradox of money but no grain – due principally to a technological incapacity for the speedy large-scale movement of foodstuffs – was the converse of subsistence crises in the twentieth century.

Kano city suffered from several famines during the nineteenth century: those in 1863, 1873, 1884, and 1889 were slight, reflecting poor rainfall and partial harvest failures within the Emirate. The famines of 1847 and 1855, referred to locally as *dawara* and *Banga-Banga,* were much more severe and overwhelmed the limited capability of urban granaries and the regional grain trade to sustain Kano residents. In the *birni* during the 1855 famine: 'For thirty days at a time no gero (millet), no dawa (sorghum), wheat or rice were to be had in Kano. People ate vultures' (Gowers, NAK SNP 7K2151). Many of the rural famine victims (*yan cin yunwa*) drifted into the Emirate capital in the hope of locating short-term casual employment, a benevolent patron, or the doubtless erratic alms provided from state granaries. These Hausa migrants were, of course, readily assimilated into a niche in the urban system but northern refugees of different ethnic origins, referred to as *rafto,* established identifiable communities and wards in Hausa cities like Kano. Ultimately, these famines which afflicted the city – and in some instances the entire desert-edge – were crises of actual scarcity; they were, as Robert Brenner (1976) has suggested, crises typical of pre-capitalist modes of production reflecting the difficulty of dealing with major harvest fluctuations. Those who depended on the urban food market were subject to its volatile character and the burden of periods of absolute shortage. But during these periods of collapse due to harvest failures, coupled with the limits of grain movement, the wealthiest of households – those capable of storing large quantities of sorghum and millet – could be assured of survival and might strengthen their clientage networks.

2. PEASANTS, MERCHANTS AND FOOD SUPPLY: KANO CITY 1903–60

The British captured Kano in 1903 and established their headquarters in Nassarawa and Bompai, to the east of the old city. While the walled city and Fagge remained the domain of the Emir of Kano, Sabon Gari was laid out in 1913 for Southern Nigerians and the non-Nigerian Africans. Over the following half-century the township grew to include Western commercial and industrial areas and a large, sprawling built-up area to the east (Waje). But Kano maintained a dual character; the old city and its markets based on 'traditional' norms and polity, and the new city (Waje) synonymous with greater ethnic heterogeneity and 'Western' government (see Figure 5). Kano emerged in the colonial period as the premier city of the North. It quickly became a large, vital mercantile urban centre principally for the bulking and shipment of groundnuts and cotton, for the cattle trade and for a flourishing petty commodity economy.

The first British census was taken in 1911 and Kano city was estimated to have a population of 39,368.[9] A decade later a rather flimsy census estimated that there were 49,938 residents in Waje and the old city, an average annual rate of increase of 1·4%. The population of Waje in particular had grown from a few hundred to over 4,000 in 1921, a result of the influx of Europeans, Syrians and southerners following the completion of the railway from Lagos in 1912. Over the next ten years Kano grew rapidly as the groundnut trade expanded; the *birni* population increased by 36,251; roughly 6·1% per year. The city attracted large numbers of artisans, labourers, clerks and traders but the relative prosperity of the 1920s was broken by the cataclysmic collapse after 1929. There is some evidence that the old city was marginally depopulated in the 1930s, Waje conversely grew quite rapidly (9·1% per year between 1931 and 1935) after the completion of the rail connection to Port Harcourt in the South-East. In the post-war period both Waje and the old city expanded at between 4·0 and 4·8% per year but in the five-year period prior to independence, the growth of new industrial and manufacturing sectors drew new waves of migrants into Sabon Gari, Fagge and Gwagwarwa. Frishman (1977) estimates that Waje grew at the rate of 17·4% per year during this period, much faster than the old city. For the first time, there were colonial murmurings of an urban labour surplus. By independence the population of Kano city *in toto* (the old city plus Fagge and Waje) must have been between 170,000 and a quarter of a million (see Figure 6). The city had swallowed some 20 sq km of farmland since conquest, and was second in size only to Lagos.

The bedrock of the colonial state in Nigeria was peasant-based export commodity production, principally cocoa in the West, palm-produce in the East, and groundnuts and cotton in the North. For complex historical

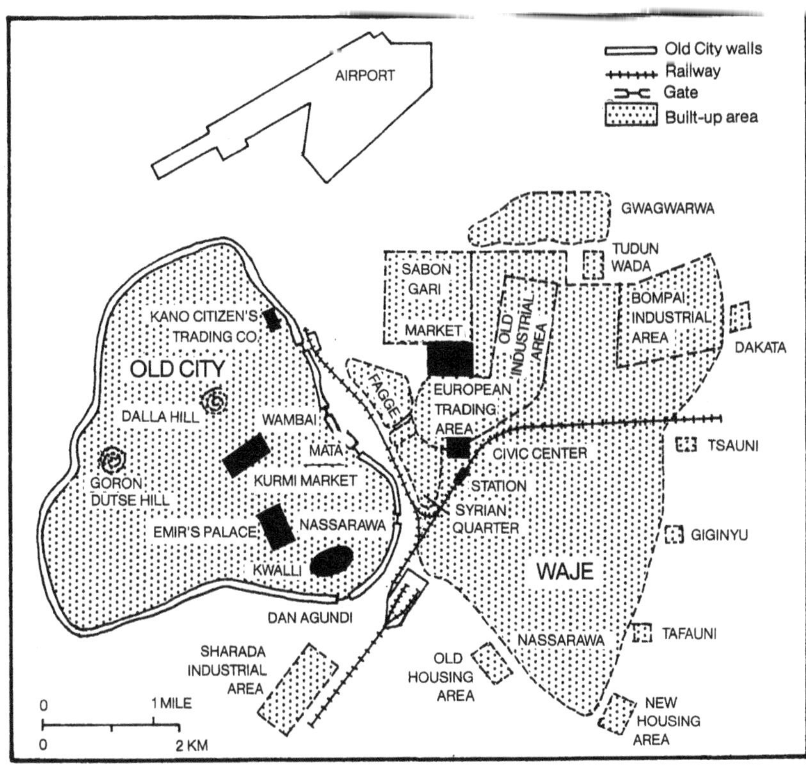

Figure 5 Kano: the Old City and the New *c.* 1960
Source Frishman 1977.

reasons, British imperialism in Nigeria did not entail an abrupt transformation of the prevailing relations of production in the countryside (Shenton 1985). Rather, the colonial state employed a series of rather blunt political and commercial instruments – for example, direct taxation, forced cultivation, expanded operations by European merchant firms – to 'induce' peasant producers to expand their output of those export commodities required by British industrial capital (Watts 1983).

Since land had been 'nationalised' in 1907, thereby effectively blocking land accumulation or large-scale plantation agriculture, either by Nigerian farmers or by European settlers, the household remained the fundamental unit of production. There were several important implications of this form

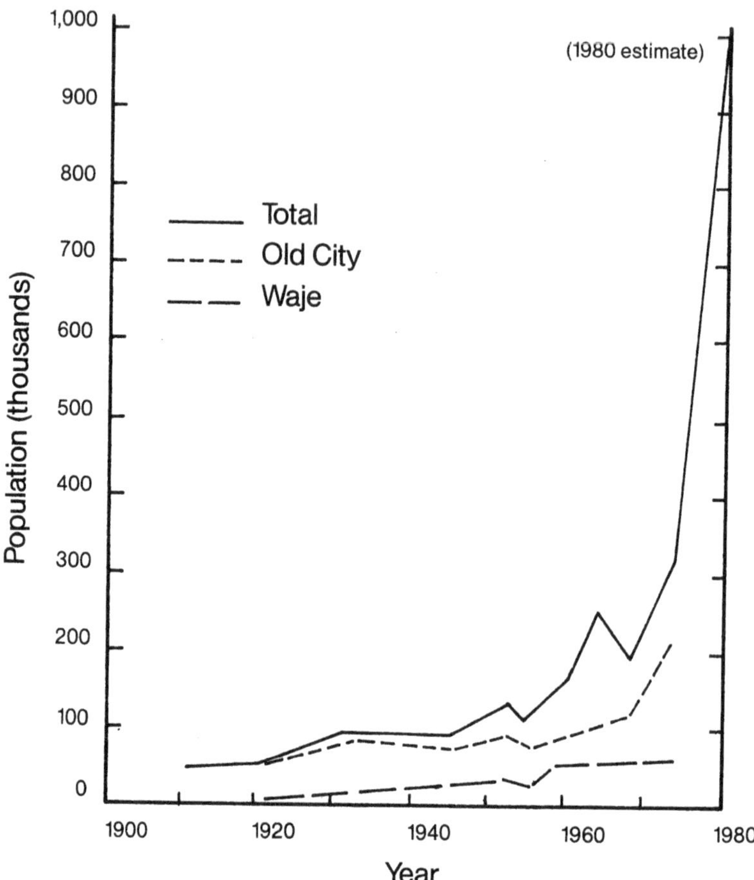

Figure 6 The population of Kano City, 1900–80
Sources Adapted from Frishman 1977; Federal Office of Statistics (Nigeria), population estimates, Lagos, 1981.

of political economy in the Nigerian context. First, fiscal self-sufficiency for the colonial state translated into a type of colonialism on the cheap, in which actual expenditures and direction by the colonial government was minimal, not least in agriculture, until 1945 (Watts 1983). Secondly, colonial overrule initiated the gradual expansion of commodity production and the incorporation of rural producers into a world economy and the global circuits of capital. The new patterns of price fluctuations, changing terms of trade, for the peasant farmer and the impositions of the state, especially taxes, broke the old pattern of famine and plenty and rendered many rural producers vulnerable to the uncertainties of both the market and the weather.

And thirdly, the development of capitalist relations in Nigeria did not involve a process of 'linear proletarianisation' (Kitching 1985) and was anything but smooth and predictable. And this was necessarily the case, because in any system in which a centralised state armed with superior but limited military, fiscal, and political capability presides over millions of individuated rural producers, the whole arena of labour control becomes highly problematic. Some peasant producers in Africa have managed to preserve a measure of autonomy and resist the market, by virtue of their control over their labour process (Hyden 1980). In Nigeria, peasant producers were increasingly drawn into market relations, yet the commoditisation of land and labour proceeded unevenly; hence many aspects of rural life were progressively eroded rather than washed away by an imperial deluge. As a consequence, after a half-century of colonialism the broad contours of Nigerian rural life in the 1960s remained intact.

Food provision, and specifically feeding a burgeoning city like Kano, must be located in terms of this general political economy, and specifically the intersection of the contradictory demands of the colonial state and the effects of expanding commodity production based on peasant households (see Spitz 1981). While the colonial state was interventionist – though not necessarily strong – it attempted simultaneously to ensure the continued extraction of export commodities for the merchant firms and ultimately British capital, revenue for its own reproduction, the provision of strategic raw materials (notably tin), and the maintenance of a class collaboration with indigenous elites as a prerequisite for political stability. These 'functions' were, however, not necessarily readily compatible with a reliable food system in spite of the improved communications infrastructure. Expanded export commodity production, under conditions of household production and limited wage labour, reduced the volume of food surpluses available for urban non-producers, especially in Kano Province. The grain traders found a partial solution by increasingly turning to the Middle Belt for staple supplies to provision the work force on the Plateau minefields, the rapidly growing cities and to meet the institutional demands of the colonial state and the Native Authorities. Regional marketing systems, however, had to meet most of the need. The state, given a general reluctance to meddle with the market, did not, indeed could not, systematise either food supply or famine relief in spite of the vulnerability of peasant production to environmental hazards such as drought. In the early years, the colonial administrators did maintain the *zakkat* but it was rapidly monetised (thereby dissolving native granaries). During World War II, the state temporarily resorted – with much political trepidation – to direct grain requisition from peasant producers. But for the most part, the strategic colonial food demands were met through private channels: the European firms and local merchant capital.

The vulnerability of peasant producers to price and weather fluctuations, the difficulties of controlling household production and the increasing control exercised by merchants over grain circulation all made for a highly volatile food system. Indeed the Kano food system *did* collapse altogether on several occasions and the city faced famine in 1908, 1914, and 1927 and lesser crises in 1943 and 1954 (Watts 1983). The colonial state, for reasons that transcend simple administrative incompetence, was neither able to regularise the conditions of pre-capitalist production nor to resolve the food security issue.

The fundamental problems of how Kano – and indeed the entire colony – was to be fed were highlighted early on in colonial rule in the period 1908–16. In 1908 there was a severe pre-harvest famine in Kano city and the surrounding districts – referred to in the North as *Yunwar Kanawa* – which persisted for roughly six weeks prior to the millet harvest following a poor harvest in the previous year. On that occasion, the Governor did not appeal to the Colonial Office for famine relief for the very good reason that he only learned about the famine in 1909 on reading the Annual Report. The acting Resident was unashamedly frank: 'Yes, the mortality was considerable but I hope not so great as the natives allege – we had no remedy at the time and therefore as little was said about it as possible' (NAK SNP 9 472/1909:18). The previous Resident, Mr Festing, while no less shamefaced in his candour, was at least better informed: 'the talakawa have suffered greatly . . . [due] to our not having realized how great was their want, and for the last few months the old people, the women and children have literally been starving' (NAK SNP 7 5490/1908:2).

The Kano cereal harvest had been one-third of normal; grain prices in the city leapt eightfold to 4*d* per pound and *zakkat* – still levied in kind at this point – made the taxes claimed by the NA 'as much as half of what was grown'. The failure spanned a fifty-mile radius of *birnin* Kano and was not simply attributable to drought as Festing himself acknowledged, but to 'the constant call for . . . labor and human transport' and to the predation of District Heads making up tax arrears. 'The big men cornered the market (for food) in Kano and the big towns and called on the talakawa to bring in more . . . it is of course not possible to prevent this' (NAK Kadminagric. 14429/1908).

In what came to be standard colonial rhetoric, the peasantry were accused of innate 'improvidence', squandering what little they had and refusing to provide for an indeterminate future. Alarming reports were spread about ensuing famine for the following year, prompting a rash of looting in the city but, as Festing confessed, it was 'by our own people'. In a sombre conclusion Festing surmised that he had been misled by a local *populus* of inveterate rural liars and duped by their administrative agents who hoped for a remission of *zakkat*. Duplicity aside, he was not mistaken in his observation that 'people have [never] realized how much corn has . . . come from the North nor that Kano Province . . . is hardly self-supporting as regards corn' (NAK Kadminagric 14429/1908). Kano was in part dependent upon *Yan Kwarami* plying millet from the North, notably from Gobir and Damagaram. These desert-edge granaries, which had been so critical in the pre-colonial period, were in fact in their twilight years; the French Administration was, as Festing remarked in 1908, in the process of regulating the now international grain trade, a trade which was undermined by the heavy capitation levies of the French and the growth of cotton and groundnuts.

The ability to feed Kano was clearly dependent upon the delicate balances within the northern Nigerian rural economy which, after 1908, had begun to look decidedly shaky. The impact of high rural taxes, conscripted labour for railway construction, the demands of the Plateau mine economy – which by 1912 absorbed 12,000 workers per month (Freund 1981) – and the effect of a new *taki*[10] tax which took land out of cultivation, all made heavy inroads into food production. On top of this, there was the overnight sensation of the groundnut trade. Purchases by the Niger Company vacillated around 1,000 tons between 1907 and 1911. 1913, however, was the watershed in groundnut cultivation: the completion of the Kano-Baro railway, the competitive prices offered by the firms, and the peasants' desperate need for tax money all conspired to produce conditions conducive to an enormous expansion in the area devoted to groundnuts, especially in the Kano close-settled zone. Bush and fallow farms were brought under cultivation, significant proportions of domestic labour time were devoted to groundnuts, and there were even rumours that cattle Fulani participated in the frenzied planting activities. Not without good reason, Emir Abbas of Kano expressed deep concern for the city's food supply. As Okediji describes it:

> The planting season of 1913 is remembered at Kano as an extraordinary year. Mohammad Ilori recalled a decline in planting of grain . . . the condition was such that . . . Abbas became worried about food supply . . . but the appeal (to grow more food) was not effective and before the end of the year there was shortage and traders tried to buy grain from non-traditional areas . . . at high prices. (Okediji 1973:194)

The production figures speak for themselves; a tenfold increase in marketed groundnut production in Kano Province between 1912 and 1913. Not surprisingly, in view of the underproduction of foodstuffs and the succession of generally poor harvests, very little of the groundnut crop actually appeared on the Kano market for the very good reason that the city and the countryside faced starvation.

The trigger for the collapse of the food system in 1914 was a severe drought during the 1913 wet season which caused a considerable harvest

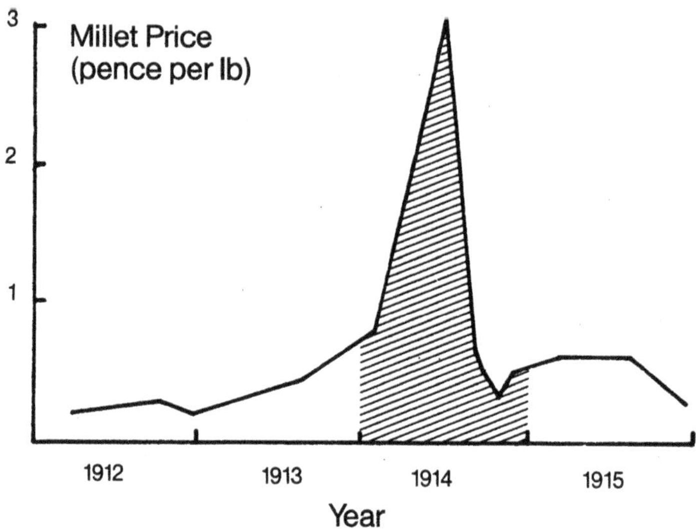

Figure 7 Kano Province: price of millet, 1912–15

short-fall throughout the Central Sudan. As domestic reserves were consumed or snapped up by grain merchants anxious to hoard for a price rise, millet of 0·1*d* per pound had risen to the unprecedented level of 3*d* per pound in July 1914. Prices in 1914 throughout the Province were uniformly high; of a sample of twenty rural markets, eighty-five per cent experienced grain prices at least ten times above the 1911 level (see Figure 7). Hogendorn (1978) believes that the relatively attractive prices offered by the firms earlier in the year induced the peasant to sell groundnuts, but in reality they were almost unobtainable: 'seven unshelled groundnuts cost one-tenth of a penny. . . . It is almost impossible to buy corn . . . and there is no longer any standard price' (NAK Katprof. 1 3146/1913).

The logic which reigned in the market place – the fact that cereals could not be obtained 'at any price' as the Kano Resident put it – simply meant that the vast majority were entirely without food and the means for obtaining it (NAK Katprof. 1 1978/1914). The urban poor and fixed-income groups suffered terribly from the food price inflation; the prevailing wage labour rate of 3*d* per day, which remained at that level into the 1920s, was clearly incapable of providing half the daily grain requirements for one individual at 1914 prices. The fixed annual costs for a Kano family of five during 1909 was roughly 11*s* which, at the zenith of the price spiral, would have covered grain costs for one and a half months only. The terms of trade moved sharply against the rural and urban poor, and in the ensuing instability, theft and highway robbery proliferated.

The colonial relief effort failed entirely to provide immediate and large-scale assistance. The 1,000 tons of imported rice, ordered several months too late and arriving in Kano in October 1914, well after the peak of the crisis, failed to provide any support; as a British person put it, in a marvellous piece of understatement, the relief was 'tardy'. Generally, the quantities of foodstuffs were so small in relation to the huge demands for free relief and market rigging that colonial relief, chaotic in its organisation right from the start, was doomed to fail miserably. The Administration failed to appreciate that the collapse of entitlements was inadequate even to cover subsidised corn purchase. One month prior to the arrival of official relief, millet actually reached the unprecedented level of 60*s* per bundle, in excess of 1*s* per pound, a price roughly equivalent to the prevailing sale price of one cow! Hastings in Kano laconically concluded that, as a consequence of the tardy relief,[11] 'the number of deaths . . . were very heavy' (NAK Katprof. 1 1978/1914).

From the ashes of the 1914 famine came the first real discussion of relief and a realisation that 'in the case of a [major] famine . . . the railway would be of little value' in saving the lives of 250,000 starving peasants and city dwellers (Secretary, KM 109/1920). A proposal offered by several Residents during this period involved the establishment of local granaries at each district headquarters; in practice, district self-reliance could be obtained through the conversion of the *haraj* tax to grain (NAK Kadminagric. 12805/Vol. III 1922). Naturally, to a colonial administration obsessed with financial parsimony such an effort spelled fiscal disaster or, even worse, the threat of welfarism, and hence Governor Goldsmith aborted the scheme on the grounds of its purported complication and its proneness to 'petty oppression'. In its place came a hefty dose of moral pressure 'to urge farmers to produce food' (KM 109/1922). Yet other voices spoke of a much graver situation:

> If you ever at all had a widespread famine in the northern provinces, your honor would find I fear that even a good deal more than 10,000 tons of rice . . . would be the proverbial pill to cure the earthquake. . . . I see nothing improbable in the occurrence of a famine on a really big scale . . . and large cash balances in the NA treasuries will not avert a serious calamity. (Clifford, KM 109/1922)

Indeed, such a calamity was only narrowly averted in Kano in the 1927 famine following a mediocre harvest, and compounded by the practice of 'hoarding' by merchants who had 'cornered the market' (Famine Relief Report 1927:12). In Kano city, four tons of grain were distributed at subsidised prices for several months but hardship was considerable as prices doubled in the open market between December 1926 and June 1927.

Mortalities were quite high, most especially in the rural districts (Watts 1983).

The colonial state never resolved the tensions inherent in a strategy based on smallholder production in which productivity per unit area remained quite low, while demands for staples and export commodities were simultaneously placed on households in which domestic labour was finite and for whom wage labour was often in short supply. The recurrent threat of food shortage forced the Government at least to reflect on a famine policy, but the first scheme (1927) was hardly ever referred to since the magnitude of the relief effort, the numbers at risk and the quantities of grain required vastly exceeded the capacity of the state. The highly ambitious scheme for five northern provinces would, had it ever been instituted, have cost more than *the total annual revenue* of the two wealthiest provinces in the colony! In a region in which drought was endemic, each year was something of a lottery and the period prior to the new harvest was invariably one of much concern. Seasonal price rises, usually peaking immediately prior to the upland harvest, were probably amplified by the deepening of commodity relations and the extended activities of merchants because the opening of the peripheral areas had the effect of evacuating harvest-time 'surpluses' which were snapped up by merchants capitalising on low prices.

The tensions within the food supply system were thrown into relief during the economic depression of the 1930s. The price of groundnuts fell by forty per cent between March 1928 and March 1931, recovering slightly in 1932 only to plummet again in 1934. In a desperate attempt to stabilise their income, peasants expanded their output, exports rising from 135,000 tons in 1928–9 to almost 200,000 tons in 1932–3. The cotton statistics show a similar trend. Yet in both cases direct tax revenue in relation to export price indices remained quite stable. Expanded production occurred in the traditional export zones but the railway and buying agent competition had pushed the frontier of cultivation deep into the peripheral districts. In the annual report for 1933, the Resident of Kano observed that: 'Economically, groundnuts provide a lifestream for the Province. A falling price last year stimulated the extension of cultivation. . . . Roughly this year it takes the peasant twice as much in groundnuts to meet tax and there has been little time left over for expenditure' (NAK SNF 7 21326 Vol. 1/1933). Pressures on producer incomes were such that in the northern divisions, pastoral Fulani were reported to have planted groundnuts to obtain tax monies.

The squeeze on producer income was felt by the firms as declining profits in their import trade. As more peasant surplus labour was appropriated for taxes by the colonial state, domestic demand for cotton, craft and European wares necessarily diminished. Faced with declining rural income, renewed commercial competition and a demand for cash in the countryside, the companies and middlemen responded with a huge expansion of the advance-crop mortgaging system to secure a satisfactory portion of peasant production. During the depression, the *yan baranda* system of cotton mortgaging flourished. The system involved the establishment of buying clerks ('*fuloti*') who were advanced money by the firms for whom they purchased on a commission basis. The *fuloti* in turn advanced to his *yan baranda* employees, who negotiated with individual producers and received a percentage of the *fuloti's* commission. The farmers took loans from the *yan baranda* using the cotton crop as collateral. The practical implications of the mortgage were that

> the dan baranda has . . . an absolute monopoly until the loan is paid off . . . the middleman takes advantage of this and the farmer sells one bundle of cotton before he is told that he has repaid the 10/- debt. Although the farmer could repay in cash, the lender will not take his money unless the crop has failed . . . [hence] the *dan baranda* makes money by manipulating the scales while the farmer is paying off his debt in cotton. (KM 234/1934)

As the tax burden absorbed an ever greater proportion of peasant income – estimated at thirty-eight to forty per cent of total income by Jacob (1934) – cash advances took the form of the middleman paying the producer's tax and withholding the receipt until crop delivery. According to a conservative estimate in the 1930s, middlemen were estimated to absorb at least twenty per cent of the total f.o.b. price for export commodities excluding usurious appropriations.

The proliferation of debt and the advance system hinged in many respects on the critical role of tax in the cycle of peasant reproduction. The vicious pressures effected by the conjunction of high tax and low export prices is clearly illustrated in Parsons's assessment of groundnut cultivation in Kano during the mid-1930s when export prices had fallen from an index of 100 in 1926 to thirty-seven in 1933: 'The average farmer producing 10 baskets of groundnuts was just and only just able to pay his tax out of his groundnut [revenue] this season, for 10 buckets at 9d is 7/6d [and tax] is . . . 7/-' (NAK Kanoprof. 20007/1937). Parsons observed that the price of groundnuts per bucket fluctuated from 5*d* to 1*s*, being generally higher near the railhead at Kano and Danbatta. The minimum price for groundnuts to cover tax was £12 12*s* per ton but every drop of 5*s* a ton below this amount meant almost 2*s* off the farmer's income. Farmers thus sold millet and sorghum regularly to cover tax arrears. In this sense, Hill (1982) is quite correct to suggest that food entering the grain trade was not a rural 'surplus' but quite mistaken to imply that this surplus extraction was a 'withdrawal' from the countryside, an abandonment which left the rural sector stagnant and unchanging.

Food availability in the 1930s was further complicated by the renewed demands of the Nigerian Chamber of Mines for forced labour and grain requisitioning, which had been irregularly continued since World War I. As a matter of principle, the state was generally loath to interfere directly in food distribution and direct assistance for fear 'the native would use his surplus corn for brewing beer or come to depend on the Government for assistance' (NAK Kadminagric 14429/1931). In view of the shortages, however, the Southern Provinces resorted to the European firms for cereal provision and quickly discovered that virtually all Residents, in a vain bid to hold what grain they had, prohibited the export of grain across provincial boundaries. Grain was difficult to acquire and Zaria Province certainly could not obtain the 2,500 tons it required for relief in its southern districts. To make matters worse, most of the provincial Administration had invested their capital in England during the 1920s and could not liquidate their assets for grain purchase because, as Resident Nash put it, '[the depression] would not appear to be a propitious moment for realizing investment' (NAK Kadminagric. 14429/1931).

In sum, the depression had three important consequences for food supply. First, the growth of indebtedness and the advance system resulted in both the reduction of food self-sufficiency among peasants and the export of food 'surpluses' to the cities by rural producers who, in the face of price collapses, had to make up tax demands through the sale of millet and sorghum. Secondly, the heightened vulnerability of peasants to food crises as a result of market and/or environmental perturbations brought periodic scarcities of food in the cities. And thirdly, the expansion of the groundnut trade drew Levantine traders – Moronite Lebanese – and southern merchants increasingly into competition with Hausa merchants; indeed, the Lebanese succeeded in displacing some of the middle-order Hausa buyers and gradually assumed an important place in the groundnut/grain supply networks. In 1949 the Northern House of Chiefs attacked these Levantine trading communities for their speculative grain hoarding in Kano (Paden 1973:323).

An important exception to the *laissez-faire* attitude to food supply occurred during World War II, which placed extra demands on subsistence, and the Government anticipated major problems of food availability. The administrative dicta handed down to regional and local-level officers were specifically to monitor price trends and promote provincial self-sufficiency in cereals as a matter of wartime policy. The Department of Agriculture rightly predicted a dislocation in international shipping and accordingly promoted a grain reserve scheme in anticipation of emergencies. In practice, the colonial programme during the war was a complex, and at times chaotic amalgam of price control and grain requisition coupled with a vigorous forced commodity production policy. The axis about which much colonial policy revolved was, in fact, food. By 1942, at least, an allocative priority for grain purchased by or on behalf of the Government had been agreed upon (NAK Gwandu NA 1253d/1942) which identified the military as the priority recipient, followed successively by the mines, government institutions and export and famine reserves.

The good intent of wartime policy was, however, jeopardised by the fact that the aims and needs of the colonial state and imperial capitalism were often at cross purposes. With one hand, the Government exhorted the Kano peasant to 'grow more food' and to aspire to the noble goal of surplus food production to supply obligatory grain requisitions, and with the other hand placed unrealistic demands on direct producers for compulsory cash-crop production and conscripted military and mines labour. As farm technology remained unchanged, forced labour siphoned from rural and urban areas alike to fulfil the wartime demands of the Plateau mines was of more than marginal significance. During the war the number of staple foodstuff consumers increased as the number of food producers correspondingly declined, further fuelling the inflationary spiral. The Kano labouring poor were especially vulnerable to wartime consumer inflation since the cost of living allowance (COLA) only emerged toward the end of the war.

The Food Price Control Scheme, initiated in March 1941 under the direction of A. P. Pullen, had the specific intention of stipulating and enforcing ceiling prices for domestic foodstuffs. The translation of theory into practice was, however, fraught with difficulties because as the Government had no real means of enforcing its dictates this would have necessitated another huge bureaucracy. In any case, many of the merchants and traders avoided co-operation since this was against their own interests.

> It seems clear therefore that it was more rational for the dealer to go idle than to get ruined by selling at an impossible price. He did not in reality go idle. He just ignored the price regulation and sold at a price which guaranteed his own profits. And as long as ready buyers were available, the market performed smoothly, although illegally. (Oyemakinde 1973:419)

Rather than resolving problems of regional food scarcity, price control introduced panic psychology (Olusanya 1973). Several northern provinces, keen to preserve whatever grain surpluses they possessed, made every attempt to limit the interregional movement of basic foodstuffs. There was a proliferation of legislation designed explicitly to forbid private sale of millet and sorghum to inhibit the movement of food commodities outside Native Authority (NA) frontiers. These restrictive measures, passed in Sokoto, Katsina, Kano and Bornu during 1942, reached absurd proportions when Sokoto officers seriously proposed monitoring, controlling and prohibiting each individual donkey in the interest of minimising the *kwarami* trade (NAK Sokprof. C.87/1943). On balance, there is every reason to believe that food price control actually compounded the wartime food crisis by discouraging farmers from further production. It was a naked attempt to milk farmers and dealers 'to feed the more vocal clerks and artisans in their arrogant municipal habitation' (Oyemakinde 1973:420).

A necessary adjunct to price control was grain requisition. In 1939 the

Food Control Commission had proposed large-scale grain reserves either through requisition of a then unspecified village storage scheme. Provincial Residents, like the Emirs, were generally in agreement that central granaries were 'impractical' and conductive to peasant complacency (NAK Kadminagric. VI 31657/1940). The farming household was to be the backbone of any reserve system in spite of the reticence of dissenting voices like the Kano Resident: 'What we have to provide for is a crop failure. I doubt very much whether . . . household reserves [given current demands] would be sufficient to cope . . . It might be possible to do so by increasing household reserves at the expense of cash crops but this is not desirable . . .' (NAK Kanoprof. 5/1 3404/1940). The Council of Chiefs actually passed a resolution in 1940 advising NAs in cash-crop regions to maintain reserves sufficient for government institutions. But it quickly became clear that requisition was the only realistic storage strategy, given wartime demands. Government agents or trading companies operating in the open market would have contributed to an already inflationary situation while raising grain prices would have drawn peasant producers out of cash-crop production altogether, which was a strategic part of the war effort.

During the early 1940s the colonial Government began to requisition grain on a small scale from peasant producers at fixed prices, particularly for military requirements and the Plateau work-force. From 1942 the requisition programme was stepped up in conjunction with the establishment of a Grain Bulk Purchasing Scheme (NAK CSO 26 36289/S.15 1942). By this time, the acute wartime strains were brought sharply into focus as a crisis arose over grain supply to the Nigerian mines. During 1942 provincial requisition targets were agreed upon and, in an attempt to minimise competition between minefield and military purchasing, the West Africa War Council established a government supply authority for both. In many cases, for example in parts of Katsina and Kano Provinces, requisition was simply too heavy and caused considerable hardship in the context of a poor 1942 harvest (Watts 1983).

Stimulated once again by the aversion of a local famine in 1943 (see Figure 8) and the self-evident shortcomings of *ad hoc* relief, the colonial Government resurrected storage and famine reserve policy toward the end of the war. Both the Governor and the Secretary to the Northern Provinces believed nonetheless that a famine reserve was out of the question: '[For] there is not the requisite amount of grain in the Northern Provinces to make the formation of such a reserve possible' (NAK CSO 26 36289/S.18). The Food Controller, Dr Bryce, opted for a city-based reserve designed to control urban food inflation and the threat of 'city-famine'. To this end, five permanent stores were erected in four northern provinces with a total capacity of 10,000 tons. In Kano city, the Emir was firmly against any central storage system which would, in his opinion, encourage dependency

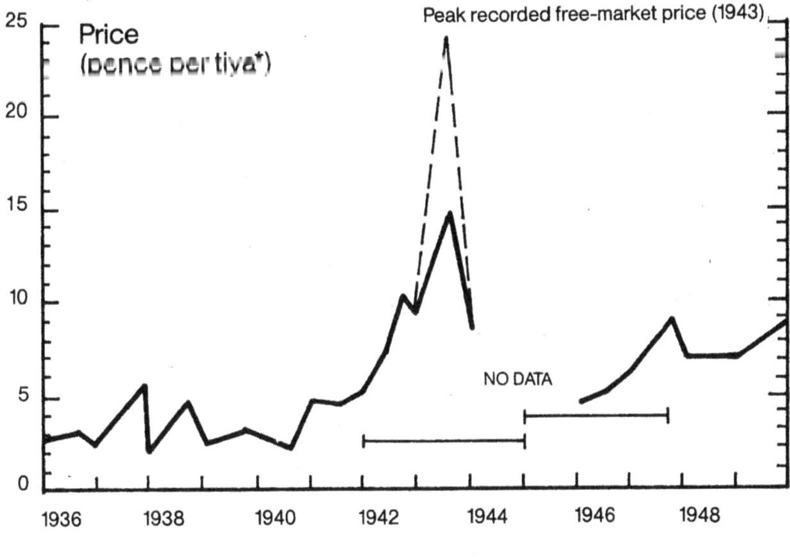

Figure 8 Kano Province: grain prices, 1936–48

on the state (NAK Kanoprof. 5/1 3404). A 2,000-ton granary was in fact constructed in Kano but ran at an enormous loss (£118,318 in 1944–5 and £117,784 in 1945–6) due to massive grain damage and rot, and losses on grain sales (NAK Kanoprof. 5/1 4975). In practical terms a reserve could only function on requisitioned grain, for government bulk purchases on the open market would have immediately hoisted cereal prices. Yet by 1946, requisition was already subject to much criticism. Among the peasantry requisitioning had always been unpopular in view of poor prices offered (see Figure 8) and for many bureaucrats any talk of village or state storage was coloured by their assumption that NA reserves bred smallholder complacency. Amidst much relief, during November 1947 the policy of grain requisition was abandoned, and with it the short-lived reserve system in Kano. As the Secretary of the Northern Provinces put it, the time had come when 'the laws of supply and demand should again be permitted to function'.

In the post-war period, groundnut production rose dramatically from 328,000 tons in 1948–9 to 872,000 tons in 1962–3. At independence, Kano

Province grew ten times more nuts (by weight) than in 1914 (Hogendorn 1978:134). Part of this growth was accounted for by the reduction of fallow and an intensification of manuring (up to 3·3 tons per acre, according to studies in the close-settled zone in the 1960s (Mortimore 1965)), but more importantly by a *specialisation* of commodity production. In some central Kano districts, up to fifty per cent of cultivated area was devoted to groundnuts (Mortimore & Wilson 1965) and up to thirty-eight per cent in surrounding provinces such as Katsina (Luning 1963). The outcome was, of course, a reduction in household self-sufficiency in foodstuffs; Smith's study of a relatively non-specialised rural area in Zaria in the late 1940s, for example, revealed that farming families purchased on average twenty-five per cent of total staple foodstuffs consumed in the household (1955:180). In Kano and Katsina this figure was unquestionably higher (Vigo 1957). In 1953 Governor MacPherson, disturbed by the spectre of a major food crisis in the Province in his address to Kano officials, proposed a 'nationwide drive for increased [food] production' (NAK Kanoprof. 5/1 7552). Grain was also scarce in Bornu, a traditional grain bin, by the mid-1950s, due to over-concentration on groundnuts, and according to Luning (1963), Katsina was importing almost one quarter of its provincial grain needs by independence.

In summary, the growth of a commodity economy from World War I had three important consequences in Kano. First, the search for staples – that is, the food supply catchment area – was pushed farther afield geographically. Millet and sorghum were again brought to Kano from South-Central Niger via the large border markets such as Maiaduwa (Collion 1982). This expansion, in conjunction with the inevitable local variability of the cereal harvest each year, produced enormous instability and variability in the Kano supply areas each buying season. Secondly, the groundnut boom, coupled with drought, produced an archetypical boom-bust pattern, both regional and local in scope. Exports grew, food crops were neglected and drought triggered a harvest shortfall which produced, in the following year, a return to foodstuff cultivation, but invariably accompanied by a price collapse due to over-production (Lennihan 1984:472). And thirdly, population growth, land shortage, and permanent cultivation compounded soil fertility problems, most especially in the close-settled zones on holdings already deficient in livestock droppings.

The political economy of colonialism in northern Nigeria was, to paraphrase Keith Hart (1982:25), a pre-industrial combination of indigenous smallholders and large European trading monopolies. As in all state systems in which a good deal of revenue came from the land because the majority of people lived there, the maintenance of centralised political control in Nigeria was invariably problematic. Ironically, in its attempt to deepen commodity relations through taxation, monetisation, and local merchant capital the colonial state often eroded its own fiscal and political security. Famines in this regard were not only crises of production but were equally seen as consumption crises – particularly in the market for European manufactures – and direct threats to political legitimacy. In her study of colonial Tanganyika, however, Bryceson (1981) has argued that without colonial commodity production the peasant 'would have [been] prone to sporadic food shortfalls' (p. 94) while the colonial state actually enhanced and regularised food supply through famine relief. I have argued conversely that the retarded form of capitalist development in Nigeria blocked any form of accumulation based on increased rural productivity and a transformation of the forces of production. Furthermore, commoditisation weakened in a variety of ways the position of rural producers in the face of drought; faced with the double burden of providing food and exports under conditions of market and climatic uncertainty, something had to give. In short, there were obvious structural contradictions within this system, as the famines testify. Under these circumstances the state did indeed intervene with relief to regularise supply, but the magnitude of the problem was far beyond the means of the colonial Government while administrative incapacity of the state apparatus left rural producers with little but their poverty. In contrast to Bryceson's suggestion, there were no regularising functions since expanded commodity production was achieved without raising peasant productivity and without a state capable of provisioning requisite food relief. In this sense, feeding Kano was much more problematic than many conventional analyses suggest.

MERCHANTS, NETWORKS AND THE POLITICS OF FOOD

Kano city's food supply in the colonial period was organically linked to, and inseparable from, two fundamental aspects of political economy in the Northern Region of Nigeria: the first is the dominant role of merchants' capital, associated with the deepening of commodity production among Hausa peasants; and the second is the political struggles between influential indigenous mercantile capitalists (usually closely aligned with Muslim clerics – *ulema* – and scholars) and the traditional office-holding aristocracy of the Caliphate who were converted under colonial rule into Native Authority bureaucrats. At independence in 1960, the Kano grain trade was dominated by huge, city-based, patrimonial merchant enterprises – referred to locally as the *manyan gari* – whose economic centrality in a number of mercantile and real estate ventures was matched by their strategic site on state executive and Kano emirate councils which they effectively controlled.

The rapidity with which groundnuts became a major source of revenue for the state, merchant and peasant alike has, of course, been claimed as a major triumph for local entrepreneurship (Hogendorn 1978). The

European firms could not readily operate in the countryside among millions of disparate peasants and accordingly, through the intermediary of the aristocracy, they worked through and with local traders who established buying points and outlets (canteens) throughout the export-producing zones. In the course of the growth of groundnut and cotton production, the numbers of traders and middlemen mushroomed. Some were already influential merchant families – such as the Dantatas and Sharabutus – who at the time of conquest were heavily involved in long-distance trade and large-scale grain production, but were badly hit by the loss of slave labour. Other 'new traders', however (including many from the South), latched themselves onto the European firms as rural agents. In the 1920s and 1930s the influx of Levantine merchants – the Arkle Brothers, Mohammed Chiranci, Aliyu Gwarzo – displaced some of the local Hausa traders from their hegemonic position in the rural areas, particularly in the realm of transportation. In sum, then, there was an explosion of mercantile activity which filled the interstices of the colonial economy, from the single Ibo bicycle trader advancing cloth on short-term credit, to rural women, to the commercial empires of Kano traders such as Sanusi Dantata, Musa Gashash, Uba Ringim, or Alhaji Danbappa.

The focal point of the Kano grain trade were the city merchants who not only advanced huge quantities of money each buying season to support the platoons of hamlet and village wholesalers, but also acted as local buyers even for the European firms such as UAC, who were often contracted by the state to supply the mines or the NA institutions. A brief analysis of the Dantata empire in the post-war period shows quite dramatically how these household-based systems were in effect patrimonial systems cemented by ties of clientage, association and kin and welded together by complex patterns of advances, debt and the circulation of money capital. Equally, the Dantata case is exemplary in so far as it demonstrates the diversified character of these enterprises; grain was simply one of several lines of activity through which buying, selling, accumulation and investment might be simultaneously undertaken (Shenton 1985, Lovejoy 1978a; Yusuf 1975). The Dantatas were important kola traders in the nineteenth century and owned large estates south of Kano city and in five other emirates. Sanusi and Aminu Dantata, however, operated in seven principal areas: groundnuts, merchandise, kola, livestock, transport, grain and real estate. They controlled in excess of 200 agents and primary clients in their buying networks and wholly dominated the Kano groundnut trade.

These networks were polyvalent in the sense that several commodities, including both grain and groundnuts, could be acquired through them and by essentially similar means. As Tahir (1975) has documented, the supply systems consisted of at least five distinct levels of operation subsuming factors, clients, agents and business associates; each level occupied a quite different social and political space and each was granted distinctive levels of autonomy from the patron (*uban gida*), namely Dantata himself. Firstly, there was a system of direct delivery from rural speculators (*madugai*) who approached and bought directly, using advances, from the farmers, usually within a locally restricted domain. Secondly, there were so-called 'balance men' (*yan balas*) of whom the Dantata system included six, who were clients or effectively quasi-kin; they received cash and goods advances, purchased and stored commodities for the patron, and received interest-free loans for their own operations. Thirdly, there were Dantata's close business associates (*abokin ciniki*), independent and significant trade magnates in their own right, with their own networks and clientage systems but who were nonetheless tied to Dantata through loans and, not infrequently, marriage. Fourthly, there were the independent agents who were of much lesser significance in terms of size and scale of operation, but were financed through short-term credits. And finally, there were Dantata's 'boys' (*yara*) consisting of kin and houseboys who, by virtue of trust and kinship, worked closely with the patron but often ran a small-scale independent trade line financed by Dantata himself.

These ramifying networks of clientage and religious affiliation allowed Dantata to operate over long distances and to seek out and support locally influential scholars and clerics who reinforced his trading dominance in local communities (Paden 1973). The centrepiece of the system was the diversified urban-based merchant who made use of clients and business associates, rural connections and local storage to acquire staples which could yield considerable speculative profits in view of the seasonally volatile grain markets. Conversely, the middle and lower-echelon traders who resided and operated in the rural communities gained access to urban credit and interest-free loans during the buying seasons, which were the basis for their own revenues of accumulation. The buying seasons by hamlet, village or inter-village wholesalers were a microcosm of the larger system since it too depended on local ties of clientage and a flourishing capital market.

A central mechanism for the acquisition of grain in the local networks was the advance (*falle*) system in which traders loan money to grain-short households during the pre-harvest period based on their estimates of harvest sorghum prices (see Clough 1981). In other words, based on the likely quality of the future harvest and prevailing grain prices, the trader will give the creditor half of the estimated harvest price for one sack of grain in return for a full sack in November or December. *Falle* functions, then, as a means by which traders acquire devalorised grain (for themselves and their patrons) as a source of speculation and as another variant of the patron–client relations which operates throughout the entire system (Clough & Williams 1983).

To condense a system of Byzantine complexity, one can say that at the lower levels of the hierarchy rural traders acting as buyers for themselves and distance patrons employed the advance system, combined with a shrewd understanding of the relative profitability and price variability among food and export crops, to acquire commodities cheaply. At each level, the traders operated through kin and clientage ties. The local traders not only shifted commodities depending on price differentials but also exploited these differences through space and time, engaged in short-term loans (*rance*), often to other traders, and invested their profits not only in lucrative local outlets such as livestock, which yielded speculative returns, but also in expanding their patronage systems on which the commodity system ultimately rested. The local merchant could thus enrich himself through siphoning off credit from wealthy urban patrons, while the city patron could use the skills, transport and storage of his client to amass large quantitites of staples. Traders not only made the most of the growing lack of self-sufficiency among peasant producers – on which *falle* rested – but also of the annual lottery of the upland harvest and the vulnerability of the colonial state itself; the latter depended upon indigenous merchants to supply the NAs and their institutions, and the tin mines on the Plateau. Until the 1930s the grain system utilised animal transportation such as donkeys and camels, and indeed thrived on it due to the intense local competition and cost-cutting among Hausa and Levantine merchants. But the advent of the lorry on a commercial basis from the 1920s and the extension of the branch rail lines in the 1930s facilitated the large-scale movement of grain, and gradually supplemented animal transportation for other than local trade.

Feeding Kano was, then, part of a mercantile nexus in which city-centred capital funded intermediary agents from inter-village wholesaler, to village or hamlet buyer, to the farmer himself, and each echelon was cemented by debt and clientage. Considerable profit was made from storing grain over time, exploiting seasonal rises in price, and from long-distance trade plying Kano markets from Lake Chad, Minna or southern Katsina. Yet the hegemonic position of mercantile capital and the particular logic of its operation had its own limits. First, *falle*, for example, required successful speculation but traders could not always rely on seasonal grain price increases; indeed, sorghum prices actually fell in the first half of 1936, 1948 and 1964 when prices generally were expected to rise. Secondly, the over-production of export crops and the actuality or threat of famine often forced farmers back into food production with the result that food crises were followed by periods of surplus and plummeting prices (and small profit margins). Thirdly, farmers often repaid loans in cash rather than grain, which precipitated considerable conflict and unrest in the countryside (NAK Kanoprof. 2401 Vol. III 1945). Traders had little recourse under Muslim law to take such cases to the Islamic courts since, in spite of rising indebtedness, granting loans on standing crops was usurious in practice and theory. And not least, commodity price crashes often found merchants with substantial advances in the countryside that could not be reclaimed; the crash of 1921, for example, was costly to many of the firms who regularly advanced in excess of £30,000 to the Syrian agents and Hausa buyers (*yan baranda*). By the same token, in some years large traders quite literally held some provinces up to ransom; in 1951 sorghum was re-exported from Kano city to rural markets, from which it was previously bought, and sold at much higher prices (NAK Kat. Cent. Off. W468/1951).

Grain was also political in another sense. The growth of Kano city, especially after 1945, moved hand in hand with growth of NA contracts for the provision of hospitals, the military, and so on. While there has been almost no work undertaken on the linkages between local politics and the merchants, the predominance of trade interests on the emirate councils by the 1940s suggests that the grain trade was quite explicitly politicised. More profoundly, to the extent that grain was one line of mercantile accumulation, it was part of the long-standing processes of political struggle and accommodation between aristocracy and mercantile classes. Some traditional office-holders had in any case worked in tandem with large merchants since World War I, acting as buying agents. But in the 1950s the emergence in Kano of the *yan siyasa* system – an alliance of merchants, bureaucrats and aristocrats – marked a watershed in the link between commerce and politics. It was this alliance which in the 1950s privatised the public purse, and siphoned off the surpluses built up by the Marketing Boards and the Northern Nigerian Development Corporation which were rapidly and systematically run down (see Watts, forthcoming). In the process enormous quantities of money were channelled into already existing mercantile networks and into other private hands by which the trading operations (in commodities such as grain) could be deepened and expanded.

These sorts of ties between politics and trade through contracting and so on have been, of course, a fundamental aspect of the post-oil boom economy and the relations between the new Local Government Authorities and local trade interests. However, for the colonial period – and indeed much of the recent past – the ties between NAs and merchants and, indeed, the histories of the merchant families themselves, is almost wholly unknown. To grasp fully the colonial grain trade, and that of Kano in particular, would certainly, then, entail a detailed understanding of those complex lineages of mercantile accumulation in the North through which the peculiar form of Nigerian polity and economy arose.

3. FEEDING KANO CITY 1960–80: EATING OIL AND BREAD

There is no reason to assume that independence in 1960 radically transformed the Kano food supply system. Several years later the Civil War did indeed have a major impact, however, both in terms of the disruption of supply and the disappearance of many southern merchants from the Sabon Gari township. The scarcity of staples during the war pushed some enterprising merchants further afield; Yusuf (1975) gives examples of traders who made their fortunes in the late 1960s, having brought cereals from Niger in periods of extreme scarcity and high prices. For the most part, however, staple foodstuffs flowed into Kano City markets from producing areas through a variety of channels and were handled by several different orders of market intermediaries. By 1965 very little millet and sorghum was moved directly via donkey by rural assemblers or producers from the peri-urban districts. Mortimore's study of donkey traffic at seventeen points around the city in the later dry season only accounted for two tons of grain (1970:381).

Mortimore's budgetary studies of six households in Ungogo District, five miles to the north of the *birni* walls, reveals that each family bought an average of three sacks of grain each year plus a variety of cooked foodstuffs. The Rural Economic Survey in 1966 also determined that in four peri-urban villages, purchases of sorghum and millet as a percentage of total consumption varied from eight to fifty-one per cent. The Kano close-settled zone, in other words, was not a major supply area for the city and several districts were clearly in deficit. According to Gilbert's (1969) survey,[12] however, at least ten per cent of sorghum and millet requirements of urban households was still met by their own production in 1965 on farms held by city residents within the close-settled zone; for wealthy households almost one quarter of domestic food was provided from owner-operator farms.

Particularly with the extension of rural feeder roads in the 1950s, marketable surpluses of sorghum and millet were drawn from more distant and hitherto isolated districts. The trade involved a large number of initial assembly operations and rural markets functioned as critical bulking and exchange foci. Sorghum, the most important of the northern staples, was imported into the Sabon Gari market from southern 'surplus' districts (Rano, Kiru, Gwarzo) within Kano Province but increasingly, urban wholesalers looked to southern Katsina, Zaria, Bauchi, and especially Niger, Benue and Gongola (see Figure 9). Unlike the case of sorghum, Kano Province was probably self-sufficient in millet in 1965 but Gilbert (1969) noted the relative decline of traditional source areas for the city – such as Hadejia, Kazaure and Gumel – and the emergence of more distant export zones, notably north-western Bornu, Bauchi and increasingly the Niger Republic. The trade in cowpeas was quite different in so far as the Province was a major exporter. Most surplus production originated from Gumel, Kazaure and Hadejia. The two other major staple imports – rice and *gari* (cassava) – were not grown locally to any extent, the latter being

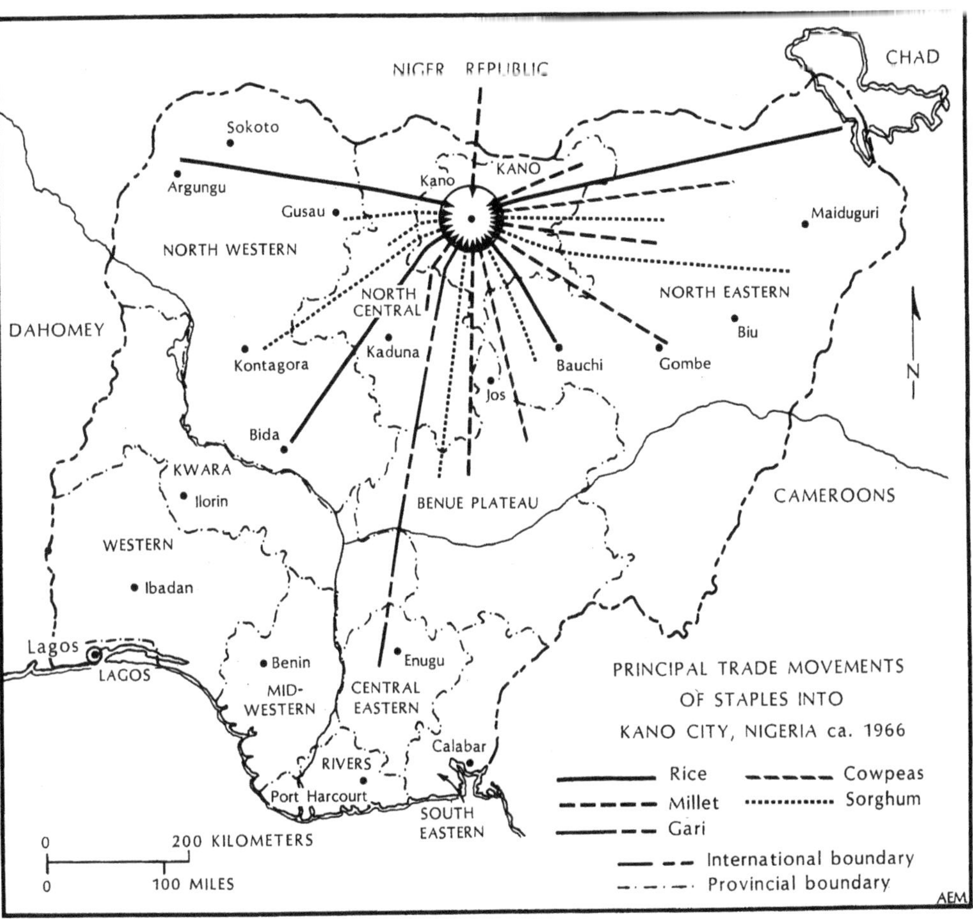

Figure 9 Principal trade movements of staples into Kano City, Nigeria ca. 1966
Source Adapted from Gilbert 1969.

imported principally by rail from the South-East. Rice of low quality was grown in the Hadejia river valley and Argungu (Sokoto Province) but large quantities of preferred Asian varieties were shipped from Bida and Minna (Niger Province), Plateau and Benue.

During the period in which Gilbert conducted his research, Kano City was growing, and indeed changing, quite dramatically. From the early 1950s onwards, the population of the old city and Waje increased by 4·8% and 25% per annum respectively; similarly between 1951 and 1965 the number of industrial establishments employing ten or more workers grew from eight to almost one hundred. This implied not only a deepening of the demand for wage foods among industrial workers, but equally among a significant informal sector work-force, and among the lumpen classes (*huntaye*), the cart pushers and the seasonally or transiently employed labourers. As a result, as Gilbert's work indicates, the growth of Kano City to something in the order of 250,000 by the mid-1960s intensified intra-regional trade within the Northern Region: 'Movements of cereals over considerable distances within the North are as important as movements North and South of gari, cassava and yams. . . . Kano [buys] . . . thousands of tons of guinea corn and millet every year from areas as far removed as Minna, Gusau and the Chad Basin' (Prest & Steward, cited in Hay & Smith 1970:55).

The regionalisation of the food trade did not of course threaten the hegemony of the urban merchants, the *manyan gari* of Kano. Nonetheless there were some fundamental developments in the post-war period. First, large-scale merchant capitalists were an integral element in the emergence of new forms of industrial production (textiles, food processing and later iron and metal-related industries) and hence there was a beginning of some sort of integration between the grain trade and nascent capitalist production. Secondly, the 1950s and 1960s was, as I have suggested, not only the period of the intensification of Nigerian political competition but of new forms of collaboration between the traditional ruling classes, the new political officials and influential merchants. The so-called *yan siyasa* class of the 1950s was a loose amalgam of bureaucrats, aristocrats and merchants centred around the nationalist politics of the North. Already by this time Kano merchants dominated local politics, and these alliances allowed merchants to gain access to state patronage, finance and contracts through local or regional government, and simultaneously permitted office-holders and politicians to enter into trade, or at least benefit from it. The growth of Kano City, for example, went hand in hand with increased government demands for staple foods to supply schools, hospitals and other institutions and this provided new opportunities for merchant and politician-bureaucrat alike. Embedded in this 'new politics' of the 1950s was the intense political competition and struggles between merchants, politicians and aristocrats which characterised the post-independence period; in practice this meant unregulated primitive accumulation within the state itself through what became known locally as the *kaso mu raba* ('kill and share') ethic (Tahir 1975). This corruption and privatisation of public monies permitted merchants – many of whom were involved in some way in grain trading – to expand and diversify their commercial corporations. In short, grain was increasingly subsumed within larger and more diversified enterprises, a process inseparable from the political struggles in the North and private accumulation funded by the (regional) public purse.

The rapid growth of Kano City after 1945 drew large numbers of southerners into the metropolitan areas. By 1965 the Sabon Gari ('new town') quarters housed some 40,000 people, at least seventy-five per cent of whom were Ibo. Furthermore, by the independence period the Sabon Gari market had surpassed the City (Hausa-Fulani) market in respect of the volume of business. Ibo traders controlled the importation of rice and *gari* from the Eastern Region and, according to Paden (1973:317), Ibo merchants had increasingly displaced middle and lower-class Hausa traders. The Civil War sharply terminated this southern presence. As Ibos fled in 1966, their trading niches were filled by Hausa and Yoruba middlemen. Similarly, the war brought the Lebanese into direct competition with large Hausa businessmen moving into light industry and especially transportation. Sanusi Dantata, Garba Bici, Haruna Kissim, Inuwa Wada and the Aminu Dantata syndicate all moved heavily into road haulage, a development facilitated by the inter-urban linkages of a greatly enlarged brotherhood system.

In briefly reviewing the period since the Civil War (1967–80), there have been two developments which, though they deserve a much more thorough analysis, are of signal importance in grasping the contemporary architecture of Kano's food system. First, Kano City was directly affected by the Sahelian famine of the early 1970s and famine conditions prevailed in a good many of the rural northern districts in 1973 and 1974 (see Watts 1983; van Apeldoorn 1981). Most commentators have noted that, in spite of two successive drought-induced harvest shortfalls, commercial channels kept even the remotest markets plied with grain. Whether the rural and urban poor could afford it was, of course, another question entirely. A somewhat unreliable set of price data suggests that inter-city grain prices varied widely and that the urban markets were quite volatile (though probably less so than more rural market-places). In Kano City prices of millet, sorghum and rice almost doubled within a single year (actually exceeding 100% in the case of millet in 1973). Over N3 million[13] was spent on relief by Kano State, principally for hard-hit rural districts, but this only amounted to 16 lb of grain per capita over a two-year period. Sharp price rises in wage foods in Kano City (for example from N4·50 per 100 lb bag of sorghum in the summer of 1972 to N16·50 in the summer of 1974) were unaffected by tardy attempts at market rigging and must have made large inroads into the already fragile budgets of the urban poor. The Nigerian state was completely unprepared for such a food crisis; government-held grain reserves were small, and the relief efforts quite deficient.

The second and much more fundamental development concerns the radical restructuring of the Nigerian economy since the oil boom (Watts 1984; Bienen 1983). Oil-based accumulation after 1973 provided the material basis for a considerable growth and centralisation of the Nigerian state and an expanded role in the productive sectors of the national economy. The recycling of oil rents funded new state bureaucracies (by 1980 the state wage-bill stood at roughly N1 billion, about thirty-five per cent of recurrent expenditures), a dramatic increase in middle-class incomes, a commodity boom of imported European consumer goods and, not least, an urban infrastructure explosion of some magnitude (see Watts & Lubeck 1982). The urban construction boom – and an impressive rate of growth in the import substitution manufacturing sector – drew labour from the countryside and provided a further boost to the informal sector. This transformation is perhaps best captured in the extraordinary growth of Kano City itself. By 1980 it had a population of perhaps one million and a formal sector work-force of 50,000, a proliferation of foreign multinationals and all the trappings of unplanned urban development: real estate speculation, urban violence, chaotic expansion, and saturated city services. The oil boom also provided new avenues for private accumulation, and generated a bourgeois class, deeply imbricated in commerce, real estate, and the exercise of administrative and managerial skills, although large-scale commercial capital has also moved, if tardily, into manufacture.

The oil boom was also marked by the sluggish performance of agriculture: export production had effectively collapsed by the mid-1970s, food production grew slowly at best, food imports grew by 700%, and real food output per capita over the period 1970–78 perhaps fell by 1·5% per annum. Per capita food production in 1981 was eighteen per cent below that of 1967–70 (Hunt & D'Silva 1981). The decline of the traditional export crops, coupled with the spectacular growth of petroleum revenues, naturally implied a transformation in the composition of Nigerian exports and the structure of GDP; in 1980, agricultural exports (by value) constituted only 2·4% of the total Nigerian exports; the corresponding statistic for oil was 96·1%. The growth of staple foodstuffs imports was astonishing. In 1980, Nigeria, with a population of perhaps 100 million, was simultaneously Africa's largest producer and importer of food. Aggregated to include food, live animals, vegetables and fats, food imports increased faster than all other import categories, rising from $130 million in 1971 (8·6% of the total) to $1·794 billion (14·2% of the total). By 1981–2 cereal imports alone amounted to 2·3 million tons. In 1970, rice imports were negligible; by 1978, imported rice totalled $92 million. Over ninety per cent of the wheat consumed in Nigeria, fifty per cent of the rice, and twenty per cent of the corn is currently imported. According to the most recent statistics (1981/2), the import bill for food is $3 billion, accounting for roughly seventeen per cent of the total caloric supply. A significant proportion of the caloric deficit is made up of cheap wheat and rice surpluses imported from North America.

Quite naturally all of this implies a complex restructuring of the Kano

City food economy. I shall attempt to illuminate some of this complexity by examining two strategic food commodities – wheat and rice – which are, and continue to be, emblematic of the politics of the oil boom and the changing political economy of food supply. The critical shift to imported staples after the Civil War prefigures the centrality of food in the politico-social dynamics of oil-based accumulation in Nigeria.

A. WHEAT, WORKERS, AND THE BREAD INDUSTRY

It seems probable that wheat was first introduced into West Africa as a result of Arab influence some time around the twelfth century. Certainly by the eighteenth century it was present as a luxury crop in Kano and Bornu, cultivated on the farms of office-holders generally in peri-urban lowland gardens or on alluvial terraces blessed with residual moisture in the cool dry season (November to March). The emergence of bread as an urban staple, however, only commenced in the early twentieth century with the settlement of Christian Brazilian repatriates in Lagos. Spurred by the growth of urban wage labouring classes, bread consumption and commercial bakery shops gradually spread inland from Lagos, Warri and Calabar. After 1915, due in large measure to technical and marketing innovations by the West Indian entrepreneur Amos Wynter-Shackleford, large-scale production of bread fuelled flour imports which actually doubled during the 1920s. Yet until the end of World War II, flour and wheat imports were quite insignificant, while the market for bread products remained relatively paltry, being confined particularly to the major southern cities.

The Nigerian baking industry and the significance of bread in urban diets were transformed after 1945. Following twenty-five years of stagnation, between 1946 and 1961 the production of bread increased nineteenfold in Nigeria as a whole; the value of flour imports over the same period rose from 136,000 to 13·232 million (see Table 2). At least ninety-eight per cent of the imports were high-protein North American hard-wheat flours. At the time of independence, the bread industry represented a dynamic manufacturing sector with a gross output valued at seven million pounds and ranking third among Nigerian indigenous industries in terms of employment and value added.

In spite of the growth of the wage food industry, it is with some trepidation that one moves to establish the role of bread in feeding Kano. According to Kilby (1963:14) there were five bakeries in Kano in 1961 – all mechanised, employing roughly fifty persons – each owned and operated by southerners and presumably catering to a largely Yoruba and Ibo demand in Sabon Gari. Twelve per cent of national flour imports (7,194 tons) was consumed in the North, of which roughly 900 tons were consumed in Kano; assuming all wheaten flour was used for bread production, this would yield

Table 2 Flour imports into Nigeria, 1900–82

Year	*Quantity (tons)*	*Value (£)*
1910	1,454·6	21,819
1930	4,000·0	108,000
1940	1,500·0	31,000
1946	2,800·0	96,000
1950	12,200·0	672,000
1955	28,950·0([a])	1,766,000
1961	61,150·0([a])	3,232,000
1970	266,400·0	15,400,000
1982	1,605,000·0	250,000,000 (est.)

Source Helleiner (1966) Kilby (1963); World Bank (1985); *The Economist* (1981).
Note (*a*) Data provided by the *Nigeria Trade Journal* (October 1961) is inconsistent with the Helleiner–Kilby data. Flour imports in 1955 and 1961 were 48,000 tons and 96,000 tons respectively, according to the former source.

a per capita flour consumption of 11·9 lb per year in the Kano metropolitan areas, i.e. perhaps a dozen loaves per capita per annum.[14] Wheat consumption was certainly skewed with respect to ethnicity but also with regard to economic status since bread was on average between five and six times more costly per calorie than traditional grains. Among labourers, artisans and clerks, bread amounted to between one and five per cent (according to income category) of total household food outlay in 1958–9 (see Table 3). In other words, outside the Sabon Gari 'middle income' wage-earner community, bread was of quite limited importance as a means of subsistence.

Doubtless a good deal of daily bread production was consumed in and around the Kano lorry parks and as a 'luxury' snack between main meals. In any event, whatever the precise significance of bread for Kano prior to the Civil War, wheat flour was wholly of North American origin. The 1,200 tons of soft wheat cultivated in Kano Province and other northern locales was of limited utility because of its low baking qualities and because its average price ($250 per ton in 1960) was almost 300 per cent in excess of US

Table 3 Urban consumer expenditure on bread in Kano and Lagos, 1958–9 (s) (as % of total household cost per month)

Town	*Labourers*([a])		*Artisans*([b])		*Clerks*([c])	
	(*s.*)	(%)	(*s.*)	(%)	(*s.*)	(%)
Kano	1·1	1·0	6·5	5·4	6·2	4·9
Lagos	5·8	5·9	8·3	6·1	9·1	5·8

Notes (*a*) Average income per person per month 50–80 *s*.
(*b*) Average income per person per month 100–10 *s*.
(*c*) Average income per person per month 100–50 *s*.
Source adapted from Kilby (1963:30).

wheat landed at Lagos.

A second, and more profound, transformation in the bread industry occurred after the Civil War and most especially during the period of the oil boom (see Beckman & Andrae 1986). The growth of food assistance during the period of domestic civil strife accounted for the growth of wheat imports in the late 1960s, but it was the consolidation of oil-based accumulation that provided the central context for the deepening of the urban bread market during the 1970s. Between 1970 and 1980 the volume of wheat imports grew by 600%; the annual rate of growth between 1965 and 1980 was 16·72%. By 1981 wheat and flour imports accounted for N231·6 million, almost fifteen per cent (by value) of the total food import bill. Of wheat imports during the year – just in excess of one million tons – seventy-nine per cent originated from the United States. The spiralling of wheat imports was, of course, not a simple function of the growth of urban incomes after 1973 but of a complex set of changes in the Nigerian political economy. Favourable oil-wheat terms of trade, an over-valued *naira,* the cost squeeze in domestic agriculture (due to a rural labour shortage as a consequence of the rapid growth of urban employment), and the importance of the food import trade as a source of rents all contributed to the 'wheat revolution'. The effect was that wheat, grown under highly mechanised production conditions in capitalist states, emerged as a central pivot of Nigeria's food policy to sustain the rapid growth of import-substitution manufacturing, most especially in the two principal industrial growth centres of Kano and Lagos. Between 1974 and 1980 official price controls on wheat flour kept the domestic price level stable at N240 per ton over a period in which consumption rose at twenty-five per cent per annum.

Kano contributed to the meteoric growth of the baking industry in the country as a whole (see Table 4). By 1980, there were 467 bakeries in Kano State (226 located in the metropolitan area) employing 5,697 persons, making this the largest single employer of labour in the State with a total annual wage bill of N25·6 million. The industry produces at least N284,000 worth of bread per day – over N100 million each year – two-thirds of which is destined for the Kano City market. All nine 'modern' bakeries, i.e. those

Table 4. Bread production and consumption in Kano City, 1961–80

	1961	*1980*
Bakeries	5	226
Bakeries employing 10+ persons	2	120[(a)]
Milling capacity per day (tons)	0	1,012·5
Per capita wheat consumption p.a. (lbs)	11	95
Average household expenditure on bread per month (*s*)	0·35	41·4

Source Computed from statistics provided by Kilby (1963) and Kiyawa (1981).
Note (*a*) This is an estimate computed from statistics in Kiyawa (1981:169)

employing automated mixers, electric ovens and cutters, are located in metropolitan Kano and one of the largest – the Golden Bread Company – produces between 5,000 and 10,000 loaves per day (Kiyawa 1981).

Since 1975, Flour Mills of Nigeria Ltd (FMN) has operated a mill in Kano which currently has a milling capacity of over 1,000 tons per day. Almost ninety per cent of their production is devoted to bread, which is supplied to bakeries either directly or via wholesale agents. The FMN milling group is a joint venture between Federal and State Governments and a US-based shipping company (The Southern Star) which also handles all wheat-freighting to Nigeria. Mills operate through a system of licensed sales agents who collect and distribute flour to bakeries at controlled prices. In practice, however, licences are sources of speculative profits and in 1980, when the official wheat flour price stood at N276 per ton, the actual open market price was N566 per ton. Some bakeries are in fact licensed agents and can obtain flour at the stipulated price of N14·60 per 50 kg bag. Many other smaller enterprises, nonetheless, are discriminated against within the networks of middlemen and agents and accordingly produce bread products of much lower quality (and lower nutritional value) at higher input prices.

In spite of general wage food inflation throughout the 1970s – the composite consumer price index for staple foods, for example, increased from 100 in 1975 to 349 at the end of 1983 – white bread remained quite cheap, retailing at fifty *kobo* or less per loaf in the early 1980s. As a consequence, not only did bread progressively undermine traditional cooked cereals such as *taushe* and *waina* but quite rapidly became a staple for the Kano popular classes. The explosion in the number of 'tea sellers' (*yan shayi*) who provide tea, bread and Carnation milk to the formal sector workers of Fiat, Union Carbide, Lonrho and Dunlop and the thousands of informal economy labourers throughout Kano City is itself a measure of, and indeed a primary vehicle for, the radical change of taste and consumption among urban dwellers during the oil boom. According to a survey conducted by Kiyawa (1981:94) in 1980 in metropolitan Kano a family of six spent an average of N1·38 on bread each day. Using different statistics based on production, I have estimated that the per capita consumption of wheat products in Kano is almost 100 lb per year, only slightly less than in Lagos.[15]

Wheat is cultivated as an irrigated dry-season crop in northern Nigeria and, partially in response to the growing demand for bread products and the famine, has undergone considerable expansion since the late 1960s and early 1970s through expensive state-sponsored river-basin development schemes (Sokoto-Rima, Lake Chad, Hadejia-Jamaare) and medium-size perimeters (for example, the 1,560 hectares in Kano State by 1975). Even under the revised Fourth National Development Plan, irrigation absorbs thirty per cent of all expenditures in the agriculture sector. Import substitution wheat production has yet, however, to emerge as a major supplier for the Kano bread industry. The Kano flour mill is wholly supplied by North American imported hard wheat; the 600 tons produced from the Kadawa, Ringim, Hadeija and Jakarade schemes in Kano State were used entirely in the local cooked-food economy (Knipscheer 1980).[16] In spite of the projected growth of irrigation in the North to 345,000 hectares by 1990 (of which 163,000 hectares will be devoted to wheat production), it is entirely unclear how adequately such schemes will fulfil the needs of the domestic baking industry. Currently, due to a variety of technical, bureaucratic and pricing reasons (Adams & Grove 1984), wheat production costs are uncompetitive internationally and wheat farmers accordingly receive enormous subsidies.[17]

Irrigation, nonetheless, continues to be a Federal priority for public investment – the expense of irrigation schemes is attractive as a source of private accumulation – but the domestic supply response for wheat remains sluggish. Following the retrenchment of oil production in 1982 and the austerity budgets thereafter, the Nigerian Government reduced trade licences and limited wheat imports, but within a year ten of twelve flour mills were effectively closed and the price of bread had increased three times (*Africa Economic Digest*, 17 June 1983). By 1984 the import duty on wheat had been reduced and some of the mills reopened the political demands for self-sufficiency because, in the words of the Head of State, 'bread has become the cheapest staple food of our people' (*Quarterly Economic Digest*, 3, 1984:13).

B. RICE AND THE RENTIER STATE

At independence Nigeria was self-sufficient in rice. Local (*O. glaberrima*) and Asian (*O. sativa*) rices were grown throughout the country but most especially in the Plateau, Benue and Niger Provinces and throughout the Eastern Region. In 1965, Kano City was supplied with local rice – a staple generally not preferred on the grounds of taste – from the Hadeija Valley and Wudil within the Province and further afield from Argungu (Sokoto), Bornu and Bauchi. Higher quality *sativa* rice was, however, imported by road and rail from the southern export zones in Plateau and Benue Provinces and in particular from the Bida and Minna Regions in Niger Province. Gilbert (1969:39) estimates that in excess of 3,000 tons of rice entered Kano by rail alone from these three provinces. A survey by the same author in 1966 estimated that in Kano City, rice constituted sixteen per cent of total caloric intake per capita per day (1969:23). While there is no available data on food expenditure for Kano, a consumer survey conducted among Hausa-Fulani households in two other northern cities (Kaduna and

Zaria) is probably suggestive (see Table 5).

The domestic rice situation was radically altered after 1970. While local production probably increased it was incapable of meeting growing demand. A large part of this internal demand reflected the explosive growth of urban centres following the oil boom and the rapid development of construction and light industries which siphoned labour from the rural sector. Nevertheless, the spectacular increase in imports (see Table 6) also signifies a preference for rice among Civil Servants and private sector employees who benefited from the oil boom salary adjustments. Between 1970 and 1980 per capita annual consumption of rice in Nigeria increased from 2·9 to 7·8 kg, an annual growth rate of 10·7%. Over the same period the volume of imports grew at an astonishing 73·97% per annum. In 1982, of a total food import bill of N2 billion, rice constituted twenty per cent by value, that is, slightly in excess of one million tons. Almost fifty per cent of this volume – perhaps fifteen per cent of total rice consumed – was supplied by the United States.

As I have already implied in the case of wheat, the reproduction of Kano labour through the increasingly dominant role of the international rice trade cannot be seen entirely in terms of over-valued currency, favourable terms of trade or the sluggish response by domestic producers in the face of

Table 5 Monthly expenditure on food staples in Zaria and Kaduna, 1955–6

Food	*Expenditure* [(a)]	*% of expenditures*
Rice	9·99	10·39
Gari	11·59	12·06
Yams	10·63	11·07

Note (*a*) In shillings per average household of 3·19 persons.
Source Adapted from Hay & Smith (1970:23).

Table 6 Rice production and imports, 1970–83

Year	*Domestic production ('000 MT)*	*Imports ('000 MT)*	*% of total supply from imports*
1970	284	2	0·69
1972	310	6	1·93
1974	348	8	2·29
1976	406	103	25·10
1978	550	770	58·47
1980	725	387	34·84
1983	1,000 (est)	700	25·30

Source USDA (1981:22); World Bank (1979); *Economist Quarterly Economic Review*, (First Quarter 1981); World Bank (1985).

limited price incentives and labour shortages. Rather – and here rice is a pre-eminent case in point – all import trade was converted into a form of rent-seeking; indeed food supply was coloured by the debilitating political economy of corruption that has immobilised state operations in Nigeria (Watts 1984). The granting of licences or import quotas by the state was the *de facto* issue of money. Accordingly established traders, and later politicians themselves operating through para-statal agencies, captured enormous rents through the food import trade. In the case of rice, imports were regulated up to 1978 through a gradually decreasing series of tariffs and thereafter through quotas and licences. In either case, however, rice landed at Lagos at thirty to fifty per cent of the price of domestic rice and was subsequently sold on the open market for at least thirty per cent above local rice prices. The scandalous 'rice-gate' affair in 1982 in which several high-ranking politicians were involved in illegal rice imports, price-rigging and profit margins in excess of 120% was perhaps the most visible aspect of the extreme privatisation of state 'regulated' redistribution of oil dollars. The result, of course, was simple: 'cheap' imports turned out to be quite expensive to consumers and, in the case of Kano City, the price of rice increased by 560% between 1971 and 1980. Yet in spite of this inflationary trend, rice proved to be economically attractive relative to other staple commodities such as *gari*, yams and beans. By the late 1970s, rice had established itself as one element in the food staple triumvirate in Kano (see Table 7).

While there are no recent consumption surveys available it is probably safe to assume that nearly twenty-five per cent of the total caloric intake among Kano City residents is provided by rice, half of which is imported. As in the case of wheat, the expansion of river-basin development is designed in part to fulfil domestic demand but costs of production remain high and variable. Imports were banned in 1979 in order to stimulate local rice production but prices tripled within several months and new licences were issued. Quotas have been progressively eased since 1980 and imports topped one million tons for the first time in 1982.

Table 7 Prices per 1,000 calories by foodstuff in Kano, 1965–79 (kobo)

Commodity	*1965*[(a)]	1978–9
Rice	2·98	18
Sorghum	1·24	10
Millet	1·24	12
Cowpeas	2·07	20
Yams	no data	60
Wheat flour	6·20	10

Note (*a*) This is a conversion from pence based on the prevailing rate of exchange in 1972 (one Nigerian pound = one naira (100 *kobo*).
Source ILO (1981: 229), Gilbert (1969: 53).

CONCLUSION

. . . a political or statist parasitism can survive only so long as it does not actively oppose or seriously inhibit the larger social process upon which it is parasitic. If it does so, either the society is plunged into crisis, or the parasitism comes under heavy challenge . . .

Edward Thompson, 1978a (p. 375)

The question of how Kano City has been fed is self-evidently inseparable from the wider issues of the jagged rhythms of mercantile accumulation in northern Nigeria and of the forms of colonial and post-colonial politics. The staple catchment area supplying Kano naturally expanded after 1903 as the export commodity boom commenced and as transport improved. New areas of commercial foodstuff production grew up, perhaps in part due to the efforts of millions of freed slaves and in response to the demands of growing cities, the mines and government institutions, but food imports constituted (until World War II at least) a relatively insignificant part of total caloric supply. If Kano was fed locally, the basis of this system was nonetheless unstable because of the double burden shouldered by peasant producers incapable of radically improving farm productivity, and of a colonial state unable to mediate and manage the multiple conflicting demands made by the Colonial Office, the European firms, indigenous elites and mercantile interests and simultaneously meet its own concerns with administrative efficiency and political stability. These tensions, which directly affected food supply in a region that suffered from recurrent drought, were never adequately resolved; the colonial state did not regularise peasant production, the famine relief system was hopelessly inadequate and indigenous merchants could make use of seasonal swings in grain prices to capture considerable profits and often corner the market. The food system occasionally collapsed and famines occurred; after 1914 they were principally rural in character: those who produced were those who died. Grain prices in Kano did rise dramatically – in 1943, for example – and low-income wage earners (the *ci-da guminka* or 'feed with your sweat' class) suffered considerably.

The entire grain and tuber system remained in private hands and large city-based merchant capital controlled the fountain-head of systems of rural buying and speculation, all sealed together by ties of credit, clientage and religious affiliation. As the colonial period wore on, however, a rural market for foodstuffs also appeared as larger segments of the peasantry – especially in the close-settled zones – were unable to feed themselves from their own domestic production. Yet the logic of mercantile interests combined with a patrimonial state were ultimately regressive forces and the peasant sector remained 'backward' and relatively stagnant; absolute rather than relative surpluses were creamed off by merchants investing in trade and patronage rather than in production. This status was already problematic at the national level by the 1950s, with the constant call for 'growing more food'.

In the oil-boom period the Kano food system has changed quite dramatically. Feeding Kano is now in some measure dependent upon international circuits of capital because large quantities of wheat and rice are annually imported as wage foods for city workers, labourers and Civil Servants. This has, however, created new links between politics and commerce because of the focal role of the state. The old merchants and businessmen remain the *manyan gari* of Kano City but the oil boom also spawned other diversified contractors, eager to capture rents from the food import trade. Food supply, in other words, is subsumed within a larger process by which the state becomes a sort of economic base; infrastructure and superstructure are thus fused together, producing the political parasitism referred to by Thompson (1978a:375). In contrast to the nineteenth century, when a sort of parallelism existed between *zakkat* and private trade, the post-colonial era has witnessed a collapse of this distinction as private accumulation has occurred through state directed food policy.

I began this chapter with a note on the 'imagination' of history and it is perhaps appropriate to close with a suggestion that food supply is no less subject to this 'historical logic', as Edward Thompson calls it. First, the tumbling of oil prices coupled with heavy debt service has plunged Nigeria into a major fiscal crisis since 1982 and this austerity will have important implications for the food sector. One tendency has been the encouragement by the state of large-scale investment (both domestic and foreign) in food production; another has been the partial withdrawal of the public sector from the northern irrigation schemes. All this suggests a dynamic political economy of food. And secondly, the fact that food prices for domestic cereals have increased faster than the consumer price index since the mid-1970s has almost certainly resulted in the commercialisation of food production in some areas covered by the 'Green Revolution' projects. Clough (1981) has demonstrated how sorghum production oriented towards the Kano market increased in one such area in southern Katsina. This commercialisation has occurred, however, in the context of a deepening of the market for staple foods in many rural areas as segments of the land poor are unable to fulfil their own food needs (Watts 1983). Furthermore, almost none of these cereals have entered the government food channels (The Grains Commodity Boards); indeed until 1984, the Board had bought no cereals at all (World Bank 1985). At the same time, one of the most striking aspects of the agricultural landscape in northern Nigeria in 1985 is the relatively recent proliferation of maize cultivation.

What is so surprising is how little is known of these developments in a country that after all accounts for a third of the population of sub-Saharan Africa. The agrarian question is a fundamental part of the political and economic architecture of contemporary Nigeria and in spite of much reference to agrarian collapse and stagnation, rural transformation in the agricultural sector is proceeding apace (see Watts, forthcoming). The feeding of Kano, and indeed all other Nigerian cities, must then be situated on this broad and changing canvas, and understood in terms of the 'millions of subjects in their struggles with their victories and their defeats' (Lipietz 1984:12).

ACKNOWLEDGEMENTS

When this essay first saw the light of day it was problematic. To the extent that it has improved, it is almost wholly due to the constant criticism and support provided by Jane Guyer. I would like to say that she is responsible for the essay's content, but she is not. The research on which this contribution is based was funded by the Social Science Research Council (Africa Committee), and the Wenner-Gren Foundation for Anthropological Research.

NOTES

1 An exception is the *azalay* trade (grain movement from the southern to the northern savannas) associated with the sustenance of pastoral communities (see Baier, 1980). But two recent volumes, for example, on trade and the city, by Coquery-Vidrovitch & Lovejoy (1985) and Cooper (1983) do not refer to the food-city question.

2 I do not devote a great deal of attention to the contemporary organisation of the wholesale-retail grain trade in northern Nigeria. Good descriptions are provided in Gilbert (1969) and Hays (1975).

3 This is the Hausa term for the old walled city.

4 In his turn of the century description of Hausa agronomy, Imam Imoru (Ferguson 1973) inventories over twenty major cereal, root and legume domesticates including peppers, indigo, groundnuts and cotton, the latter confined largely to the heavier *laka* soils and higher rainfall zones in southern Katsina, Zaria, Kano and parts of the Sokoto-Rima Valley. The particular constellation of cultigens grown varied latitudinally, sorghums predominating in the wetter southern plains while the northern limit of rain-fed millet agriculture (roughly 300 mm per year) lay in the Sahel proper, bisecting Adar and Damerghou.

5 The upland millet-sorghum complex, which provided the bulk of the means of subsistence for rural households, was complemented by three other agricultural endeavours. First was the irrigation of low-lying riverine (*fadama*) gardens devoted largely to 'luxury crops' like manioc, sugar cane, onions, tomatoes, rice, tobacco, cotton, henna and a variety of herbs. Secondly, was game hunting and the gathering of sylvan produce, including the fruits of a large number of semi-cultigens used as supplementary foodstuffs and frequently as the raw material for local craft and petty commodity production. The third was livestock production, which formed a mixed economy in association with crop cultivation. Virtually all households possessed a number of small ruminants, especially sheep and goats, which functioned both as organic (and relatively liquid) capital and sources of manure for upland farms.

6 A colonial officer referred to *chappa* as a 'confusing system of administration', but it has superficial parallels with the *uban daki* functionaries described by Low (1972) in Hadejia and to the *tarayya* system noted by M. G. Smith (1978) in Daura.

7 *Zakkat* also embraced the cattle tax (*jangali*) raised on nomadic pastoralists and levies on non-grain commodities, particularly *shuka* (on groundnuts, cassava, cotton and gourds) and *rafi* (on irrigated crops like wheat, tobacco, sugar-cane and onions).

8 In pre-colonial Gobir, for example:
'a part of the agricultural surplus of producers were appropriated by the local aristocracy who only consumed part of it. The enormous quantities of grain thus accumulated were stored in mud granaries inside the birni . . . when a drought came, it was encumbent upon the Sarki to open the granaries . . . and to redistribute their contents to his subjects. A prince who strove to avoid this obligation lost this throne [for] the local populus had the capacity to intervene in the political life of the court. If the granaries were empty, . . . the sovereign mounted an expedition into the interior . . . to bring back grain bought in exchange for his treasures' (Nicolas 1977:163, my translation).

9 This section draws on the excellent work of Frishman (1977).

10 A fixed, inelastic tax that had the effect of taking land out of cultivation and in some areas constituted almost ten per cent of gross household income (see Watts 1983:282–3).

11 (a) Relief measures in Kano city last seventy-four days. About 160,000 free rations of grain were issued and 400,000 *mudus* of rice sold at subsidised prices between July and September.
(b) Four-hundred and fifty tons of imported rice arrived two months late by which time the Native Administration, already saddled with the costs of import, could only sell it at deflated prices, incurring an enormous loss in the process. Relief did not reach the northern districts of Kazaure until August, the second consignment having been attacked near Daura and sixteen bags stolen (NAK Katprof. 1/1978, 1914).

12 Gilbert's survey estimated that the average calories from staples consumed per day in Kano City were 1,750 (1,160 sorghum, 310 millet, 280 rice and a trace of cowpeas). Since his sample excluded Sabon Gari the significance of imported cassava (*gari*) as a means of subsistence for the southern population (especially the Ibo who constituted almost sixty per cent of Sabon Gari in 1965) is under-represented.

13 The Nigerian naira (N) stood at US$0·72 in 1984 and US$1·25 in 1973.

14 According to Güsten (1967:62) the Northern Region consumed 20,000 tons in 1966, an average per capita wheat consumption of 1·5 lb (compared to 70 lb/capita in Lagos).

15 Estimated to be 130 lb/capita/annum (AERLS, 1979:79).

16 Phase I of the Kano River Irrigation Scheme (22,000 ha.) has recently been completed and will ultimately be one element in a 200,000 acre Hadeija-Jemaare River Basin Authority project. Wheat yields are, however, very low (1·9 tons/ha) due to late planting, water-distribution problems, limited inputs, greater profitability of other crops (e.g. tomatoes) and pest infestation (see Wallace 1981; Palmer-Jones 1982). Wheat production was 8,000 tons in 1983 (*Africa Economic Digest*, December 1983:56).

17 According to AERLS (1979:69) subsidies on nine wheat schemes varied between N57 and N220 per ton.

REFERENCES

KM Katsina Museum, Katsina, Kaduna State, Nigeria.
NAK National Archives, Kaduna State, Nigeria.

Abubakar, 1975. 'A survey of the economy of eastern emirates, Sokoto caliphate during the nineteenth century.' Paper presented to the Sokoto History Seminar, Sokoto.

Adams, W. & A. Grove. 1984. *Irrigation in Tropical Africa*. Cambridge African Monograph No. 3, Cambridge.

AERLS. 1979. *Report on Wheat Production and Marketing in Nigeria*. Zaria: Ahmadu Bello Univerity.

van Apeldoorn J. 1981. *Perspectives on Drought and Famine in Nigeria*. London: Allen & Unwin.

Baier, Stephen. 1980. *An Economic History of the Central Sudan*. London: Oxford University Press.

—— and Paul E. Lovejoy. 1977. 'The Tuareg of the Central Sudan: gradations in servility at the desert edge', in S. Meirs & I. Kopytoff (eds.), *Slavery in Africa: historical and anthropological perspectives*, pp. 391–411. Madison: University of Wisonsin Press.

Barth, H. 1857, 1859 (reprinted 1965). *Travels and Discoveries in North and Central Africa*, 3 vols. London: Cass.

Beckman, B. & G. Andrae. 1986. *The Wheat Trap*. London: Zed Press.

Bernstein, H. 1979. 'African peasantries: a theoretical framework', *Journal of Peasant Studies*, 6, (3): 420–43.

Bienen, H. 1983. 'Oil Revenues and Public Policy in Nigeria'. World Bank Staff Paper No. Lo P- 592.

Brenner, R. 1976. 'Agrarian class structure and economic development in pre-industrial Europe', *Past and Present* 70: 30–75.

Bryceson, D. F. 1981. 'Colonial famine responses – Bagamoyo District of Tanganyika, 1920–61', *Food Policy*, 6, (2): 78–90.

Clough, P. 1981. 'Farmers and traders in Hausaland', *Development and Change*, 12: 273–92.

—— and Williams, G. 1983. 'Grain and cotton marketing in Northern Nigeria'. Oxford University, unpublished ms.

Collion, M. H. 1982. 'Colonial Rule and Changing Peasant Economy in Damagherim, Niger'. Cornell University, unpublished PhD thesis.

Cooper, F. (ed.). 1983. *Struggle for the City*. Beverly Hills: Sage.

Coquery-Vidrovitch, C. & P. Lovejoy (eds.). 1985. *The Workers of African Trade*. Beverly Hills: Sage.

Ferguson, D. 1973. 'Nineteenth-Century Hausaland, Being a Description by Imam Imoru'. University of California, Los Angeles, unpublished PhD thesis.

Forrest, T. 1981. 'Agricultural policy in Nigeria 1900–1975', in G. Williams, P. Roberts & J. Heyer (eds.), *Rural Development in Tropical Africa*, pp. 222–58. London: Macmillan.

Freund, W. M. 1981. *Labor and Capital in the Nigerian Tin Mines*. London: Longman.

Frishman, A. 1977. 'The Spatial Growth and Residential Location Pattern of Kano, Nigeria'. Northwestern University, unpublished PhD thesis.

Gilbert, E. H. 1969. 'The Marketing of Staple Foodstuffs in Northern Nigeria: a study of staple food marketing systems serving Kano City', Stanford University, unpublished PhD thesis.

Güsten, R. 1967. *Studies in the Staple Food Economy of Western Nigeria*. Ibadan: Nigerian Institute of Social and Economic Research.

Harriss, B. 1979. 'There is a method in my madness; or is it vice versa? Measuring agricultural market performance', *Food Research Institute Studies*, 17: 197–218.

Hart, K. 1982. *The Political Economy of West African Agriculture*. Cambridge Unversity Press.
Hay, A. & R. H. Smith 1970. *Interregional Trade and Money Flows in Nigeria, 1964*.Ibadan: Oxford University Press.
Hays, H. 1975 'The Marketing and Storage of Food Grain in Northern Nigeria'. Samaru Misc. Paper No. 50, Ahmadu Bello University.
Helleiner, G. 1966. *Peasant Agriculture, Government and Economic Growth in Nigeria*. Homewood, Ill: Irwin.
Hill, Polly. 1976. 'The Relationship between Cities and Countryside in Kano Emirate in 1900'. Paper to the Seminar on Economic History of the Central Savanna of West Africa, Kano.
—— 1977. *Population, Prosperity, and Poverty: rural Kano, 1900 and 1970*. Cambridge University Press.
—— 1982. *Dry Grain Farming Families*. Cambridge University Press.
Hogendorn, J. 1978. *Nigerian Groundnut Exports*. Zaria: ABU Press.
Hunt, D., & D'Silva, B. 1981. *Go and Stop: agricultural development in Nigeria*. United States Department of Agriculture Economic Research Service, Washington, DC 20250.
Hyden, G. 1980. *Beyond Ujamaa in Tanzania*, Berkeley: University of California Press.
ILO. 1981. *Nigeria: first things first*. Addis Ababa: International Labour Office.
Jacob, S. M. 1934. 'Report on taxation in Nigeria'. Rhodes House, Oxford University: file number MSS Afr.T.16.
Jones, W. O. 1968. 'The structure of staple food marketing in Nigeria', *Food Research Institute Studies*, 8: 95–123.
—— 1980. 'Agricultural trade within tropical Africa: achievements and difficulties', in R. Bates & M. Lofchie (eds.), *Agricultural Development in Africa*, pp. 311–48. New York: Praeger.
Kilby, P. 1963. *African Enterprise: Nigerian bread industry*. Stanford: Hoover.
Kitching, G. 1985. 'Politics, method and evidence in the "Kenya Debate"', in H. Bernstein & B. Campbell (eds.), *Contradictions of Accumulation in Africa*, pp. 115–52. Beverly Hills: Sage.
Kiyawa, I. 1981. 'Indigenous Entrepreneurship in Kano State, Nigeria'. Syracuse University, unpublished PhD thesis.
Knipscheer, H. 1980. *Wheat and Sorghum*, Ibadan: International Institute of Tropical Agriculture.
Last, D. M. 1978. 'The Sokoto Caliphate and Borno 1820–1880'. Paper delivered to Bayero University, Kano.
—— 1983. 'From sultanate to caliphate', in B. Barkindo (ed.), *Studies in the History of Kano*, pp. 67–92. Ibadan: Heinemann.
Lennihan, L. 1984. 'Critical historical conjunctures in the experience of agricultural wage labor in Northern Nigeria', *Human Ecology*, 12, (4): 465–80.
Lipietz, A. 1984. 'The Globalisation of the General Crisis of Fordism', SNID Paper No. 84–203. Queen's University, Ontario.
Lovejoy, P. 1978a. *Caravans of Kola*. Zaria: Ahmadu Bello University Press.
—— 1978b. 'Plantations in the economy of the Sokoto caliphate', *Journal of African History*, 19: 241–68.
—— 1984. Review of M. Watts, *Silent Violence, African Economic History*, 13: 242–7.
—— and S. Baier. 1975. 'The desert side economy of the Central Sudan', *International Journal of African Historical Studies*, 8: 1–42.
Low, V. 1972. *Three Nigerian Emirates: a study of oral history*. Evanston: North-

western University Press.
Lubeck, P. 1986. *Islam and Urban Labor: the making of a Muslim working class in northern Nigeria*. Cambridge University Press.
Luning, H. 1963. 'An Agro-Economic Survey in Katsina Province', Kaduna: Government Printer.
Mortimore, M. 1965. 'Some aspects of rural-urban relations in Kano, Nigeria', in *La Croissance Urbaine en Afrique Noire et à Madagascar*, pp. 871–88. Paris: CNRS.
—— 1967. 'Land and population pressure in the Kano close-settled zone', *Advancement of Science*, 23: 677–86.
—— 1970. 'Population densities and rural economies in the Kano close settled zone', in W. Zelinsky, L. Kosiński & R. M. Prothero (eds.), *Geography and a Crowding World*, pp. 380–88. London: Oxford University Press.
—— 1971. 'Population density and systems of agricultural land use in northern Nigeria', *Nigerian Geographical Journal*, 14: 3–15.
—— and Wilson, J. 1965. 'Land and people in the Kano close-settled zone'. Zaria: Department of Geography, Ahmadu Bello University.
Myint, H. 1971. *Economic Theory and the Underdeveloped Countries*. London: Oxford University Press.
Nicolas, Guy. 1977. 'Remarques sur divers facteurs socio-économiques de la famine au sein d'une société sub-Saharienne', in D. Dalby *et al.* (eds.), *Drought in Africa: 2*, pp. 159–69. London: International African Institute.
Okediji, F. 1973. 'The Cattle Industry in Northern Nigeria 1900–1939.' Bloomington, Indiana: African Studies Program.
Olusanya, G. O. 1973. *The Second World War and Politics in Nigeria*. Lagos: Evans.
Oyemakinde, W. 1973. 'The Pullen Marketing Scheme: a trial in food price control 1941–47', *Journal of the Historical Society of Nigeria*, 4: 413–24.
Paden, J. 1973. *Religion and Political Culture in Kano*. Berkeley: University of California Press.
Palmer-Jones, R. 1982. 'Irrigation and agricultural development in Nigeria'. Paper presented to the SSRC Workshop on State and Agriculture in Nigeria, Berkeley. (To appear in Watts, forthcoming.)
Richards, P. 1983. 'Ecology and the politics of African land use', *African Studies Review*, 26: 1–71.
Richardson, James. 1853. *Narrative of a Mission to Central Africa*, Vol. II. London: Chapman and Hall.
Shea, P. 1975. 'The Development of an Export-Oriented Dyed Cloth Industry in 19th Century Kano Emirate'. University of Wisconsin, unpublished PhD thesis.
—— 1981. 'Approaching the Study of Production in Rural Kano'. Paper presented to the International Conference on the History of Kano, Kano, 6–10 September.
Shenton, R. 1985. *The Development of Capitalism in Northern Nigeria*. University of Toronto Press.
Smith, H. F. C. 1971. 'The early states of the Central Sudan', in M. Crowder & F. Ajayi (eds.), *West African History*, Vol. 1, pp. 158–201. London: Longman.
Smith, Mary. 1954. *Baba of Karo*. London: Oxford University Press.
Smith, M. G. 1950. 'Social and Economic Change Among Hausa Communities'. London University, unpublished PhD thesis.
—— 1954. 'Slavery and emancipation in two societies', *Social and Economic Studies*, 3: 239–90.
—— 1955. *The Economy of Hausa Communities in Zaria*. Colonial Research Series No. 16, London: HMSO.
—— 1960. *Government in Zazzau*. London: International African Institute.

—— 1967. 'A Hausa kingdom: Maradi under Dan Baskore', in D. Forde & P. Kaberry (eds.), *West African Kingdoms in the Nineteenth Century*, pp. 99–122. London: Oxford University Press for the International African Institute.
—— 1978. *Affairs of Daura*. Berkeley: University of California Press.
Spitz, P. 1981. 'Economic consequences of food climate variability', in W. Bach *et al.*, *Food-Climate Interactions*, pp. 447–64. Dordrecht: Reidel.
Staudinger, P. 1889. *Im Herzen der Haussa Lander*. Berlin: Landsberger.
Tahir, I. 1975. 'Scholars, Sufis, Saints and Capitalists in Kano, 1904–1974', Cambridge University, unpublished PhD thesis.
Thompson, E. P. 1978a. *The Poverty of Theory*. New York: Monthly Review.
—— 1978b. 'Eighteenth-century English society: class struggle without class?', *Social History*, 3, (2): 133–65.
USDA. 1981. 'Nigeria: Agricultural and Trade Policies'. Report No. FAS-M303 United States Department of Agriculture, Foreign Agricultural Service, Washington, DC.
Usman, Y. B. 1981. *The Transformation of Katsina*. Zaria: Ahmadu Bello University Press.
Vigo, A. 1957. 'A Survey of Agricultural Credit in Northern Nigeria, Kaduna'. Ministry of Agriculture.
Wallace, T. 1981. 'The challenge of food', *Canadian Journal of African Studies*, 15: 239–58.
Warren, Bill. 1980. *Imperialism: pioneer of capitalism*. London: New Left Books.
Watts, M. 1983. *Silent Violence: food, famine and peasantry in northern Nigeria*. Berkeley: University of California Press.
—— 1984. 'State, oil and accumulation', *Society and Space*, 2: 403–28.
—— (ed.) Forthcoming. *State, Oil and Agriculture in Nigeria*. Berkeley: Institute of International Studies.
—— and Lubeck, P. 1982. 'The political economy of rural and urban poverty', in W. Zartman (ed.), *The Political Economy of Nigeria*, pp. 105–44. New York: Praeger.
Wheatley, Paul. 1972. *The Pivot of the Four Quarters*. Edinburgh University Press.
Williams, Raymond. 1973. *The Country and the City*. Oxford University Press.
World Bank. 1979. *Nigeria: Agriculture Sector Review*. Report No. 2181– 21N1. 2 vols. Washington, DC.
— 1985. *Nigeria: Agriculture Sector Review*, Washington, DC.
Yusuf, A. B. 1975. 'Capital formation and management among the Muslim Hausa traders of Kano, Nigeria', *Africa*, 45, (2): 167–82.

3 *Jane I. Guyer*

FEEDING YAOUNDÉ, CAPITAL OF CAMEROON

INTRODUCTION

In 1888, when the first Europeans arrived and settled on the present site of Yaoundé, the rolling forest and parkland south of the Sanaga and north of the Nyong Rivers were dotted with the villages of the Beti people. A segmentary and mobile population, their spacious settlements of wood and bark houses ranged on each side of a central court probably never exceeded a few hundred people. The extraordinarily rich natural environment was farmed and hunted to provide a diet of great variety (Laburthe-Tolra 1970). Some foodstuffs were exchanged, but an integrated regional market system did not exist. Each community supplied its own basic needs.

In the mid-1970s, Yaoundé, now the capital of Cameroon, maintained a population of over 300,000, including representatives from most of Cameroon's 180 ethnic groups and about 10,000 foreigners. The Beti people still comprise the largest single group but are no longer in an absolute majority except in the peri-urban and rural areas surrounding the city. The rural Beti now live in administratively regrouped villages of between 300 and 700 inhabitants, and constitute one of the most important cocoa-growing populations in the country as well as provisioning Yaoundé with staple foods. The region has been a major centre of agricultural production throughout the twentieth century and, at one point during the 1920s, faced the extreme pressures of managing simultaneous expansion in the production of food and cash crops, and the provision of labour for construction.

In spite of this long-term expansion in production and commercialisation, the most recent nutrition study indicates that both urban and rural populations are still well-fed by comparison with other regions of Cameroon. In 1977 the Centre-South Province had the lowest percentage in the country of chronically undernourished children under five years of age, even when the city of Yaoundé itself was excluded. The cities had the

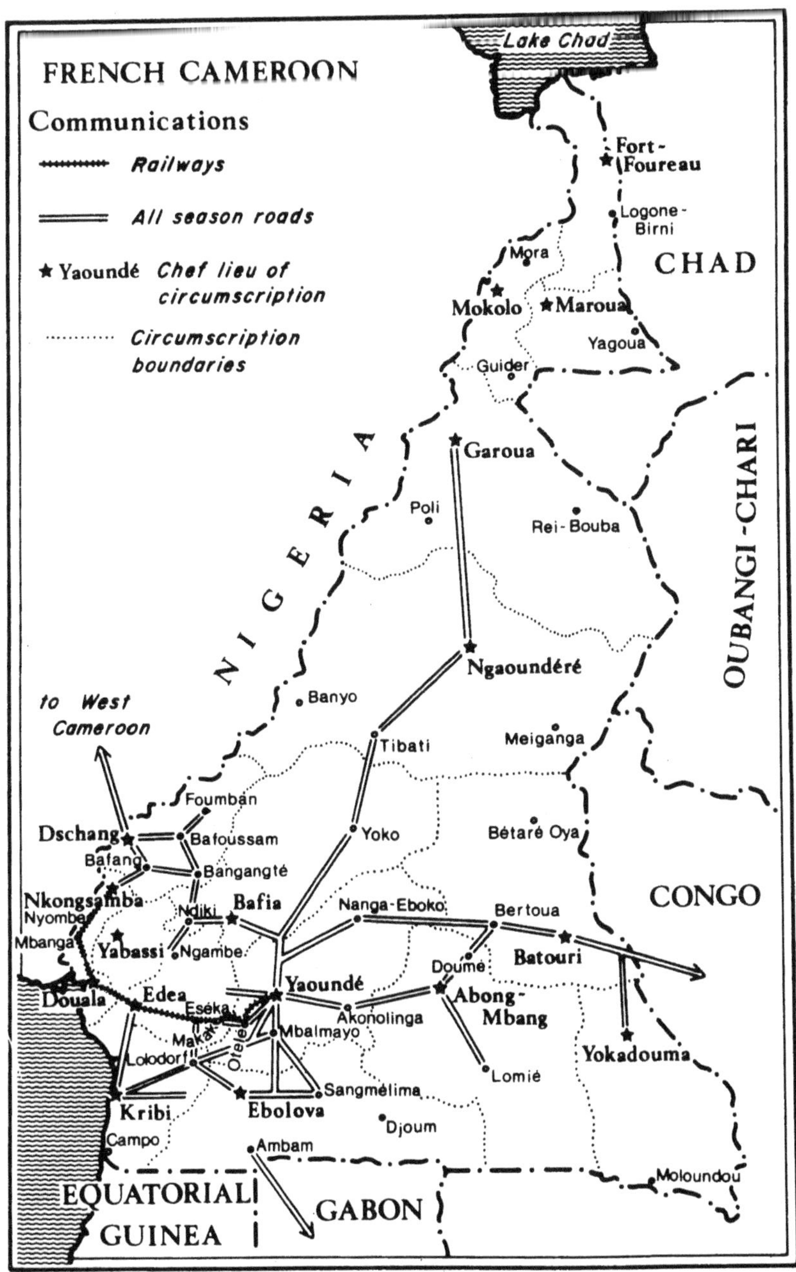

Figure 10 French Cameroon – communications

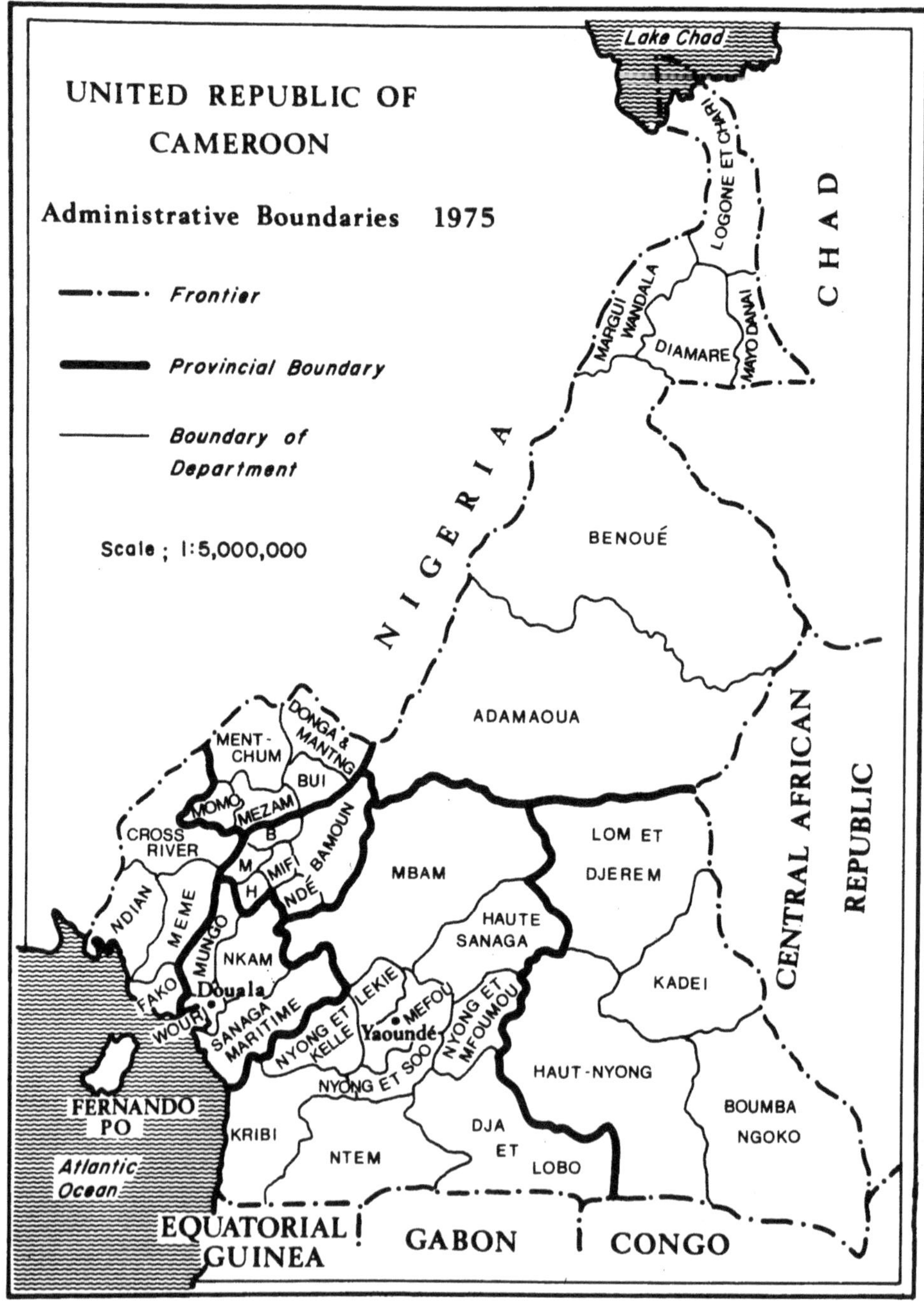

Figure 11 United Republic of Cameroon – administrative boundaries, 1975

lowest rates of all (RUC National Nutrition Survey 1978:87).[1] This is not to say that the situation is in any way ideal: in fact, all these rates were considerably higher than a control group of elite children, and historical reconstruction suggests that the rural diet is nutritionally poorer and less varied than before colonial rule. Nevertheless, these data do imply that fundamental social and economic changes have taken place without making severely detrimental inroads into a minimal standard of nutritional adequacy. Moreover, the historical record contains no mention of famine, nor of intermittent acute shortages of food which could be accounted for by environmental conditions. On the face of it, Yaoundé would seem a classic case of vent-for-surplus economic growth.

However, the apparent constancy with which basic material needs have been met is a misleading indicator of the social and political processes involved. The construction of a food market for Yaoundé has been highly problematic from the outset. Each generation of officials – German, French and Cameroonian – has viewed the food system as unreliable, its organisation anarchic and its dependability suspect. The terminology of official reports is itself recurrent; the system is *aléatoire,* implying both a lack of predictability which is at odds with the record on actual performance, and a lack of controllability which is much more to the point. Such nervousness reflects less a judgement of the technical capacity of local production than a knowledge that the institutional framework of the market has been too fragile to bear the material, social and political burden expected of it. The crises in the history of the Yaoundé food system are institutional and political crises in the complex process of constructing a controlled, differentiated social system. Two dimensions of this process are of central importance: the formation of social strata, with differential power, occupations, access to resources, and labour values, and the development of politically tangible structures which mediate the relations between strata. The almost complete lack of market institutions and relationships in the Beti indigenous economy meant that the whole system had to be constructed, prices and modes of payment arrived at, processing, transport and trade developed, the position of producers, traders and consumers in the stratification system determined, and the entire process politically and culturally sanctioned. The present history is primarily focused, then, on the construction of the institutions of a food market, its place in state policy, and the shifting position of its various functionaries during the colonial and post-colonial periods.

Examined from this perspective, the history of the food system comprises five phases, each one characterised by a different set of institutions and policies linking producer with consumer. In the early period of colonial rule, under the Germans, the provision of food supplies to the garrison and the porterage crews was a bone of contention, resolved in part by the garrison feeding itself and the crews purchasing along the route. When Yaoundé was named the capital of French Cameroon in 1922, the organisation of urban supplies became far more crucial and was handed over to the chiefs to administer. After 1945, management was ceded to the Provident Society. Direct administrative control was only lifted during the independence period at the end of the 1950s. There ensued almost a decade of 'free market' development, followed in the early 1970s by a series of state interventions.

In the view of the Government, none of these has proved entirely satisfactory; each lasted only fifteen to twenty years before requiring fairly radical restructuring. It would be too simplistic to interpret this process as an indication of a persistent antagonism between the state and an intransigently segmentary population. After all, in factual terms a system has been formed and it does function. The issue is rather, that the major aims of food policy have been very difficult to bring into consonance with one another, and when they have, it has been under conditions which eventually provoked political conflict. At the basis of the entire process is the dilemma posed by the need for low prices, which implies that the food supply functionaries will be in the lower social classes, and the desirability that they be within reach of influence, which implies greater prominence. Yaoundé has always been a white-collar town, with a large proportion of the labour force in government employment. Keeping food prices low and stable has been critical to the national budget, but it has not attracted capital to production and distribution. The various institutions established at crucial points during the last hundred years have been attempts to resolve this dilemma by experimental social engineering, aimed not only at exploring possible solutions to technical problems, but at finding those places within the social and political system which would yield to pressure and function under both conditions – low and predictable prices, and amenability to government influence. At the same time, of course, forces altogether beyond state control were reformulating social and productive relations. The present official concern with food supply must not, therefore, be seen as a new situation, a simple reflex of the international conditions of the 1970s; it is a new phase in a long process which goes back to the nineteenth century and is intrinsically part of the long-term construction of a new social order.

Here the suggestion of Lonsdale and Berman is very helpful, that the state in Africa be looked at as the arena in which, during the entire modern period, structural contradictions of articulation are most openly faced and solutions explored (1979). The history outlined below is centred on successive governmental attempts to overcome the potentially contradictory requirements of a cheap and controllable food supply. The term 'potential', however, is used advisedly. In working with Lonsdale and Berman's approach, the concept of contradiction may need to be limited in its application and made more analytically precise. In each phase of its development, the dilemmas of the Yaoundé market were, in fact, resolved enough for people to be fed. But each 'solution' shifted the actual cost and the perceived responsibility for blame in ways which ultimately created or exacerbated conflicts. Fundamental structural contradiction, dilemma and conflict are all part of the process of radical social construction, of which the food market is a critical element. The particular sociological characteristic of the history of the food system is that its continual material realisation has been socially discontinuous and contingent; that is, the contradictions were bridged, but at a cost whose focus was continually shifted within a changing social and political order.

Before tracing this history, a brief digression is necessary on the range of coverage. The concern here is almost exclusively with the staple food economy, and not with the whole range of products which comprise the diet. The major limitation this represents is that the other items – oil, meat, fish and beverages – dominate the budget to a greater extent than they dominate the protein-calorie complement.[2] The trade in the latter commodities tends to have been more capital-intensive and organised on a larger scale than the staple food trade. At times when local people could enter trade, these and other consumer goods were often a greater attraction than the staple food system.

Oil and meat were established quite early as ethnic specialities and seem to continue on these lines. Palm oil used to be produced by the Beti population, but for several decades production and trade has been dominated by the Bassa in the forest to the south of Yaoundé. The meat market is almost exclusively northern, more or less monopolised by peoples known as *Haoussa* in pidgin, but who are generally Fulfulde speakers. There is no study of the organisation or history of the northern community of Yaoundé, but it is very old. Established during the early colonial period, trade primarily dealt in kola and a kind of musk from the forest antelope known as *elut dzoe* in the Beti language. By the 1930s, at the latest, cattle were being brought down from the North, and continue to be transported, by rail or on the hoof. As in the rest of West Africa, the cattle trade demands complex social and financial arrangements and considerable capital.

Dried fish is another important dietary item in both the urban and rural areas. It is brought in from abroad or from the artisanal and industrial fisheries of Douala, Cameroon's largest city, on the coast. Finally, various beverages are produced and consumed locally. Palm wine is tapped and sold to dealers for the numerous urban bars. A kind of distilled liquor known as *arki* was developed during the colonial period when the French restricted alcohol sales to wine, and this is now sold to the urban areas, although its production and trade is illegal.

These items are the most important complements to the relatively rich variety of staples and fruits which the Yaoundé diet comprises: yams, manioc, banana-plantain, maize, cocoyams, sweet and Irish potatoes; beans and groundnuts; citrus fruit, *saa*, avocados and a range of other fruits and vegetables.

YAOUNDÉ AS A MILITARY POST, 1888–1917

Under German rule, Yaoundé was a military post of some importance, but not the administrative or commercial capital of Cameroon. Founded by a civilian, Georg Zenker, it was run as a military and administrative headquarters for the Germans after his replacement by Major Dominik in 1895. Suppression of insurrections against German authority involved a series of campaigns, as well as the persuasive diplomatic mediation of a Beti man, Charles Atangana, who was installed as superior chief of the whole region just before the outbreak of World War I.

According to Beti history, the headmen of local villages, and in particular a notable named Esono Ela, provided the early German settlement with land and food. For about a year this system seems to have operated as if the newcomers were guests. They were supplied through the headmen, who controlled the bulk surpluses over and above subsistence needs and allocated them to ceremonial and other political purposes. The women, who did most of the farming, may also have sold small, personal surpluses on an intermittent basis. After the year of grace was up, however, the settlement was sent a bundle of seeds and cuttings to help, and remind, its people to start their own gardens.

From this moment on, the process of negotiation became much more difficult. For some time purchases of food could be paid for in buttons, if bought from men, and beads if bought from women (von Morgen 1972:29–30). Under this system both men and women were at liberty to refuse to sell, and by 1891 people were turning down these media of exchange in favour of the cash, in larger denominations, which they were earning from rubber-tapping. Short of food in the midst of tropical plenty, Zenker complained that, as Laburthe-Tolra paraphrases it, 'he had great difficulties in provisioning, and was obliged to go from door to door to persuade people to accept his buttons in exchange for food' (1970:101). In the course of a dispute over payment for food purchases, two of his Dahomean soldiers were kidnapped (Quinn 1971:77). Ultimately Zenker established his own farms, drawing on his training in botany and a life-long interest in the tropical environment. Nevertheless any kind of commercial transaction with the Beti proved frustrating, including efforts to acquire farming tools. As Zenker wrote:

'it was not possible to obtain from the blacksmiths the gardening tools in local style which were so necessary, even by paying well; they promised to supply them, but did not keep their word, and if one insisted their final excuse was that they were free men (literal meaning of Beti) and not the slaves of Whites. With such a mentality, it is obvious that no commerce can develop' (Laburthe-Tolra 1970:99, my insertion).

The control of substantial amounts of wealth, in any form, was monopolised by village headmen for whom the quintessence of power was to do as, and when, they pleased.[3]

After 1895, when Major Dominik took over the post, the military presence was expanded, disciplinary sanctions were imposed on local headmen, and they were forced and co-opted into providing support functions for the Germans and their troops. Village 'mayors' were appointed and instructed to supply food, both to the settlement itself and to the caravans of porters along the tracks between Yaoundé and the coast (Quinn 1971:72). The Germans called the settlement Yaoundé, after the name of the local Beti sub-group, Ewondo. The Beti, for their part named it after the Germans, Ongola, meaning an enclosure and referring to its military nature, a name which it retains to the present.

By the time the Germans lost Cameroon at the end of World War I, Yaoundé consisted of a military enclosure, some formal buildings, and stately avenues of mango trees, but a very small population. In 1914 the military and police forces included 2,700 men, most of them Beti, and 215 officers (Quinn 1971:77). Other occupations were probably limited to trade and transport. It was still a provincial centre, a simple administrative post, with the brief distinction of being designated the provisional national capital after the coastal towns had been lost. The post was taken by the British army in 1916.

Few sources of information exist on such mundane matters as provisions for the next five years. The Beti men who had been installed as chiefs under the Germans fled with them to Fernando Po, leaving the countryside without an integrated hierarchy of leadership. The combination of the effects of war and epidemic influenza undermined the administration which the Germans had gradually been building. Villages retreated deep into the forest, and under the crisis conditions politico-religious secret societies sprang up. Central control disintegrated and it is unclear who or how many people remained in Yaoundé.

Only in 1922 was the international status of Cameroon defined as a mandated territory of the League of Nations, to be governed by France. Yaoundé was declared the capital, since the old capital at Buea now came under British sovereignty. The new strategic importance of the city resulted in an increase in the Civil Service and civilian populations. The issue of a regular and cheap food supply reappeared with new urgency.

YAOUNDÉ AS COLONIAL CAPITAL, 1921–39[4]

The town of Yaoundé was the administrative centre for both Yaoundé Circumscription and the national Government, headed by the High Commissioner. In 1921, even before the full installation of the French Government, the head of the local administration advised the High Commissioner that he doubted the region's capacity to provision even a relatively small foreign population. In his assessment, this was not because of poverty but because of the disinclination of the rural people to respond to the market (CNA APA 11896/C). Again, it was not a question of the quantities involved but of the means of tapping into the production system on acceptable terms. The next indication of the problem appears in the Annual Report of the Government to the Permanent Mandate Commission of the League of Nations for 1924: 'The difficulties of provisioning the Yaoundé Market are the object of the concern of the administration. Measures have already been taken, which provoked the arrest and imprisonment of several natives, under the system of discliplinary punishment' (AR 1924:170).

The precise nature of the difficulty is not described, but it clearly involved the problems of relying on the incentives of a free market because the decision was made to institute requisitions. By this time the Government already had experience in levying food from the Beti population to supply rations to the labourers working on the completion of the Douala-Yaoundé railway. The same model was applied to the urban system. 'At the moment a total reorganisation of the system of delivery to the market following a pre-established schedule, by region and by village, is under way' (AR 1924:170).

It was no small undertaking for the local Administration to assume this responsibility, one which it retained until World War II. The urban population consisted of 5,500 Cameroonian and 365 foreigners in 1926 (Franqueville 1979:323) and 6,190 and 261 respectively in 1933 (Kuczynski 1939:97). In addition there was an average daily work-force on *corvée* labour duty of 800 to 1,000, a prison population of 300–400, and a hospital population of at least 200. Many more people came into Yaoundé as porters, workers for private traders, litigants in court cases and in a variety of other capacities. The total dependent population could therefore be estimated conservatively at about 8,000.

However, the challenge was organisational and structural rather than material. The working population of the Circumscription of Yaoundé was large, at about a quarter of a million in 1931 (Kuczynski 1939:97), and the dependency ratio was low, at about two workers for every one dependent.[5] A few thousand extra dependents is a negligible number; in fact, since much of the agricultural work was done by women and most of the urban population of workers was male, the effective change in the demands on production may have been even less than the numbers imply. And the food system was rich and varied. The problem, from the government perspective, was in finding a way into it. The rural population was dispersed throughout numerous small villages, and the only feasible means of transport was porterage. Furthermore, control of the harvest remained divided between the women, who could sell in small quantities, and the men, who alone controlled transactions in bulk.

In the event, food supply became just one part of a comprehensive plan to create an elite in the rural areas which would mediate the relationship between the state and the people, and which would manage the mobilisation of resources for colonial development. The key people were the indigenous chiefs, chosen and appointed by the Government. Giving them the responsibility for urban food supply served several functions at once. It strengthened the chiefs' administrative power as well as their economic involvement in the colonial enterprise by requiring levels and kinds of organisation which had not existed in the pre-colonial system. The chiefs were assigned quotas for delivery at Yaoundé, on a fixed schedule, were required to organise the production of new crops, such as rice, to feed construction crews, to levy goods from their subject villages, to summon porters to carry them for what was often a two-day trip each way, and provide an escort for the caravan to maintain discipline. Prices were kept down because the freedom of supply and demand was eliminated, and at the same time, the colonial officials shifted the entire problem of dealing with recalcitrance into the indigenous system. With a single policy, the food supply was rendered cheap, reliable and politically tangible, and was made to serve the greater aim of constructing a 'middle class' between the state and the people.

However, the indigenous institutions on which the chiefs could depend either to legitimate exactions or to enforce compliance were limited. The solution imposed by the French bureaucracy passed the cost and the conflict on to Beti society itself, as the chiefs drew on every possible symbolic and material resource available to them to stay in control.

The framework of the French chieftaincy system, and ultimately most of its personnel, had been taken over from the Germans. There existed no organisational basis in the pre-colonial social structure for such large administrative units with a graded hierarchy of command. The first generation of chiefs, created by the Germans, was the only group to have worked in such a system at all. With some misgivings, the French brought them back from exile. At the top, under the direct orders of the French, were the superior chiefs, with the chiefs of administratively defined and regrouped villages under them. Canton chiefs, at a middle level of the hierarchy, were added in 1925. The central area of the Circumscription of Yaoundé (later the region of Nyong-et-Sanaga) was divided into seven superior chieftaincies, thirty cantons and a thousand villages. The most important superior chief was Charles Atangana, who resumed his critical position as a broker between European and Beti. Atangana ruled the largest single chieftaincy, a population of 120,976 (Eze 1974:97–101). Canton chiefs administered populations of between 5,000 and 20,000. These units were far outside the range of group size in the indigenous structure.

The main weapon of control at the chiefs' disposal was administrative discipline, the *indigénat*. This allowed anyone with the legal status of *indigène* to be imprisoned for fifteen days and/or fined 100 francs, without any judicial procedure. The chiefs were granted the right to recommend people for punishment under the *indigénat,* and generally there was no recourse against their decision. Food cultivation and provisioning the cities and workers was obligatory and sanctioned by the *indigénat* very early in the French period (Arrêté, *Journal Officiel du Cameroun* 31.12.1920), and, clearly, sanctions were applied. During the 1920s, when the rural population was producing rice for construction workers on the railway as well as food for the urban population, it was noted that 'those who are indifferent (to rice cultivation) are the object of disciplinary sanctions'. 'Everything has been put into effect to obtain the 60 tons assigned. Threats to the chiefs. Guards sent into all the regions, disciplinary sanctions. Surveillance during official tours' (CNA APA 11894/A). There was no hesitation to bring in the police when sanctions on key individuals failed to produce the required goods. Many villages leaders were imprisoned.

Under the protection of the *indigénat,* the chiefs improvised on Beti themes of legitimacy to develop the allegiance of their subjects. They built up clientage networks through outright patronage, protection from their own exactions, and the control of bride-wealth. As a result, production took several forms of organisation: collective village plantations worked by *corvée* labour, chiefs' farms worked by wives, prisoners, servants and clients and, at the base, family or individual plots worked by independent farmers. Agricultural labour in all three cases was controlled through indigenous and administrative sanctions, neither of which could operate entirely without the other.

The village or co-operative plots were imposed by government order and were used almost exclusively for experiments with new crops such as rice, cocoa, coffee, potatoes, and new varieties of oil palm. In the Beti area, rice was the most important crop grown on co-operative plots; it was introduced in the 1920s as a convenient, storable staple with low transport costs, to feed those working on the building of roads and railways. Rice production was very unpopular for technical as well as political reasons, and was abandoned as soon as pressures were removed, but village plots persisted in many places. The possibility of raising a *corvée* labour service had been developed and the chiefs took advantage of it even long after it was officially required.[6]

The chiefs' own farms were the largest and most complex agricultural enterprises, and they produced for the most conspicuous and lucrative sector, the supply of food to Europeans. The food was either delivered directly to colonial institutions such as the hospital and the prison, or was sold in a shop, the *économat,* access to which was limited to Europeans and *évolués*. The chiefs were required to produce some European food for administrators on tour and were therefore given access to new techniques and seeds. But many of them went far beyond their duties, to become entrepreneurs, participating in agricultural fairs and expositions, and sitting on the Administration's Agricultural Commission. The impression one gains of their farms suggests a size, diversification, and devotion to systematic experimentation in both crops and processing technology which may still not be equalled, and certainly bears comparison with the heavily capitalised ventures presently supported by rural development credit. Chiefs such as Zogo Fouda Ngono and Max Abe Fouda were genuinely interested in agriculture as a science and a business. Zogo Fouda had almost 400 hectares of cocoa alone, according to the inventory of his property when he died in 1939, in addition to smaller areas of coffee, oil palm, rubber and local foods, and experimental developments in poultry, small livestock, and the processing of groundnut oil (CNA at Saa). Most of the produce was sold to augment his own income, but he also supplied the local mission and Administration free of charge and shrewdly used this as a political lever. Max Abe produced large quantities of export crops, supplied the construction crews, and experimented with European vegetables such as Irish potatoes. Atangana is reported to have had 500 hectares devoted to indigenous staples, plantain, cocoyam, manioc, maize, sweet potatoes and pineapple (AR 1924:186), in addition to export crops.

Labour for the chiefs' farms was generally carried out by unpaid wives, clients, and subjects. Zogo Fouda was an extreme example of a more general principle; his wives, who numbered hundreds by the 1930s, were organised into work crews to cultivate, store, and process the crops, and headcarry them to market at Yaoundé. Max Abe, though a monogamous Christian, also resorted to various forms of unpaid labour; workers were recruited through clientship and some through additional *corvée* impositions on his subjects, over and above their basic annual obligations to the Government. The harshness of his methods of labour recruitment and control led to an unprecedented outcry and his dismissal from office in 1934. These enterprises were undoubtedly highly lucrative businesses which, because of the unpaid labour on which they depended, could guarantee cheap services to consumers while still providing their owners with investment funds and personal enrichment. Although some of the labour relations were phrased in terms of marriage and clientage, the amounts of labour involved, and the depth of the differential power, are a direct result of the colonial force which stood behind the chiefs.

The bulk of the traditional food requisitioned for Yaoundé's urban population came, not from chiefs' plantations or co-operative farms, but from the farms of individuals or families. Farmers and family heads were simply ordered to bring a certain quota of goods on the scheduled day, and to provide porters to headload it to Yaoundé. The team of porters was then led by the chief's functionaries, and the goods were delivered to the Yaoundé market. At the retail level the requisitioned food was, in fact, sold for cash, but like the control, the returns were also concentrated at the top. During the inter-war period, most workers received rations as part of their wage, rather than cash to purchase food on the market, so that a high proportion of the food sold in the market was sold to employers rather than to individuals. Villagers complained at the time (Buell 1928:327) and still report that they received no cash for the goods they brought. The price itself was controlled by the Government *mercuriale,* and remained remarkably stable, even though other agricultural prices fluctuated widely.

Not only did the producers lack incentive, but exchange outside the politically-controlled channels was heavily discouraged. The measures instituted to restrict market trade applied primarily to export crops and consumer goods. They included direct control on movement, such as the institution of passes for people travelling beyond their own regions, punishment for *vagabondage,* and repatriation of illegal settlers in urban areas and at private plantations. Trade itself was restricted by licences and controlled access to European commercial centres. Cameroonians were limited in the amount of money they could deal in. Under the protective umbrella of a formal position in the employment of a foreign trader, some local people did manage to engage in trade in kola, palm oil and other high-return foodstuffs. But the trade in staples was dominated by the requisition system in the 'wholesale' sector, and by the small-scale activities of women farmers in the immediate hinterlands of towns and commercial centres.

This 'anti-market mentality' on the part of the colonial Government persisted well beyond the initial crisis of the early 1920s for several reasons. First of all, the administration itself was the main employer in Yaoundé, and was therefore concerned about food prices since they affected Civil Service wages and, through this, the national budget. The 1920s and 1930s were characterised by dramatic fluctuations in the value of the franc and the price of commodities, while French policy required that the government in Yaoundé be independent of metropolitan aid. Certain kinds of control on wages and prices were inevitable. Secondly, the Beti and Bulu populations in the Centre-South were critical to the export crop economy, concentrated at that time in palm products and other forest crops, including some cocoa. The other demands on their labour and produce held greater priority and were themselves heavily administered. A free market in food was hardly possible under these circumstances.

Finally, food control was just one of many functions which the French used in building a rural middle class around the chiefs. The threat of anarchy on the doorstep of the capital seemed quite real. As one report put it, 'here in the south we will soon be faced by a dust of individuals (*une poussière d'individus*)' (AR 1922:59). The erosion of authority was of constant concern to the Government, and extended logically from immediate needs such as tax collection, to a fear of uncontrolled mobility – without which a free marketing system is impossible. The chiefs themselves lobbied for market control, partly in economic self-interest, but also because they saw people's unrestricted mobility as a threat to their political control. They were the bulwark of the colonial enterprise, 'a landed middle class which will constitute in indigenous society the element of order, calm and reason' (AR 1923:77).

In the long run, the requisition system rose and fell with this social and political strategy. During the Depression the chiefs found themselves at the heart of the structural contradictions, discredited in the eyes of the people by the extreme measures employed to meet colonial demands, punished by the Government for the inadequacy of these measures, and blamed by all for the conflicts generated at every level. Their power was undermined by administrative restructuring in 1934, their voices in public affairs became muted, and their power was gradually eclipsed (Guyer 1981). During World War II, the chieftaincy system was infused with new life because it offered the only viable structure for rapid and forced mobilisation of resources. One suspects that it also provided a convenient and acceptable scapegoat for intensified and oppressive demands: rice cultivation for the troops in North Africa, labour recruitment for the gold mines in Betare Oya and the rubber plantation at Dizangue. The only organised resistance to a superior chief occurred during the war, with the refusal of the Eton and Manguissa to go in forced labour to the gold mines. By this time official reports reflect the low status to which the chiefs had fallen: punished, as they had not been in the 1920s, under the *indigénat,* and described, as Max Abe and Zogo Fouda never were, as exploiters of their people (CNA APA 12022). By the end of the war, a new political and economic order would be established, consonant with the greatly increased levels of personal freedom on which local populations insisted and to which European ideology had turned. One immediate issue was how a cheap and dependable food supply could be re-established on a different institutional basis.

The requisition system had been part of a remarkably coherent policy which foundered on the very clarity of its logic; it was a blueprint for social construction which shifted the entire cost of change into the indigenous system, and gave its organisers an inflexible social prominence. When the levels of force required rose too high, and the cost too great, the chiefs had no room for political manoeuvre and became the obvious target for conflict. The institutional framework which replaced their food-supply functions was far more subtle in the way in which cost and responsibility were allocated, but it also faced a fundamentally restructured rural economy. The bitter conflicts of the inter-war years resulted in a change in orientation; on the whole, people no longer expressed freedom and autonomy through withdrawal from the market altogether, but through involvement in it. The state was dealing with a population ready to produce for the market, but still free to choose the conditions and the crop.

THE PROVIDENT SOCIETIES AND YAOUNDÉ FOOD SUPPLY, 1945–60

The abolition of the *indigénat* in 1946 led at one and the same time to a final collapse of chiefly power and to a new mobility of labour. The urban population increased from 9,080 in 1939 to 17,311 in 1945 and 36,786 by 1953 (Franqueville 1979:323), thereby tripling within a fifteen-year period (see Appendix 1). The chieftaincy system no longer had the power to provision it and there was no strong tradition of marketing, nor specialist intermediaries, except the foreigners who monopolised the trade in export crops. During the war, Greek traders had gained ascendancy in agricultural commodity markets and had built up businesses with strong relationships 'in the Interior' (CNA APA 12022). In the context of the post-war cocoa boom, however, food was simply not the most advantageous proposition. The solution to urban food supply was found in another colonial institution, the Provident Society (*Société de Prévoyance*). Understanding the implications of this policy demands a digression on the Provident Societies in general.

These Societies were important institutions in French colonial policy throughout Africa and Asia. A British colonial officer, writing in 1950, suggested that 'In some ways the Société Indigène de Prévoyance (Native Provident Society) has been as characteristic of French Colonial administration as the Native Authorities of our own' (Robinson 1950:29). The Societies were instituted as insurance and co-operative organisations at the local level, whose structures and policies were directed by the French Government. The original plan had been developed during the Algerian drought of 1891–2, for seed storage. The first Societies in tropical Africa were introduced in French West Africa in 1910. In Cameroon, the legal structure for the institution of Provident Societies was established on 7 June 1937. Although some activities were undertaken during the war, the great era of expansion began in the late 1940s. As a report noted, the Provident Societies 'have been conceived with multiple functions in view' (CNA 679/A), and by this time the possibilities for using such a flexible instrument for local economic planning had been well explored in French colonies throughout the world.

The legal and political framework for the Provident Societies in Cameroon differed little from the model described by Suret-Canale (1971). Under the umbrella of a national bureaucratic and banking structure, they were set up as savings and credit societies for indigenous small producers in the primary sector. These individual societies at the local and regional levels came under a committee of directors at the national level, which administered the Common Fund. Members paid an annual subscription, part of which was used locally and part invested in the Common Fund. Further resources were available to the Common Fund from the colonial budget and later from FIDES funds from the metropolitan Government.[7] The local Societies invested their own funds in collective projects or loans to individuals, as well as raising loans and grants from the Common Fund. The Government objective was to build an investment system which could support national policy while leaving maximum local flexibility.

The Societies therefore combined public and private elements. Membership was universal and compulsory. Annual dues and loan repayments were collected by administrative authorities as if they were taxes, and the local chapters corresponded to administrative subdivisions, 'the smallest commanded by a European' (*Journal Officiel du Cameroun*, Decree, 7 June 1937). The local French administrator was its president, and the National Governing Committee was composed of French administrative personnel. On the other hand, the Societies undertook profit-making commercial activities, benefiting from their access to interest-free or low-interest loans and their tax-free status, even if they suffered from an inability to raise money from purely commercial sources. Their mandate was 'to replace commerce wherever it was lacking, by opening purchase centres and by organising the collection of products in the countryside by lorry' (UN 1952:124). The Societies were therefore primarily financial and organisational institutions in a system which was otherwise, nominally at least, an open commercial system.

In fact, the Provident Societies provided the Government with a structure which could perform a variety of functions beyond the purely commercial: extraction of funds from the rural people, injection of capital into the rural economy for specific purposes, the creation of new demands and associated debt among the producers, provision of a slush fund for the local administration and, during the 1950s, a framework for rural political control (see Kom 1971, 1977). As a result the Societies grew very wealthy. During the expansion of investment in the 1950s, they constituted the single most important recipient of funds for rural development. In 1946 their total income was 31 million francs; in 1956 it had reached 2,000 million (UN 1951:112; 1956:352). In 1955, the total resources of the Provident

Societies amounted to a sum five times as high as the regular agricultural services of the administration (UN 1955:104). It is difficult to imagine that foreign private business did not benefit also, through increased demand for corrugated iron for buildings, tools, consumer goods, vehicles and repairs. The Provident Societies were a powerful administrative and economic resource.

The feeding of the capital city could hardly fit more closely the criterion for Provident Society activity: a weakly commercialised, but essential, sector of the agricultural economy. By 1946 the function had been ceded to the Nyong-et-Sanaga Provident Society: 'the provisioning of Yaoundé, in indigenous food, small livestock, fresh vegetables and rice are the main activities of the Provident Society' (CNA 679/A). The plan was ambitious, namely to stimulate production, set up a wholesale trade and transport system, and keep prices to the urban consumers down. The means of achieving this was to organise each stage of the supply system into units which were larger than indigenous producer and consumer groups and more predictable in their activities.

The Societies themselves provided the political and financial resources to deal with supply in the rural areas. They purchased from the women farmers, stored the crops, negotiated sales contracts and often provided transport. But to keep the intermediary chain as short and controllable as possible the organisation of the consumers became a priority. In Yaoundé two large consumer co-operatives were created, both concentrated on the wage and salary earners. The *Coopérative des Travailleurs de Yaoundé* had two thousand members and about four thousand users, transacting an annual business of forty-seven million francs in 1951. The *Coopérative des Fonctionnaires et Militaires du Cameroun* was mainly European in membership and did an annual business worth sixty million francs, about one-third of which represented imports from France (UN 1951:112, 114). Smaller co-operatives were set up in the provincial centres as well; for example in N'Tem 'The consumer cooperatives were created to make up for the weakness of local commerce in the area of food supply to the African civil servants' (CNA 679/A). Similarly, businesses and plantations with large work-forces placed standing orders with local Provident Societies; the SEITA tobacco plantation at Batchenga purchased most of its staple food supplies from the Society chapter at Saa. In 1955 the municipal Government of Yaoundé became a large customer for food supplies to its cafeteria, serving about 500 workers per day at subsidised rates (Billard 1961:401).

The consumer groups drew on a variety of regional Societies for their total provisions and, in so doing, greatly enlarged the catchment area for Yaoundé's supply. Well outside the old catchment area for Yaoundé, which more or less coincided with Beti territory, Societies reported spending large amounts of money to purchase local food for resale. The co-operatives ordered from the Provident Society's modern dairy in Meiganga, the rice mill at Nanga Eboko, and the specialised vegetable growers at Dschang. In addition, the Yaoundé Provident Society organised rural food markets which were held three times a week and for which it provided at least one truck for transport (CNA APA 11819/D).

At the production end, the Societies dealt mainly with smallholders direct, but two important attempts were made at restructuring production itself. The first involved taking over the prisoners' farm at Mvog Betsi, which had always been experimental in theory and a source of European foods for the *économat* in practice. After 1946 it produced milk, vegetables, meat and oil on an annual interest-free advance from the Provident Society, employing wage labour (CNA APA 11819/D). Eventually this enterprise foundered, due to rising wages. The use of Provident Society funds to underwrite European productive enterprise was contrary to the Charter, so that when rising wages resulted in a financial loss in 1948, it drew attention to the fact, and the farm was closed down.

The other Provident Society enterprise, the rice project in Nanga Eboko, operated successfully for several years, although it never produced as much rice as was imported from Indo-China. The modern hulling machinery installed at the mill was the largest single capital investment in food production by the Provident Society of Yaoundé. The enterprise was run by a European, and employed eleven extension workers to supervise production by farming families throughout the region, where nineteen paddy storehouses were built to keep the crop. From 400 tons sold in 1949, production rose to 1,100 tons in 1953, worth more than ten times the business of the next most important Provident Society in the Yaoundé area (CNA 679/A; Antoine 1954: 120,36). The production was carried out on family farms, and it seems likely that a high proportion of the rural people must have been rice cultivators to account for such high production figures in a generally low population-density area. The whole enterprise quite closely resembled more modern rural development schemes in that it engaged small-holder peasants, and attempted technical and financial innovation. Its decline in the early 1960s was far more to do with the fate of the Provident Societies in general than with the political or economic viability of this particular project. However, two sources, taken together, suggest that it would eventually have suffered the twin problems of underpaid farmers (Tissandier 1969) and an enormous staff of seventy-three employees (BD, B118).

The integration of a larger hinterland and the intensification of market activity within the old hinterland depended crucially on the ability of the Provident Societies to subsidise transport. Local Societies purchased from the producers and, therefore, like commerce and unlike the requisition system, paid the producers and assumed the risks of trade. By the early

1960s, they had become far more involved with transport than with production (Barboteu *et al.* 1962:101–2). Financing with Provident Society capital was one way of keeping consumer prices down without displacing the entire cost directly onto the peasant sector. While it is unlikely that the Provident Societies actually monopolised the food trade in Yaoundé, their ability to subsidise transport costs did influence market conditions. According to the UN 1950 (p. 118–19):

> (T)he consumer cooperatives continue to play their role in the provisioning of the urban populations, as much in the subdivisions far from the large centres where they are the only institutions capable of supplying the mass of non-producers, as in the great urban agglomerations like Douala and Yaoundé, where they permit Europeans as well as Africans to be abundantly provisioned at prices below those practised by local commerce.

In his review of the system, Antoine gives the following example: 'In 1953, in a rural market, the market-boys were selling palm-oil at 100 to 124 francs a bottle of 75 centilitres, while the Provident Society, by buying oil from a neighbouring Society, could sell it at 55 francs a litre and still make a profit' (1954:127).

African trade faced stiff competition under these circumstances, and evidently no strong local element emerged in the Yaoundé food trade during this period. African traders constituted a political lobby in Yaoundé, but there is no hint of an attack on the food supply system. The contrast with Douala, the commercial and industrial capital, is striking. In Douala, the independent food wholesalers instituted the *Coopérative des Fournisseurs de Vivres de Douala* as early as 1946, with a membership of 388 traders. They worked primarily along the railway line from the Bamileke region in the West down to the coast, and themselves dealt in the wholesale trade with certain specialist Provident Societies (CNA 679/A). The Bamileke have experienced a quite different social history from the Beti (see Joseph 1977), but Douala's employment patterns and wage structure are also much less tied to the administrative budget and the politics of the bureaucracy.

The other form of food trade which emerged in Yaoundé during this period was small-scale independent trade within the immediate Beti hinterland. The only category of trader exempted from market taxes was that of producers selling their own goods in amounts weighing less than thirty kilos or worth less than 250 francs, that is, one small headload (Municipal Archives). Food traders could only reach the farming populations on all-season roads, and even there they could not compete with the cocoa industry for the interest of the male farmers. Women's sales were relatively small, and limited by the poor transport system, long journeys and the restrictions of domestic control. According to Binet's family budget study conducted in the rural areas in 1954, 'food does not find a market except in small amounts and in very limited areas' (1956a:60).

The reasons for the decline of the Provident Societies were entirely political. With decolonisation, the Provident Societies became a target for anti-French sentiment. The dues had constituted a form of taxation for which the majority of people saw no direct return. According to Binet, 'at the moment taxes appear to the peasant to be a punishment: they are convinced that the governor can fabricate money whenever he wishes' (1956b:144). In addition the Societies had lost legitimacy because the Government used the Provident Society structure to maintain control over any spontaneous co-operative development in the rural areas; after 1954 all co-operatives had to be affiliated with their Provident Society, in theory for the supervision of their finances, but in practice to place them within a government structure at a time of intense political activity. The aim of stabilisation was explicit: to encourage 'the promise of stability at the same time as a means of raising the standard of living of the rural population' (UN 1955:80; Kom 1971).

Resolution of the political conflict left the Provident Societies tainted in the eyes of the people and no longer useful to the Administration. The precise dynamics of their abolition remains somewhat unclear, partly due to lack of local records, partly because it was included in a process within the French colonial world as a whole, and partly because vestiges of the structure remained long after Barboteu treated it as defunct. In some rural areas people continued to pay the special taxes until 1965, and four years later, in 1969, another obligatory savings fund was instituted, explicitly to replace the Provident Society (SOMUDER, see Benjacov 1970). The major event was the suppression of the credit facilities (*circulation fiducaire*) of the Common Fund, whose resources dropped to nearly 10 per cent of their former value.

In contrast to the requisition system, the Provident Society had encouraged market incentives among the producers, but it had hindered market response in commercialisation. In order to keep food prices low and still pay the farmers, it had to draw on its status as a public corporation to gain access to credit and subsidies, most of which it used to capitalise transport. Its public status also obviated the need to finance risk through commercial mechanisms. The costs of cheap food were diffused: peasants accepted the low prices, which were a considerable improvement on the previous system; consumers bore the cost, not so much of food prices themselves, but of maintaining the consumer co-operatives; and foreign capital must have underwritten the cheap transport. The focus for class antagonism is ambiguous with this strategy, but as highly conspicuous political institutions the Societies attracted the conflict which was raging in the South as a whole.

The subsequent system must be seen as a result of forces released by the civil conflict and the larger configuration of political dynamics, rather than following any orderly sequence of market evolution which may have been envisaged as part of the justification for the Provident Societies' intervention. Ironically, a state mechanism intended to promote commercialisation was in fact replaced by a free market. The organisation of that free market, however, entailed a radical shift in personnel. For the first time, the operatives in the Yaoundé food market were inaccessible to direct government influence or control.

INDEPENDENCE AND THE FREE MARKET, 1960–72

The structures of both supply and demand were altered by the process of decolonisation. On the demand side, there was rapid growth in the urban population and change in its ethnic and occupational structure. On the supply side, the political and economic contingencies of that era brought new categories of intermediaries into the gap left by the demise of the Provident Societies. An indigenous market system developed, and for the first time in its history, the Civil Service was supplied by a system over which it had no direct control. The rationale for the shift in policy – confidence in the market orientation of peasant producers, lack of institutional capacity to regulate market activities, or absence of political incentive to continue colonial controls – is unclear without access to the documents. However, the expectation that supplies would continue to be inexpensive and the system highly responsive to policy was deeply entrenched, and experiences in the early post-independence years did nothing to jeopardise this assumption.

Increased demand was basic to the development of the independent food market. Census figures (see Appendix 1) show that between 1957 and 1962 the urban population rose from 54,343 to 89,969 (RUC 1970). Since then the rate of growth has speeded up, resulting in a population of 165,810 in 1969 (Franqueville 1979:323) and 313,706 in the mid-1970s (RUC 1976). A high proportion of this population was employed in the Civil Service and salaried occupations associated with government and education. In 1962 the occupations of the adult male population could be divided roughly into three categories: one-fourth unemployed, one-fourth in agriculture, transport and 'other traditional' activities, and the remaining half in formal sector employment or domestic service (RUC 1970). Only 10·5% were in modern industrial employment in 1962 (RUC 1970:112), and even in the 1970s industrial employment was dominated by very few enterprises: a cigarette factory, a beer factory, and printing.

Yaoundé therefore retained and solidified its identification with white-collar, government employment. A study on the standard of living in 1964–5 concluded that 'In the Yaoundé market, demand comes essentially from the Cameroonian public sector and from foreign households which together account for 62·4% of total cash consumption, 30% of households and 37·3% of the total population' (SEDES 1964/5:49). It was a differentiated population, but with a high average standard of living. Household budgets reflected both the relative affluence of its population and their separation from supplementary agriculture activities. Only thirty-two per cent of household expenditure was devoted to food and drink (SEDES 1964/5:30), by comparison with the fifty to seventy per cent found in other, more proletarian African towns (see Introduction). An insignificant proportion of food was supplied in kind (SEDES 1964/5:32).[8] Average dietary standards were higher than in the surrounding rural areas, especially with respect to animal protein, and have remained superior up to the present.

The construction of the supply system involved two different social processes and a reorganisation of relations with the hinterland. Certain of the more distant supply areas whose viability had depended on Provident Society support, such as Nanga Eboko and Meiganga, declined. The two major supply sources which dominated the market were the immediate Beti hinterland and the Bamileke area in the West. These corresponded to the two categories of traders which emerged to dominate the market. While these two categories differed in scale and organisation of operations, and in ethnic origin, their emergence was in both cases contingent on particular historical conditions.

According to Franqueville, of the approximately 180 ethnic groups in Cameroon, 129 were represented in the Yaoundé population by 1957 (1979:336). But the local Beti people and the Bamileke and Bamoun groups from the West together accounted for over seventy per cent of the total population (RUC 1970). In 1957 the Beti had an absolute majority, at fifty-five per cent of the urban population, whereas the Bamileke accounted for eighteen per cent. By 1962 the Bamileke population had more than doubled, raising their proportional representation to twenty-four per cent., while the Beti had dropped to forty-seven per cent. The only other group with a comparable growth rate was the Bassa. The Bassa and Bamileke were the two ethnic groups most involved in the anti-colonial struggle, and it is likely that the violence in their home regions was a major cause of migration (RUC 1970:43). More important than the actual numbers is the fact that the Beti and Bamileke occupied quite different positions in the urban economy: two-thirds of the Civil Service positions were held by Beti, while fifty-two per cent of those occupied in commerce, transport and 'artisanal activities' were Bamileke (SEDES 1964/5:71).

With respect to the food trade, two processes converged. The Bamileke opened up their home area to the Yaoundé produce market, in spite of the daunting state of the road system, as they had done much earlier to the more accessible Douala market. By contrast, the Beti expansion was almost entirely a female affair. The rural male population was engaged in cocoa farming and the urban population in professional occupations. At this time, and throughout the mid-1960s, cocoa prices were declining and rural women needed to generate an income. The dynamics within and between these two sectors, and their different responses to both policy and changing conditions, is the central theme of the post-independence development of the food market.

The absolute importance of the Western Provinces for Yaoundé food supply is difficult to assess. According to N'Sangou's interpretation of the figures for 1965, the majority of the yams, maize, cocoyams and sweet potatoes came from the West, as well as one-third of the plantain. The area around Yaoundé predominated only in manioc supplies. (N'Sangou 1977b:62). On the other hand, manioc was by far the most important urban staple at this time, accounting for over a third of all local vegetable consumption by weight (SEDES 1964/5:44). In any case, the Bamileke presence in the Yaoundé food system was strategic and critical, expanding at a time when the local infrastructure was still minimally developed.

The particular niche which Bamileke dealers moved into was the provision of institutions: schools, the army, and other large organisations. Bamileke trade had been a major factor in the supply of Douala since 1945, so that modes of commercial organisation and control of capital and credit had already been developed on a significant scale. According to Passelande, for example, the food traffic to Douala by rail was dominated by large Bamileke traders, who accounted for sixty-four per cent of the tonnage but only twenty per cent of the expeditions (1972:214), suggesting that individual traders were dealing in substantial quantities. The internal organisation of this sector is not well-documented; there may well be internal differentiation in the size of enterprise, but it clearly operates with substantial capital by comparison with the system which emerged in the Beti area.[9]

The expansion of Beti trade in food involved large numbers of women taking on trading as a part-time or full-time activity. Binet had written in 1956 of the effect on women of men's rising cocoa incomes: 'they cannot help but envy men and look for ways of equalling them, by farming for themselves or by running away to town' (Binet 1956a:60). The conditions of the early 1960s offered both the opportunity to sell food crops to the market and the need to generate an income. The decline in cocoa prices, which reached its lowest point in 1965, pressurised married women into the market. At the same time, the generally bad economic situation seems to have lowered the marriage rate, resulting in many unmarried women having to find a source of cash income to support themselves (Franqueville 1976:124). The new intermediaries were both rural women who combined farming and trading, and specialist traders who were mainly urban-based and often independent. A few men also entered the food trade at this time, and others expanded food production for the market, generally in various tree crops (fruit, avocados, plantains). In his study of the *Marché Centrale* in 1973, Franqueville found that eighty-nine per cent of the traders were women, about equally divided between rural and urban-based (1976:124).

By comparison with Bamileke trade, it appears that Beti enterprise was small-scale. A study in 1976 reported that the average sales per food seller in the market were 200 kg per day, and that the chain of intermediaries was very short, involving only two intermediaries between producer and consumer (MIDEVIV 1976). About one-fourth of customers bought from an intermediary who bought directly from the producer. Women in peri-urban villages still headloaded goods to market and most produce was transported in small vehicles. Diarra's detailed 1974 study suggests that few traders owned a vehicle and, although collective rotating credit associations were common, there was little accumulation of capital. Bulking was done on a very limited scale, partly due to the dispersal of the farming villages, the paucity of rural markets and the poor condition of the roads.

These two groups constituted the *bayam sellam* (pidgin term from buy/sell) who became the brunt of attack when inflation in food prices set in around 1968. Within a short period of time they had created solidly-rooted, mediating structures between producers and consumers, but which, unlike the Provident Society, had class alliances which set limits on the absorption of the cost of cheap food.

This brief period of free-market activity had definitively broken the state's ability to set up institutions which would insulate the local food market from wider social and economic forces, as the subsequent development shows.

INTERVENTION, 1972–9

The actual pattern of inflation in food prices is as controversial as interpretations of its causes. Apparently, prices in Yaoundé more than doubled between 1965 and 1972 (RUC 1977:113), but the sources are at variance about the relative contributions of 'manufactured items' and local foodstuffs to the price rise (N'Sangou 1977a:7; *Note Annuelle de Statistique 1974–5*:70; see Appendix 2). The cost of transport rose faster than any other single item, and well before the 1974 escalation in oil prices. In any case, the cost of living was rising rapidly, and locally-produced food was an important component of the increase.[10]

The implications of an open market were beginning to be played out. The size of the urban population was increasing rapidly, significantly altering the rural/urban ratio in the immediate hinterland (see Appendix 1) at a time when the supply hinterland seemed to be shrinking. By the mid-1970s there were indications that an increasing proportion of the total food supply was coming from the immediate area, and in particular from the Department of the Lékié. N'Sangou suggested that as much as forty-five per cent of the traditional food coming from the Beti hinterland originated from this Department (N'Sangou, *Cameroun Tribune,* 11.5.1975). Even here, there was competitive pressure, as old supply areas were beginning to support other urban centres. During the 1970s Libreville, the capital of Gabon, was increasingly fed from Southern Cameroon (Lebigre 1980); the western peoples started to sell to Nigeria; and the growing urban centres of the West itself were attracting local food supplies. How early these processes appeared is unclear, but in 1973 Franqueville was struck with the apparent restriction of the Beti hinterland since his first study in 1968 (1976). From later developments, it seems likely that this was the beginning of greater regional integration by the large operators for whom Yaoundé was just one of several possible markets.[11]

At the same time, the producers and traders in the small-scale sector became more assertive about a 'just price', that is, they were resisting disadvantageous shifts in cost through the bargaining of the market rather than through opposition to particular institutions. Diarra's interviews with food producers and traders in 1974 are full of complaints about the rise in price of consumer goods, school fees, and agricultural tools. Even more pointedly, one trader commented 'The important people want to make money and feed themselves for nothing' (Diarra 1974:Annexe 3.51). In fact, by comparison with many other African urban populations the 'average' Yaoundé consumer was eating well and cheaply during the early and mid-1960s. A new sense of polarisation by class interest was clearly developing, with a lower class urban and rural 'moral economy' focused on prices and standard of living, rather than on non-economic dimensions of differentiation. Jeanne Henn (1978) has argued persuasively that the decade between 1964 and 1974 saw a significant decline in the real incomes of both the peasants and the lower-class urban workers, which were, of course, for the Beti population, related groups. The relationship between consumers and providers was phrased in class terms, with the rural producers and traders identified as providers and the professional middle-class as consumers. The response of the authorities, the re-imposition of price control, was justified by an entirely different model of urban-rural relations, but was seen by the food traders as a defence of class interest.

The rationale for price control was based on the expectation of cheap food, which had been built up over the entire history of Yaoundé, and on a corresponding economic and social ignorance of the actual organisation and cost in the food supply system. The SEDES studies in 1964/5 had established that producer and rural market prices were approximately half and two-thirds respectively of the urban price, and simple observation in their home villages suggested to urban dwellers that production itself was not the major constraint (Onambele 1969). What was lacking on the part of the Yaoundé officials was any realistic model of the current operation of the food trade: the costs of transport, petrol, credit, risk coverage, market fees and so on, and the relationship of all these to the other opportunities for production and investment. The long-term implications of food supply through the market, with inevitable price fluctuations and interregional competition, seems not to have been totally assimilated. Local officials in smaller towns still thought in terms of the civic obligation of their people to support them, regardless of the price level in other accessible markets. Villagers on a road linking Yaoundé with a smaller town reported that they were instructed by the police as to which of the two markets they were supposed to service (personal communications, 1979).

Consequently the official blame for the price rises was laid squarely on the 'excessive' margins of the *bayam-sellam,* often unambiguously designated as feminine by the French term *revendeuse*. The imagery associated with the public debate evokes and condemns independence and/or disloyalty on the part of the traders: 'A form of commerce which is complex, non-integrated, independent, traditional and primitive' (N'Sangou 1977:7); 'the most anarchic sector because of its lack of organisation' (Governor of the Centre-South, in Diarra 1974:Annexe 6); later, a commentator would remark on 'the disloyal competition' of the traders against a government enterprise (*Cameroun Tribune,* 24.9.77:4).

The fact that it was largely a female sector is by no means irrelevant to the conceptualisation of the issue in terms of loyalty, nor to the authoritarian measures initially taken. The market control imposed in 1972 was part of a broader-ranging attempt by the Government to bring the entire 'informal sector' under direct control. Ordinances were passed against *vagabondage* and prostitution. People without homes or means of support were liable for prison sentences of six months to two years, and prostitutes could be fined between 20,000 and 500,000 francs and sentenced to six months to five years in prison (Franqueville 1979:353). Such measures represented an attempt to shift costs back into the peasant and female sector by imposing a family or civic interpretation on a situation which the traders themselves seemed to be interpreting in straightforward class terms.

The attempts at control took the form of strict police enforcement of the *mercuriale* for food prices in September 1972. The result was startling: people simply refused to sell, and the volume of commerce in all urban markets dropped sharply. It seems very unlikely that what amounted to a market boycott was organised by any particular group. It was more a reflection of the institutionalisation of the position and interests of those involved in the food market. The Governor of the Centre-South Province clearly recognised this fact of political life in his recommendations following the crisis:

> Under the threat of risking disorder or a crisis in urban food supply, it seems appropriate neither to impose the mercuriale, with the example of the general

discontent aroused by its application in the Mefou (Yaoundé) to inspire us, nor to bully these shady intermediaries who are the sellers, who, so completely integrated into the peasant masses that they have won them over to their cause, deserve more to be taken in hand with a view to constructing real cooperatives for purchase and sales. (Diarra 1974:Annexe 6)

With this phraseology, he essentially conceded that the traders and farmers had an identification of interest, and implied that cheap and tangible sources of supply would have to be created by piecemeal interventions which rendered them more accessible to influence.

Targeted scapegoating of the traders diminished after this in favour of a series of measures which included greatly increased investment in production. Subsequent policy documents focused heavily on the insufficiencies of production in the rural areas, rather than on unacceptable trading margins. In particular, attention was turned to the lack of specialised production for the market. The document written in 1973 to launch a 'Green Belt' policy for the cities noted simply that food production was not keeping up with urban growth, and that rice imports had tripled from only ten thousand tons in 1970 to thirty-two thousand in 1971 (RUC Min. Agri. 1973:6). In fact, as others pointed out, the bottlenecks were far more complicated than this: the road system was very poor (Lefebvre 1972), transport was increasingly expensive (Diarra 1974) and the costs of food preparation, in terms of time, fuel, and water in a congested urban environment, made rice an attractive alternative to the tubers and plantains which dominated the diet in 1964. Some of these issues were addressed in other ways: the development of rice cultivation in the North and West, and plans for road improvement. But within the Yaoundé hinterland the main policy emphasis was on developing a significant number of specialised producers who would sell food staples through some kind of 'modern' structure. The emphasis was both technical and organisational, to encourage the departure from 'the excessive mixed farming evident in traditional agriculture' (RUC Comice Agricole 1974:40), and to set the terms of market involvement through credit provisions. It was also pursued in such a way as to draw men into the food supply system, as I will discuss later. Rather than control the current system directly, this was an attempt to set up parallel and competitive structures.

The 'Green Belt' policy had two main components: a credit system (FONADER), and a multi-functional organisation for promotion of the food economy through technical research, production, extension, and commercialisation (MIDEVIV)[12]. MIDEVIV was created in September 1973. By 1979 its production and commercialisation branches were running so poorly that its operations had to be heavily subsidised and its sphere of action strictly limited to technical research and seed propagation. In 1977–8 it received a subsidy of over $300,000 'which permitted it to resolve important financial difficulties' (RUC Min. Ec. Plan. 1978:45). The failure of MIDEVIV to dominate or even compete with the indigenous sector in either production or commercialisation reveals a great deal about the system as a whole.

The branch of agriculture most directly undertaken or supported by MIDEVIV was plantain production. The reason for this emphasis is never explicitly stated even though it is written into the title of the 'Green Belt' programme for the South: 'Project for the creation of village plantations of plantain-banana in the hinterland of Yaoundé' (RUC Min. Agri. 1973). Plantain production makes sound ecological sense in the forest environment, but there can hardly be a crop for which the costs of transport in relation to calories is so high, or for which the losses from spoilage are so great. The choice of plantain reflects a conjunction of two considerations: there was an established experience of growing bananas and plantain on large farms with modern technical inputs, and plantain is the only basic staple to which the male population of the forest will devote themselves. Plantain is treated as a tree crop and is grown without the use of the essentially female tool, the hoe. Implicitly, then, MIDEVIV represented an attempt to involve men, particularly young men, in the production of basic staples for the market, in organised and specialised productive units.

Production took two organisational forms: MIDEVIV's own plantations which employed wage labour, and peasant groups referred to as GAMs (*Groupes d'Agriculteurs Modernes*). The plantations were a complete failure in economic terms. At the plantation at Mbankomo, eighty-five hectares of plantain were worked by 154 employees. Since the original plan projected a total labour requirement of 206 man-days per hectare (RUC Min. Agri. 1973:25), there were clearly far too many employees. The costs of production were extremely high, the yields lower than expected, the workers undisciplined, and twenty per cent of the produce plus an undetermined amount of inputs and tools were stolen (MIDEVIV 1978:28).

The peasant groups (GAMs) were just as problematic. By 1977 there were only twenty of them in the entire Centre-South, Littoral and South-West Provinces, and FONADER had refused to advance further credit because the repayment rate had been only four per cent (MIDEVIV 1978:40, 43).

These failures are not a simple reflection of unresponsiveness. Within the peasant sector farmers were making innovations and expanding production. Women farmers were growing various foodstuffs for the market, although still within the general framework of home provisioning (Guyer 1984). Men were also going into food production, but of market garden crops rather than staples. Tomato production had expanded rapidly, with farmers using many of the inputs and forms of group organisation which were being promoted by MIDEVIV for plantain (Morinière 1972; Guyer 1984). One of the critical problems for MIDEVIV was their pricing policy which directly reflected the official mandate to bring urban prices down.

To summarise commercial policy briefly, the intent was to produce efficiently, maintain a low producer price and therefore sell on the Yaoundé market, at their own outlets, at a price which would severely undercut the independent traders. The MIDEVIV prices were approximately seventy per cent of prices in the urban markets (interviews at MIDEVIV, 1979).

The independent sector undermined this plan at three points. First, traders were ready to pay the producers at a higher rate and could therefore capture the market, literally in some cases, since traders visited villages the night before the MIDEVIV truck had a scheduled pick-up and bought up all the produce. This kind of competition was severe within 40–50 km of Yaoundé, and particularly in the Lékié, where many producers were themselves traders. All the MIDEVIV markets in the Lékié had been closed down by 1978. Secondly, as a result, MIDEVIV was forced to buy at increasing distances from the Yaoundé market, which in turn led to inflated transport costs and the necessity of subsidies if consumer prices were to be kept down. And finally, the urban traders realised that they could present themselves as consumers, buy at seventy per cent from the MIDEVIV outlet, sell at the going rate, and earn a good profit. Hence the newspaper article about the 'disloyal competition of the *revendeuses* against MIDEVIV', with its rhetorical question: 'what can one do to distinguish a housewife from a trader?' (*Cameroun Tribune*, 24.9.77:4).

The possibility of MIDEVIV selling in bulk to institutions was also thwarted. Supplies to the military and other large groups of consumers had been established soon after the demise of the Provident Societies by westerners with substantial capital and resources. The military diet consists primarily of maize and Irish potatoes, reflecting the regional networks through which the provisions come rather than the natal, millet-based diet of the majority of soldiers who tend to be northerners. MIDEVIV could not break into the institutional side of the Yaoundé market. It did, for a while, supply the workforce at CAMSUCO, a large, new sugar concern north of the city, but at least some of the food sent there was actually purchased by MIDEVIV on the open urban market.

The institutions of the Yaoundé market were already too established, by the mid-1970s, for a semi-governmental organisation to make any headway against them, in spite of huge subsidies and foreign advisers paid from international aid. The small-scale sector was uncontrollable because it was organisationally highly-dispersed. The larger interests were entrenched and difficult to control because they dealt in other markets as well, not only regional but international. In the late 1970s the larger interests in the food trade appeared to be shifting resources away from the domestic market and moving into exports. The trade to Gabon became a major factor influencing the Yaoundé market. In 1976 and 1977 lorries were loading up food products, even perishables, within 20 km of Yaoundé in its old supply hinterland for transport to Libreville. For a time an official attempt was made at closing the major roads across the border, but in 1979 it was said that wholesalers were buying in Yaoundé itself and that urban prices in Libreville could go as high as three times the Cameroonian price (interviews at MIDEVIV, 1979). It seems clear that rice is being exported to Southern Nigeria from the West, at the same time that rice imports from Asia have risen. One implication of the final emergence of capital-intensive, profit-oriented operations in the food system is that they contribute to food price inflation in Yaoundé, not just because they shift the costs of operation to the producer and consumer if they are powerful enough to do so, but, above all, because they effectively integrate the Cameroonian market with the markets of Southern Nigeria and Gabon where other conditions prevail.

Following the failure of MIDEVIV, government policy still encourages plantation agriculture, but in the private sector. Land law and credit provisions favour the development of large farms, but the beneficiaries of private registration in land and the recipients of FONADER credit have tended so far to be employees in the formal sector rather than farmers. One study shows that of all the credit extended to individuals in the Centre-South, in distinction from groups and organisations, eighty-two per cent was extended to *fonctionnaires* (INSTRUPA. 1978:v). The newspaper regularly reports on the agricultural enterprises set up with these funds; for example, one M. Ndoungou Billy Black set up a farm of 426 hectares, 90 km from Yaoundé, at the cost of twenty-two million francs CFA (approx $100,000), to produce latex, cacao, plantain, egusi-melon, groundnuts, eggs, chickens, rabbits and pigs, with a wage labour force of thirty (*Cameroun Tribune*, 7.12.1976). The capital invested in such projects is enormous and their long-term prospects unclear.

There are also agro-industrial schemes involving capital on a much larger scale and open to foreign investment. An article in the *Cameroun Tribune* outlined nine such projects (11.12.1976). But out of the nine, only one, for maize production in the Bamoun region, was for a staple crop, and even this may be destined for the brewery rather than the food market. The others were for fruit to be used in preserves, pineapples, a cocoa butter factory, fresh milk products, soluble coffee, malt for the brewery, baby foods, and pork products. The very low profile of staples is striking. The single staple food which benefits from high levels of public expenditure is rice (RUC Min. Ec. Plan. 1976b:113).[13]

However, Cameroon is one the few African countries whose imports are fairly restricted and whose population enjoys a nutritional status which is close to adequate. It is hard to avoid the conclusion, therefore, that small-scale, diversified production and market trade have actually fed Yaoundé, not as cheaply as in the past, but probably at considerably lower margins than larger businesses would accept. The continuing reluctance of larger enterprises to penetrate the Yaoundé market except as institutional suppliers, reflects the low margins involved in working a conspicuous and politically important market. But the dependence of Yaoundé on what is perceived as an artisanal supply is still considered extremely problematic. 'It is not possible to base the provisioning of the capital of Cameroon on a subsistence agriculture which produces little marketable surplus. The costs of transport would be too high . . .' (INSTRUPA:33). On the contrary, it seems to be the only system which can keep the Yaoundé prices somewhat insulated from the extraordinarily high food prices in places like Libreville.[14] At the end of his work on the informal sector in Yaoundé, N'Sangou recognises this by quoting a proverb, 'Do not kick away the canoe which has brought you across the river' (1977:49). The spirit of this is more sympathetic than most writing on the food trade, but on one issue it is misleading; the canoe is still in mid-stream, the artisanal system still feeds the city.

Thus far, I have put aside the issue of productive capacity because I believe it to be largely irrelevant to the early history of the regional food system. But whether, and under what circumstances, there could be enough accumulation in the small-scale sector to increase phyical productivity and returns to labour through technical and organisational innovation rather than through price pressure or incentives alone is becoming a crucial question.

The traders whose activities are based in the villages operate with small amounts of capital, on an intermittent schedule, and tend to combine trading with farming. In the villages in which I conducted fieldwork in 1975–6, the largest trader made four trips to Yaoundé during the month of November, a peak month in the consumer economy because of the influx of cocoa money. She purchased at 16,250 francs CFA ($81), sold for 27,750 francs ($139), and incurred transport costs of 4,150 francs ($22). Her margin, for returns to labour and profit, was therefore 7,350 francs (about $36), or twenty-six per cent of the sale price. She is not representative in any statistical sense, but is an example of the kind of enterprise which, multiplied many times over, brings food into Yaoundé.

The producers who sell to this level of trader are all primarily engaged in production for home consumption. This judgement is not based on the scale of their activity so much as on the actual pattern of farming. The field system is a modification of intercropping sequences which go back to the pre-colonial past, and include the entire variety of crops necessary for the Beti diet: groundnuts, root crops, plantain, leaf vegetables, egusi melon and palm nuts. This does not mean, however, that the internal plan of farming carries no market component. Fields are now considerably larger than they were in the past and are more closely intercropped with marketable crops (such as manioc for processing), one of the major field types is worked twice a year instead of once a year, and the former slack season is often used for growing vegetables in irrigated fields. This complex process of intensification has resulted in a heavy workload. Even so, sales per woman farmer tend not to be very large; they are estimated at approximately twenty-five per cent of the total crop (Weber 1974). In their November budgets, the twenty-six women in my own budget study reported an average income from the sale of their own produce of 2,167 francs CFA, or about $11. The amount is small, but then everyone was involved in the market at one level or another.

Perhaps institutional arrangements for pooling resources will develop, but Diarra's work suggested that powerful women's organisations had not yet emerged in the early 1970s, as they have in the food trade in other parts of West Africa (Trager 1980). This is not to say that such organisations will not develop, and to see the system as 'traditional' in a static generic sense obscures the fact that it has developed quite fast, in response to the opportunities of the post-colonial transition and under the constraints of declining real incomes from cocoa. The directions in which it is changing, developing further intermediary steps such as processing, pooling capital, or organising into larger units is at present unclear, but its image as a 'traditional' system, inflexible or stagnant, is clearly historically inaccurate. That vision has its own history in the distrust of uncontrolled social processes, which successive governments of three different nationalities have associated with anarchy.[15]

DISCUSSION

The history of Yaoundé's food supply is one dimension of the growth of social differentiation – by class, by occupation, and by regional specialisation. Successive governments have seen, in both the wider social process and the specifics of market development, a matter of central importance to their economic and political viability and to any programme of social and national construction. They have not, however, found the 'evolution' of the market to be a process which took care of itself, nor have they been presented with straightforward solutions from within the indigenous or the colonial/modern traditions. Neither, finally, has the process been a constant battleground, with fundamentally opposing principles locked in intransigent mutual resistance. There has rather been a series of experiments in social engineering, each with its moment of maximum realisation, but each both setting up and being conditioned by dynamics which were much broader than any plan could contain. The characteristic dilemmas which emerged time and again from the various interventions derive from the great difficulty of constructing a situation in which the class implications of maintaining low consumer prices, and therefore low margins and returns to traders and farmers, can coexist with the social control implications of needing an accessible, and therefore socially prominent, category of producers and traders. Under the conditions of production prevailing throughout the century, 'cheap' and 'predictable' were aways in potential tension, brought together by force or by subsidy, but, in the long run, not by the development of mutally accepted institutions.

From earliest days, the Beti population in the immediate hinterland of the capital, by virtue of a radically segmentary indigenous social structure, provided only elusive and fragmentary bases on which to build dependable organisational links between rural producers and urban consumers, between peasant and Civil Servant. This space between the two was not, however, a sociological vacuum into which successive governments could simply insert whatever sort of blueprint they chose. An initial period of freedom in the food market made it clear that food could never be cheap or predictable enough if it were delivered through the local headmen who controlled the large surpluses. The requisition system, imposed in the 1920s and run through the chieftaincy hierarchy, enjoyed a decade or so of legitimacy on both sides, largely by virtue of its ambiguity and the relatively low level of extraction in the food sector. When the economic and political costs of the force needed to maintain the two conditions of 'cheap and predictable' rose beyond a certain point, however, the entire blame could be placed squarely on the chiefs, from both sides.

Requisitions were replaced by another government structure, the Provident Society. Here the costs of maintaining low prices were diffused amongst several groups and never, in fact, surfaced as a political issue. The Government was willing to subsidise transport from its own resources, less because of pressures within the food system itself, but because of the advantage which the Provident Societies afforded of helping to maintain economic and political predictability, and an administrative presence, in the rural areas at a time of great unrest.

After independence, direct methods of controlling the food supply were no longer possible to impose. Like the other distribution systems, the free market 'worked' to provide both cheap and predictable supplies over several years, not, however, from some kind of inertia but because of the confluence of several forces, including increased demand, low cocoa prices, and the influx of Bamileke into the capital. Once other prices started to rise, however, neither condition seemed dependable. Producers and traders had other options besides the food market, and were therefore ready to become more elusive in the interest of higher returns. The large-scale traders could move to other markets and the small-scale operators could withdraw their services. Behind official concern about price inflation in the late 1960s lay the more serious fear that Yaoundé could be cut off altogether.

There has been government intervention of one kind or another in urban food supply throughout the 1970s, but the form has been piecemeal and eclectic. Tangible organisations have been promoted through the extension of credit to groups and individuals and the development of a parastatal food agency. Through these means, it was anticipated that prices to the urban consumer could be forced down. In the event, the costs to government and foreign funders has been enormous, with no clear effects on the market, and many of the initiatives have been abandoned.

The successive phases of this history show how contentious the development of the food market can be in a situation characterised by quite definitive limits on the physical productivity of labour in agriculture, on the use of direct force and on the capacity of government to subsidise food to consumers. Political and economic dilemmas are recurrent, resulting in various more or less short-lived measures to bridge their potential inconsistencies. Cutting across this circular motion of shifts in costs and patches in policy, the striking fact remains, however, that market institutions have been formed and that the actual record of supply shows less fluctuation in market prices or volume than one might expect from the convulsive politics of market control.

APPENDIX 1

Population

Table 1 *The population of Yaoundé, and its immediate hinterland (Departments of Mefou, Lékié, Nyong et Kelle, Nyong et Soo), 1965–80 (ratio)*

	1965	*1970*	*1975 (est.)*	*1980 (est.)*
Total ('000)	111:460	178:413	288:458	464:477
Ratio	1:4·1	1:2·3	1:1·6	1:1

Source RUC Min. Agri. 1973:5–6.

Table 2 *The growth of the population of Yaoundé, 1926–76*

Year	*Cameroonians*	*Foreigners*	*Total*
1926	5,500	365	5,065
1933	—	—	6,500
1939	8,500	580	9,080
1945	15,000	2,311	17,311
1952	29,451	2,332	31,783
1953	33,786	3,000	36,786
1957	54,343	3,756	58,099
1962	86,871	3,098	89,969
1964	105,985	3,200	109,185
1965	110,328	—	—
1967	144,723	—	—
1969	159,685	6,125	165,810
1976	303,688	10,018	313,706

Source Franqueville 1984:12.

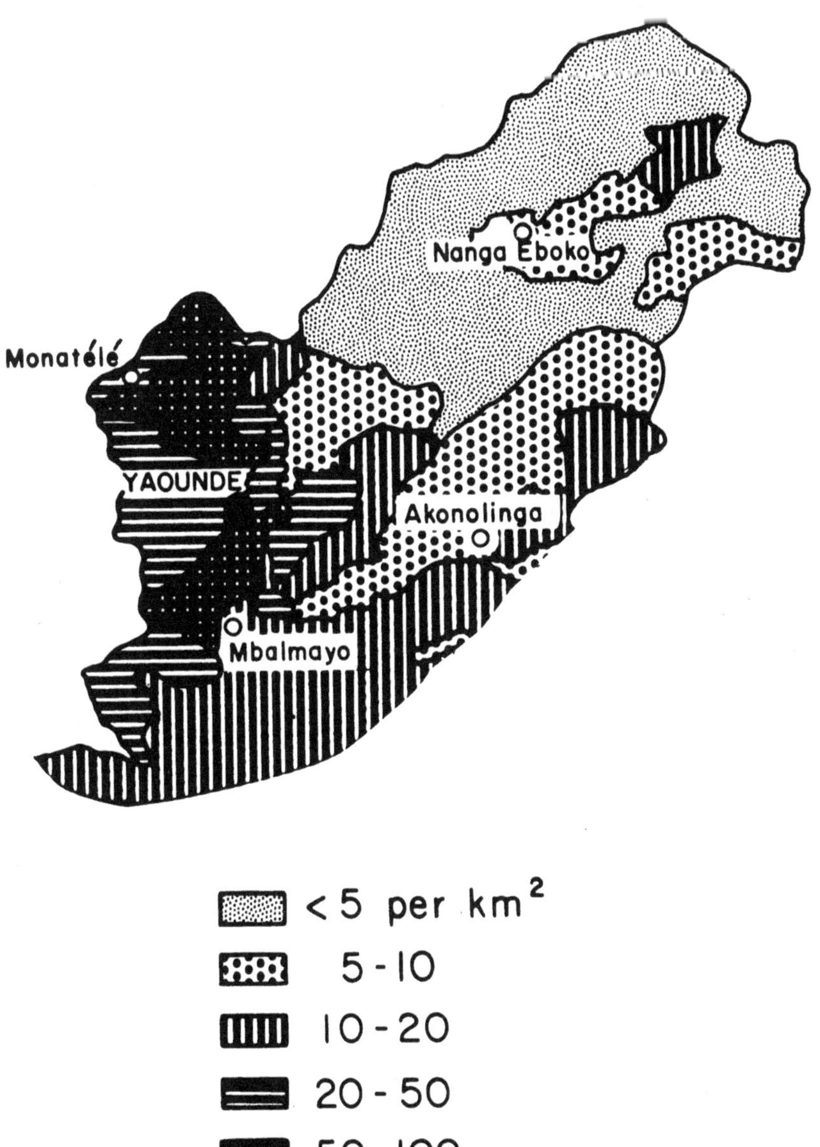

Appendix 1 Population densities in the Yaoundé hinterland

APPENDIX 2

Food prices, 1965–76

Table 3 Price index of staple foods in urban Yaoundé 1965–72

Year	*Plantains*	*Cocoyams*	*Yams*	*Manioc*
1965	100·0	100·0	100·0	100·0
1970	140·0	142·7	94·6	180·0
1972	210·8	224·5	134·9	290·0

Source RUC Min. Agri. 1973:6.

Table 4 Price index of consumer goods, 1968–76

Year	*Food*	*Transport*	*Services & other*	*Clothing*
1968	100·0	100·0	100·0	100·0
1972	130·3	108·3	120·4	115·4
1976	209·8	254·6	203·6	184·6

Source RUC Min. Ec. Plan. 1976:80.

Table 5 Real prices of staple foods, 1970–72

Year	*Plantains*	*Cocoyams*	*Yams*	*Manioc*
1970	0·43	0·41	1·17	0·34
1972	0·65	0·63	1·3	0·44

Source N' Sangou 1975:16.

Table 6 The evolution of the prices of several food products, 1972–5 (%)

Imported products		*Local products*	
Wheat flour	+ 23	Sugar	+134
Nestlé milk	+ 63	Rice	+123
Canned tomatoes	+140	Eggs	+120
Stockfish	+197	Cottonseed oil	+ 93
Red wine	+ 21	Beef (with bones)	+ 71
Sardines	+ 75	Manioc (ball)	+ 55
		Palm oil	+ 50
		Yams	+ 42
		Chicken (live)	+ 42
		Salt	+ 29

Source Franqueville 1984:118.

APPENDIX 3

Urban budgets, 1964–5

Table 7 Expenditure by category, % of total

Food	25
Drink	7
Clothing	11
Construction	11
Services & other	9
Gifts	9
Personal vehicle	6
House and upkeep	6
Transport	4
Household	4
Rent, water, electricity	2
Cash held over	2
Health	2
Total	99

Source SEDES 1964–5: 30.

Table 8 Expenditure on food by category, % of total

Local vegetable foods	
Tubers	10·0
Plantain	5·5
Maize	3·9
Vegetables, fruit, condiments	11·4
Oils, oil seeds	7·5
Total	38·3
Meat, fish	44·8
Manufactured products	16·9
Total	100·0

Source SEDES 1964–5:44.

ACKNOWLEDGEMENTS

The field and archival research on which this paper is based were financed by grants from the US National Institute of Mental Health and the Joint Committee on African Studies of the Social Science Research Council and the American Council of Learned Societies. While carrying out the research the author was an associate of the National Advanced School of Agriculture, Yaoundé. The support of the School, and of Boston University African Studies Center, where a version of the present paper was given in a seminar, is gratefully acknowledged.

NOTES

1 The 1978 National Nutrition Survey concluded that the prevalence of chronic under-nutrition (under ninety per cent height for age of reference median), in children aged 3–59 months, in the country as a whole was 22·1%. In the Centre-South, excluding the large cities, the prevalence was 18·8%, the only region where the percentage fell below twenty (RUC 1978:87).

2 As shown in greater detail in Appendix 3, the urban food budget in 1964–5 was spent in the following proportions: local vegetable foods: 38·3%; meat and fish: 44·8%; manufactured products: 16·9%.

3 The association between disciplined predictability in the commercial system and forms of servitude has by no means died along with the elders of the first colonised generation. Options and concomitant freedom of action are still highly prized, particularly by men.

4 The history of this period is dealt with in considerably more detail in Guyer 1978.

5 According to the census, the working population of 266,737 supported a dependent population of children, the elderly and invalids of only 147,229. While these figures may seem implausible, there were serious epidemics during this period which may have seriously affected child survival.

6 Dugast mentions that in the Ndiki area north of Yaoundé, the chief was still benefiting from 'co-operative' labour in 1953, even though 'this organisation having been created a long time ago, we have not been able, in 1953, to ascertain exactly what it is supposed to be'. We are told that '. . . in 1940–1941, the women were devoting long days (in co-operative plots) to the detriment of their own food plots'. Total duties included 'several days per month on cooperative plots, and one day a week by the women in the chief's coffee' (1955:380, 390, 404). Such lingering of older institutions into new eras is not unusual. As mentioned later, the Provident Societies did not entirely disappear either. The membership fees continued to be levied in the rural areas, and the structure was ultimately transformed into SOMUDER. Such interpenetration makes clear periodisation questionable, especially for the people themselves, who are inclined to see one kind of organisation drift indistinguishably into another.

7 FIDES (*Fonds d'Investment pour le Développement Economique et Social des Territoires d'Outre-Mer*), created in 1946, was the most important form of metropolitan investment in the colonies.

8 The degree of self-provisioning of the urban population may have changed in recent years, as the proportion of non-professional urban workers has risen, and as many professional people have revived interest in their villages of origin or have acquired land elsewhere. The insignificance of self-provisioning in the early 1960s is unusual for an African city.

9 Bamileke commercial enterprise is renowned, but its operation in the food

trade has not been described in detail. One commentator has gone so far as to suggest that the official neglect of the transport infrastructure throughout the South during the presidency of Ahidjo was an attempt to 'put a brake on the characteristic expansionism of the South, in particular of the Bamileke' (Willame 1985:70).

10 The tables in Appendix 2 come from different sources and are not altogether consonant with one another. It may be a mistake to try to resolve any of the ambiguities, or to pull out a particular interpretation. Diarra's informants amongst the food traders claimed that rising food prices were a result of the increased cost of essential items such as transport and stockfish to rural producers (1974). According to price series, local food prices may have crept up faster than other prices at the end of the 1960s, but they were quickly overtaken by the price of transport and stockfish in the early 1970s. In any case, there is flimsy evidence to support the isolation of local food prices as particularly responsible for the rise in the urban cost of living.

11 Between 1960 and 1980, Cameroon has been one of the few African countries experiencing decreasing primacy of its largest city (World Bank 1984:260). This is due in part to the separation of economic and administrative capitals (Douala and Yaoundé respectively), and in part to the growth of important regional centres in old chieftaincies (Marguerat 1984:65).

12 FONADER is the *Fonds National de Développement Rural*: MIDEVIV is the *Mission pour le Développement de la Culture Vivrière*.

13 Policies and practices on rice production and import have been, like much of Cameroonian food policy, eclectic in conception and mixed in results. Cameroon's cereal imports grew only forty-four per cent, to 117,000 metric tons, between 1974 and 1982, and hardly any cereals were given in food aid (World Bank 1984:228). Domestic rice schemes have provided half of the total rice consumption, but at high prices and through an organisational structure which allows importers to 'purchase their quota' of national rice, without taking delivery, and continue to import rice from India and Pakistan' (Willame 1985:48–9). How this possibility then affects the official statistics on rice consumption by source within Cameroon (as opposed to neighbouring countries) is quite unclear.

14 In a recent book on Yaoundé, Franqueville captures the same profound ambivalence about the food supply system. From one point of view, 'and this is probably the gravest in the eyes of the Government, total anarchy reigns in the organisation of this commerce, susceptible to all kinds of abuses', while from another perspective, 'the 'buy'em sell'em' system seems better tolerated and its virtues even seem to be recognised. Does it not function in a perfectly competitive market, with no monopolies, open to all?' (1984:120, 122).

15 Due in part to the sense of increasing political liberalisation following the change in national leadership in 1982, there has been a surge in local organising in recent years. The rapid spread of women's rotating credit associations throughout the South has been dramatic enough to have political repercussions, as the single political party and its women's branch attempt to come to terms with an apparently spontaneous social movement. The implications for economic change have yet to become apparent, but they could be considerable.

REFERENCES

Reports and publications

Antoine, Philippe. 1954. 'Les Sociétés Africaines de Prévoyance au Cameroun'. Univérsité de Paris, unpublished *theŝe pour le doctorat en droit.*

Barboteu, G., U. Poisson & P. Vignal. 1962. *Etude des Structures Rurales.* Yaoundé: Ministère de la Coopération.

Benjacov, M. 1970. 'The statutes of SOMUDER in the Eastern Cameroun', *Cooperative Information,* 55–60.

Billard, Pierre. 1961. *La Circulation dans le Sud Cameroun.* Lyon: Imprimérie de Beaux Arts.

Binet, Jacques. 1956a. *Budgets Familiaux des Planteurs de Cacao au Cameroun.* Paris: ORSTOM.

—— 1956b. 'Les Capitaux Autochtones et leur Mobilisation dans l'Economie Rurale: Mobilisation des Capitaux dans l'Economie Rurale du Sud-Cameroun'. Paris: *Troisième Symposium Internationale d'Économie Rurale Tropicale.*

Buell, R. L. 1928. *The Native Problem in Africa.* New York: Bureau of International Research, Harvard University & Radcliffe College.

David, M. 1956. *La modernisation du Paysannat au Cameroun et en A.E.F.* Paris: Centre National de la Coopération Agricole.

Diarra, Fatoumata A. 1974. *Commercialisation des Products Vivriers de la Lékié par les Béyam-Sellam.* Yaoundé: UN and Ministry of Planning.

Dugast, I. 1955. *Monographie de la Tribu des Ndiki.* Paris: Institut d'Ethnologie.

Eze, L-F. 1974. *'Le Commandement Indigène de la Région du Nyong et Sanaga (Sud-Cameroun) de 1916 à 1945'.* Université de Paris, unpublished thesis.

Franqueville, André. 1976. 'L'évolution du marché centrale de Yaoundé. Comparaison de deux enquêtes', in *La Croissance Urbaine dans les Pays Tropicaux.* Paris: Memoirs CECET, CNRS.

—— 1979. 'Croissance démographique et immigration á Yaoundé', *Les Cahiers d'Outre-Mer,* 128:321–54.

—— 1984. *Yaoundé. Construire une capitale.* Paris: ORSTOM.

Guyer, Jane I. 1978. 'The food economy and French colonial rule in Central Cameroun, *Journal of African History,* 19, (4): 577–97.

—— 1980. 'The Provident Societies in the Rural Economy of Yaoundé 1945–60' Boston University: African Studies Center, Working Paper No. 37.

—— 1981. 'The administration and the depression in South-Central Cameroun', *African Economic History,* 10: 67–79.

—— 1984. *Family and Farm in Southern Cameroon.* Boston University African Studies Center, African Research Studies No. 15.

Henn, Jeanne K. 1978. 'Peasants, Workers and Capitalists: The Development of Capitalism in Cameroon'. Harvard University, unpublished PhD thesis.

Joseph, R. 1977. *Radical Nationalism in Cameroun.* Oxford: The Clarendon Press.

Kom, David. 1971. *Le Cameroun. Essai d'analyse économique et politique.* Paris: Éditions Sociales.

—— 1977. 'The cooperative movement in the Cameroons', in Peter Gutkind and Peter Watermen (eds.), *African Social Studies. A Radical Reader,* pp. 281–94. New York: Monthly Review Press.

Kuczynski, Robert R. 1939. *The Cameroons and Togoland. A Demographic Study.* Oxford University Press.

Laburthe-Tolra, Philippe. 1970. *Yaoundé d'après Zenker.* Yaoundé: Extrait des Annales de la Faculté des Lettres et Sciences Humaines de Yaoundé, No. 2.

Lebigre, J.-M. 1980. 'Production vivrière et approvisionnement urban au Gabon',

Les Cahiers d'Outre-Mer. 130: 167–85.
Lefebvre, André. 1972. *Conditions d'un Développement Intégré dans la Lékié*. Yaoundé: UN & Ministry of Planning.
Lonsdale, J. & B. Berman. 1979. 'Coping with the contradictions: the development of the colonial state in Kenya 1895–1914', *Journal of African History*, 20: 487–505.
Marguerat, Yves. 1984. 'Réflexions sursives sur l'évolution des réseaux urbains en Afrique noire', in Philippe Haeringer (ed.), *De Caracas à Kinshasa*, pp. 51–65. Paris: ORSTOM.
von Morgen, Curt. 1972 (1893). *A Travers le Cameroun du Sud au Nord*. Yaoundé: Université Fédérale du Cameroun, Archives d'Histoire et de Sociologie.
Morinière, Jean-Louis. 1972. 'La région maraichère intra et peri-urbaine de Yaoundé'. in *Dix Etudes sur l'Approvisionnement des Villes*, pp. 47–79. Paris: CEGET, CNRS.
N'Sangou, Arouna. 1975. 'La consommatioin alimentaire dans la région de Yaoundé', *Le Cameroun Agricole, Pastoral et Forestier* 148, (10): 19.
—— 1977a. *Secteur Refuge et Développement Economique au Cameroun*. Yaoundé: ONAREST.
—— 1977b. *Offre et Demande des Produits Vivriers dans la Région de Yaoundé*. Yaoundé: ONAREST.
Onambele, Xavier. 1969. 'Distribution des biens de consommation et les problèmes urbains à Yaoundé'. Université de Paris, unpublished thesis.
Passelande, Vincent. 1972. 'Le ravitaillement vivrier de Douala par la voie ferrée', in *Dix Etudes sur l'Approvisionnement des Villes*, pp. 207–16. Paris: CEGET, CNRS.
Quinn, E. F. 1971. 'Changes in Beti society – 1887–1960'. Los Angeles, University of California, unpublished PhD thesis.
Robinson, K. 1950. 'The *Sociétés de Prévoyance* in French West Africa', *Journal of African Administration*. 12, (4): 29–34.
Suret-Canale, Jean. 1971. *French Colonialism in Tropical Africa, 1900–1945*. London: C. Hurst.
Tissandier, J. 1969. *Zengoaga*. Paris: Mouton.
Trager, Lillian. 1980. 'Customers and creditors: variations in economic personalism in a Nigerian marketing system', *Ethnology* 20, (2): 133–46.
Weber, Jacques. 1974. *Structures Agraires et Evolution des Milieux Ruraux. Le Cas de la Region Cacaoyère de Centre-Sud Cameroun*. Yaoundé: ORSTOM.
Willame, J-C. 1985. 'Cameroun: les avatars d'un libéralisme planifié', *Politique Africaine*, 18: 44–70.
World Bank. 1984. *World Development Report*. Washington, DC.

Government documents

INSTRUPA (Insitut fur Strukturforschung und Planung). 1978. Étude sur l'établissement d'un système de distribution de crédits agricoles au sein du FONADER.
MIDEVIV (Mission pour le Développement de la Culture Vivrière). 1976. Grandes Lignes d'une Organisation Commerciale de Produits Vivriers.
—— 1978. Rapport Annuel d'Activités, Exercise 1977–78.
Ministry of Agriculture. 1973. Operation Ceinture Verte: Projet de création aux environs de Yaoundé de plantations villageoises de bananes plantains.
Ministry of Economy and Planning. 1970. La Population de Yaoundé: Résultats définitifs du recensement de 1962.
—— 1974. Comice Agricole, Ngaoundéré, 10–11 December.
—— 1974–75. Note Annuelle de Statistique.

——1976. Combien sommes-nous?
—— 1976b. Fourth Five-Year Economic, Social and Cultural Development Plan, 1976–81.
—— 1978. Rapport sur la situation économique de la Province du Centre-Sud (1976/1977–1977/1978).
SEDES/Direction de la Statistique (*Société d'études pour le Développement Economique et Social*). 1964/65. Enquête sur le Niveau de Vie à Yaoundé.
—— 1965. Les Prix des Produits Vivriers dans les Marchés de la Zone Cacaoyère Centre.
—— 1966. Trafic Routier Autour de Yaoundé.
United Republic of Cameroon (RUC). 1978. National Nutrition Survey. Final Report.

Archival sources

AR Annual Report of the Government of Cameroun to the Permanent Mandate Commission of the League of Nations.
BD Ministry of Economy and Planning: Bureau de Documentation (BD). Monographies Départementales.
CNA Cameroon National Archives: Yaoundé, Saa.
UN Annual Report of the Government of Cameroun to the Permanent Mandate Commission of the United Nations
JOC Journal Officiel du Cameroun

Newspaper
Cameroun Tribune.

4 *Deborah Fahy Bryceson*

A CENTURY OF FOOD SUPPLY IN DAR ES SALAAM

FROM SUMPTUOUS SUPPERS FOR THE SULTAN TO MAIZE MEAL FOR A MILLION[1]

INTRODUCTION

In 1866 Sultan Seyyid Majid of Zanzibar Island set about building a settlement of extravagant design in a sheltered harbour on the East African mainland. Dar es Salaam, the 'harbour of peace', idyll in name – nonetheless its establishment was a pragmatic venture intended to secure the Sultan's firmer influence over the mainland caravan trade. By 1870 a palace had been constructed on the site, but Sultan Majid's death brought a halt to the project. His successor, Sultan Bargash, let the settlement revert to bush. The deep-water harbour, however, attracted both Asian trade and the interest of European explorers. In 1891 the German Government, seeking to establish formal control over its newly acquired territory, designated Dar es Salaam as its capital. Once the central railway line was constructed into the hinterland with Dar es Salaam as its terminus, Dar es Salaam became the major port of German East Africa.

Although Dar es Salaam's original founding was rooted in nineteenth-century mercantile interests, its growth fed on the forces of the twentieth century: the railway, modern shipping, and later, the advent of automobile transport. Dar es Salaam was to maintain its supremacy as the seat of government and major port throughout the colonial period under the Germans and, beginning in 1919, as a British mandated territory. Since independence in 1961, it has continued to serve in these capacities[2] as well as being the main site for Tanzania's embryonic industrial development. In response to the metropolitan character of Dar es Salaam, the youth of Tanzania have gravitated to the capital from the rural areas. In the 1970s the population grew at the rate of almost ten per cent per annum, burgeoning to over a million inhabitants by 1982, just a little more than a hundred years after Sultan Majid first embarked on building his dream city.

The present residents of Dar es Salaam, most of whom are migrants from the rural areas, have their own dreams and aspirations when they arrive in the city. Although they are a diverse population, hailing from all parts of the country and hence accustomed to various staple foods of their home areas – maize, cassava, rice, plantains, sorghum, millet, sweet potatoes – there is a very strong tendency for the so-called 'preferred cereals', namely maize, rice and wheat, to predominate in the city due to acquired urban tastes, relative availability and convenience of preparation. Cassava serves as the staple food of last resort. Sorghum and millet, the drought-resistant staples indigenous to East Africa, have been steadily displaced by maize in many places in rural Tanzania. But this tendency is taken to an extreme in Dar es Salaam, where sorghum and millet have no place at all in the official urban market.[3]

Dar es Salaam's population constitutes five per cent of the total Tanzanian population and roughly forty per cent of the total urban population in a country where eighty-seven per cent of the population is rural (1978 census). Tanzania's population growth rate between 1967 and 1978 was 3·3 per cent, whereas the urban growth rate was 9·3 per cent, Dar es Salaam being 9·9 per cent (see Appendix 1). Dar es Salaam is a primate city *par excellence*, with a population seven times greater than that of the next largest city. Situated on the coast of a huge, relatively sparsely-populated territory, it would pose logistical problems of food supply even if it were not so large.

Urban population growth represents an expanding proportion of the country's total population who are non-food producers, making increased output of grain from rural producers imperative. But the conditions of staple food production prevailing in the rural areas do not favour the rapid attainment of increased grain output. With the exception of wheat, the vast majority of grains and starches are produced by peasant smallholders dispersed throughout the country. Most peasant households aim to be self-sufficient in grain production. Marketed grain represents a small and uncertain margin over and above annual household consumption, making the collection of grain crops by marketing agencies extremely difficult.

Peasant production is highly vulnerable to weather variability and soil degradation. Drought is not uncommon. The source of eighty-five per cent of farm energy is human labour using hand hoes. Only ten per cent of production is based on oxen and ploughs and another five per cent using tractor mechanisation. In 1980, 104,600 tonnes of fertiliser were distributed, amounting to 0·02 tonnes of fertilizer per hectare in Tanzania as a whole.

Staple food yields fluctuate widely from year to year around a low average. Depending on the area of the country, yields range between 550 and 1,100 kg/ha for maize, an average of 400 kg/ha for paddy, 600 kg/ha for white sorghum/bulrush millet and 1,400 kg/ha for cassava. The labour days per hectare required to produce such yields are estimated to be between 97 and 122 days for maize, 120 days for paddy and white sorghum/bulrush millet and 142 days for cassava (Stainburn 1982). World average yields for maize are 3,000 kg/ha, 2,600 kg for rice and 1,300 for sorghum (World Bank 1981:169).

Assuming that all adult Tanzanians eat 180 kg of grain per year (Food and Agricultural Organisation standard), children under fifteen years of age eat 90 kg, and only the adult rural population produce grain, then each of the 7·8 million rural adults in 1978 producing an average maize yield of 800 kg/ha would have to produce 300 kg to feed themselves as well as rural non-adults and the urban population. This would require forty-one days' effort per producer, cultivating two-fifths of a hectare, and would occupy forty-three per cent of the 6·8 million hectares presently under cultivation in Tanzania. By world standards, this is highly land-extensive and labour-intensive.

During the 1970s Dar es Salaam residents experienced shortages of the preferred cereals. Beginning in 1974 after a bad harvest, wheat flour was in almost perennial short supply, rice in sporadic supply and even maize meal, *sembe*, the major staple, became a problem in the early 1980s. Food shortages are not new to Dar es Salaam. Demand and supply factors have combined to produce critical shortages for extended periods of time in previous decades, but there are indications of an increasing tendency towards a shortfall in the national supply and the extent to which Dar es Salaam's increasing demand for food contributes to this shortfall is suggested by the fact that Dar es Salaam accounts for roughly fifty per cent of officially marketed consumer purchases of maize meal, rice and wheat flour (see Appendix 2).

The sections that follow delineate three stages of population growth and food demand in Dar es Salaam. These stages represent different orders of magnitude in city size and rate of population growth, the changing accessibility of the city's hinterland, as well as different organisational forms of production and marketing. While the main actors in the evolution of the city's food supply have been the urban consumers and peasant producers, marketing agents have been the vital go-between. The changing nature of marketing agents, as well as state policies aimed at circumventing peasant production by encouraging grain production from commercial farms, both private and public, lend complexity to the central issue at hand, that of matching rural food supply with urban demand. Historically, the tendency has been for demand to be disproportionally larger than supply, necessitating imports and, when extreme, engendering food crises. Three periods of food crisis are identified and compared.

DAR ES SALAAM 1866–1906: NUCLEUS OF A NEW ORDER

THE ECLIPSE OF THE SLAVE ECONOMY

At the time of its founding in 1866, Dar es Salaam was populated by the Zeramo tribe as well as a few Indian and several Arab traders. A hierarchy of slave and master relations characterised this community. The agricultural slaves cultivated on their masters' plantations for four days and could cultivate their own food for the remaining three (Baker 1931:3). Given the low population density there was free availability of land for all. Usufruct rights prevailed. The agricultural complex was one of coconuts and rice. Rice flourished in the various swampy areas surrounding the harbour and coconut groves fringed the beaches extending inland for some distance. The cultivation of cassava, sorghum, sweet potatoes, beans, millet, maize, mango and sugar-cane rounded out the agricultural picture.

Sultan Majid encouraged the continuation and extension of existing cultivation (Seward 1866). As early as 1867, he was entertaining diplomatic guests in Dar es Salaam. No doubt locally produced food bedecked the banquet table on such occasions.

In 1887 the Germans took control of Dar es Salaam from the Sultan and in 1891 they designated the city as the capital of their newly-acquired German East Africa colony. The German period initiated three structural changes: first, the slave economy was destroyed and replaced with the beginnings of a rural peasant and an urban wage economy; secondly, the social division of labour on racial grounds was established, giving rise to differentiated standards of living; and thirdly, the foundations of the colonial economy were laid, both in the sense of infrastructure building, i.e. construction of government buildings and the establishment of a transport network and in agricultural experimentation. In the context of these developments Dar es Salaam grew rapidly.

Rates of in-migration were very high during the German period, causing population growth to be the highest on record (see Appendix 1). This quickly led to grain deficits in the city. Historically the Dar es Salaam area had been a net exporter of grain to Zanzibar. In 1888–9, at the outset of German rule, production in and around Dar es Salaam accounted for approximately forty per cent of German East Africa's total rice exports, twenty per cent of the maize exports and ten per cent of the sorghum; by 1894 the situation had drastically changed. Net imports were three times the value of 1888–9 exports, and constituted 68 per cent of the territorial deficit by volume (Wright & Butler 1979). Roughly one-third of all grain requirements for the city were being imported; a substantial amount in view of the overwhelmingly agricultural character of the country. Rice constituted the bulk of the imports.

CHANGING FOOD TASTES

Why was rice the most popular staple? Three racial groups who hailed from distinct culinary traditions were resident in the city: the Africans with a variety of sorghum/millet, banana and maize-based diets, the Asians generally with a rice diet and the Germans with a wheat and rye diet. Since the Asians were a minority, constituting less than ten per cent of the population, it was unlikely that their presence dictated the shift in staple food. Rather, it had more to do with the acculturation process that African migrants experienced in Dar es Salaam. Three-quarters of the city's inhabitants in 1903 were migrants from up-country (Raum 1965:166). Islam and its attendant Arabisation had prevailed as a strong detribalising force on the coast since the ninth century, and the Germans did not discourage it. The incoming tribal migrants found themselves being labelled *washenzi*, uncouth, backward natives, whereas the assimilated Swahili-born of up-country parents but adopting various aspects of Islam and Arab culture were *wastarabu*, civilised people. Not only did this involve speaking Kiswahili, wearing a *kanzu*, making a token attempt at knowing a bit of the Koran and being circumcised, but also the dictum 'you are what you eat' prevailed; rice was the food of the Waswahili (Raum 1965:166).

The socio-economic form of food demand changed radically during this period. In previous times the slave had produced his own food on the days allotted to him by his master. The amount of food that a slave had to consume depended directly on the weather and the benevolence of his master. With the growth of the wage economy this began to change. Personal benevolence or malevolence on the part of the master were replaced with an impersonal wage packet; the dilemma of effective demand began to make itself felt.

LOCALISED FOOD SUPPLY

Since transport was restricted in the main to human porterage, and the tropical climate caused rapid food spoilage, Dar es Salaam's food supply had to depend on production in a limited radius from the city, and the immediate coastal areas which were accessible by boat. Cultivation in the immediate environs of Dar es Salaam was considerable. The Zaramo grew rice in the valleys. To what degree they monopolised land at the expense of the incoming migrants is not known. Most of the food produced on the innumerable plots surrounding the city was probably for home consumption, only a portion of it entering the market.

The Government actively encouraged this private cultivation, but tried to extend cultivation in collectivised forms as well. In 1902, every local *jumbe*[4] in the Dar es Salaam district had to enforce the government decision to establish common fields in each village where all male inhabitants not in European employment were obliged to work twenty-four days in the year. By 1905, these village fields covered 1,200 hectares, boosting the area's food supply.

The German colonial state endeavoured to increase peasant production, but faced an intractable environment. Natural hazards caused fluctuations in production. Drought was a serious problem affecting the coastal districts in 1907. Locusts appeared in most parts of the country between 1893 and 1895 (Iliffe 1979:125). Because of the low population density, vermin were a continual menace. The presence of ripening crops attracted birds and monkeys. Women and children guarded the fields. The men made fires to keep hippos and wild boars away at night (German East Africa 1906–7).

Political and social circumstances also militated for restricted food production. The decade of the 1890s was a period of rebellion in many parts of the country. Dar es Salaam was not directly involved, but the pestilence that followed in the wake of the violent upheaval affected Dar es Salaam. Smallpox killed a tenth of the city's population in 1893. Twelve years later, in 1905, the Maji Maji War flared, bringing virtual decimation to agricultural production in many southern areas of the country which supplied Dar es Salaam (Iliffe 1979:124; German East Africa 1907–8).

In the Dar es Salaam district itself, the German authorities held the view that the inherited slave plantation system hindered agricultural production. Twenty per cent of the total coastal population in 1900 were slaves. Immigration of men from up-country was encouraged with the intention of undermining the paternalistic slave system and its alleged low level of output.

> Although the coastal districts still are the only ones from where the exportation of most of the agricultural produce at the present state of transport is profitable these are in the least favourable position in respect to the number and zeal in work of the population, as a consequence of the immigration fostered by the administration of the Protectorate, a rejoycing (sic.) increase of the agricultural production can be observed there. . . . However, the growth of the production was not fully reflected in the exportation since the population increase created a higher domestic consumption and apparently the overall conditions of living of the coastal population are gradually improving. (German East Africa 1901–2).

Throughout the German period, slavery as opposed to slave trading was not outlawed, but slaves could buy their freedom for a sizeable sum or petition the Government for freedom if they could prove maltreatment by their owners. The Government decreed that all children born after 1905 could not be enslaved (Iliffe 1979:131). These measures had the effect of slowly undermining the coastal plantation system.

The German Administration was of the opinion that the traditional hoe used by the peasants was 'too weak and small for an orderly tillage and cultivation of the soil' (German East Africa 1901–2). The agricultural service distributed seeds and encouraged the use of the plough, not realising, in the latter case, that its adoption would require momentous change in the sexual division of labour of many tribes. So too the adoption of the plough demanded a significant monetary investment that few peasant farmers could afford in the absence of credit facilities (Henderson 1965:144; Raum 1965:188; German East Africa 1906–7).

In the forty years between 1866 and 1906, Dar es Salaam had developed from a Zaramo tribal settlement subject to the influences of the Zanzibari ivory and slave trade to become the capital of German East Africa. The small village population had expanded, under the economic stimulus of trade and government administration, to probably more than twenty times its original size. The food demand generated by this concentration of people put stress on the productive capacity of the surrounding area still heavily influenced by the legacy of slavery. Reliance on food imports, particularly of rice, for roughly a third of the city's food requirements, characterised the end of this period.

DAR ES SALAAM 1907–39: PROVINCIAL CENTRE

ORGANIC DEVELOPMENT OF TOWN AND COUNTRY

Until 1907 Dar es Salaam represented a new order incubating in the womb of a rapidly disintegrating older system. With the advent of the central railway the new order asserted itself. Railway construction was initiated in 1905, and by 1907 the track reached Morogoro, the first major up-country crop supply area.[5] The final completion of the line at Kigoma, on the shores of Lake Tanganyika, took place in 1914 on the very eve of World War I.[6] Dar es Salaam became the gateway to a vastly expanded hinterland, but a hinterland which was still unharnessed and remote. The railway opened up a corridor bisecting the country, but the multitude of branches from this main artery were still only footpaths plied by porters heaving twenty-five kg loads. Tsetse, African horse sickness and rinderpest prevented the widespread use of animal power. Lorry transport did not become prevalent until the 1930s and 1940s.

In contrast to the rapid population growth of the late nineteenth century, Dar es Salaam grew at only two per cent per annum between 1907 and 1939 (see Appendix 1). The declining rate of population growth began to manifest itself even before the dislocating effects of World War I. Dar es Salaam was not a booming urban centre. It was provincial in character.

During this phase of Dar es Salaam's development, with the exception of the war years, a fairly neutral country-wide import–export grain picture emerges with years of net import being counterbalanced by years of net export (see Appendix 2). This situation prevailed between 1921 and 1937, despite localised famines that sporadically occurred in various parts of the country. The proportion of imports consumed in Dar es Salaam cannot be discerned from the data, but the slow population growth of the city, and the greater accessibility to up-country grain supply areas, would have contributed to the achievement of proportionality between the city's marketed food demand and rural supply. The war years, however, were different, being a period of enormous food supply stress.

WORLD WAR I AND FOOD CRISIS

The relationship between heavy food imports and crisis that was to become a recurrent theme in the twentieth century first appeared during World War I. The reliance on food imports before the war put the city in a vulnerable position under combat conditions. As the war progressed, the supply of food to Dar es Salaam became increasingly difficult for the Germans and reached crisis proportions under British occupation.

Dar es Salaam was a likely target for attack, being the colony's main port. In December 1914, the British navy bombarded Dar es Salaam. A coastal blockade left the Germans with no option but to become self-sufficient in the provisioning of the population's needs. Deprived of its function as a port, Dar es Salaam became a drain rather than a facilitator of German war operations. In the face of the coastal blockade the Germans had to make maximum use of stocks and resources existing in the area they controlled. As it happened, unusually large stocks of European food were on hand in readiness for the central railway's opening celebrations. Plantations all along the line of rail switched from plantation crops to food production. Peasants in Ulanga, Tabora, Mwanza and Kigoma were reported by one German writer in the early stages of the war to have produced rice in such abundance that it was surmised that after the war it would no longer be necessary to import rice from India. Whether this was true or German propaganda is impossible to verify; the situation did, however, drastically worsen as the war intensified. To halt grain speculation the German administration adopted the policy of curbing Asian middleman trade by establishing a monthly ration for troops at fixed prices. Later, food rations were extended to the civil population (Henderson 1965:160; PRO/CO691/12/206).

In September 1916, Dar es Salaam was taken by the British and assumed the role of a huge military camp. The British as occupiers did not have the same resources nor commanding influence. Restricted civilian movements, Indian traders' qualms over the value of German currency and the eventual ban on trade spelt the decimation of normal channels of hinterland trade. In any case, as the war progressed Dar es Salaam's hinterland became virtually devoid of food surpluses for the urban population. The requisitioning of food for troop consumption; the destruction of large amounts of food as a tactical move when the enemy was advancing and the general instability of wartime conditions caused peasants to reduce their acreages. And on top of all this drought struck (PRO/C0691/5/380; PRO/C04/289; PRO/C0691/6).

The high cost of living resulting from the difficulty of procuring foodstuffs in Dar es Salaam made it necessary for the British Administration to raise the monthly cash assistance given to interned German families to twice that of those interned in other parts of the country. The African population cut off from supply links with up-country relations and not subject to the same humanitarian conventions as were applied to the interned Germans faced acute deprivation. Many migrated to their home areas (PRO/CO691/18/396).

After the war, severe food shortages continued for yet another year. The drought that had plagued the country since 1917 did not abate; by 1919 tens of thousands had died in the central area of the country, and one out of every five persons in Dodoma was thought to have died. The reduction in the Dar es Salaam district population between 1913 and 1921 from 161,500 to 149,100 implies that the coastal area did not escape the calamity. Both migration and death are behind these figures (Iliffe 1979:269; see Appendix 1).

In the wake of this devastation the upsurge of grain production and exports in the early 1920s has to be viewed as a remarkable recovery testifying to the re-establishment of a viable relationship between Dar es Salaam and the countryside in the immediate post-war period (see Appendix 2).

URBANISATION AND FOOD DEMAND

During the 1920s and 1930s, Dar es Salaam was not a centre of immigration as it had been and was later to become. Labour migration in the country was focused on the plantation rather than on the town. To meet government tax exactions, thousands of African men from marginal and remote parts of the country migrated to the sisal estates of the coast and along the central line railway, to work for 'bachelor' wages.

The absence of urbanisation tendencies amongst Africans was viewed officially as a positive factor, as evidenced in the commentary of Orde-Browne, a well-known government labour official of that time.

> The creation of large industrial centres with workers completely divorced from food production would be an entire innovation of very doubtful desirability; it appears most unlikely to occur. The African man, and still more the woman, is firmly attached to the soil, and the whole fabric of social organization is based upon the right to cultivate; it thus seems probable that the native will always aim at having his

own home among his own crops, whether in a distant village or as a 'squatter' on an estate. (Orde-Browne 1926:72)

In fact, Africans had few job opportunities in Dar es Salaam outside the port and domestic service. The city's economic activity centred on government offices and the administrative headquarters of various trading establishments where skilled labour was required. Very few Africans had the education qualifying them for these jobs. Not surprisingly, the population growth rate of Asians in Dar es Salaam far exceeded that of Africans at over five per cent per annum. Asians were often employed in clerical posts in government offices, but they were most numerous in the private trade sector. Asian family firms recruited relatives from India as their businesses prospered.

In spite of the growth of the Asian population, the Dar es Salaam district remained rural and relatively underpopulated, as indicated by the posting of more game control staff to curb the presence of elephant and hippo (Tanganyika, Provincial Commissioner's Annual Report, Eastern Province 1933:42–3).

In 1931, Dar es Salaam's population numbered 34,300, whereas the total territorial labour force was probably between 130,000 and 150,000, roughly four times greater (Tanganyika 1927–30).[7] In comparison with the heavy demand for staple foodstuffs exerted by the plantation labour force, Dar es Salaam's food demands were minimal. As Iliffe points out:

> . . . situated on the coast of a vast country, the capital never dominated Tanganyika's economy as Nairobi dominated Kenya's. Instead Tanganyika had a polycentric economy, with each export-producing region acting as a focus of exchange. North-eastern estates drew maize and fruit from Bonde, vegetables and tobacco from Usambara, and meat from Mbulu, Kondoa, Singida, Masailand, and Usukuma. Coffee-rich Buhaya bought the cattle of Sukumaland and Rwanda, the fish of Lake Victoria, and tobacco of Biharmulo. These regional economies were as yet scarcely integrated into a territorial economy. (Iliffe 1979:312)

Effective demand from the small African sector of the urban labour force was blunted by payment in kind and by low wages. Many employed Africans resident in Dar es Salaam received a portion of their wage in kind, especially house servants, who ate meals at their place of work. The rest of the African working population depended on the purchasing power of their cash wages. The real value of wages, although higher than the rest of the country in the early 1920s, was being eroded throughout the depression of the 1930s. One telling indication of this was that the Dar es Salaam beer market erected in 1926 showed reduced returns during the depression (Tanganyika, Provincial Commissioner's Annual Report, Eastern Province 1938).

Since Dar es Salaam's African population was predominately male, receiving low bachelor wages, they often depended on the food parcels that

Table 8 Comparison of maize and rice imports

	Rice		Maize		Maize and maize meal	
Year	*Vol. of imports (quintals)*	*Total grain import (%)*	*Vol. of imports (quintals)*	*Total grain import (%)*	*Vol. of imports (quintals)*	*Total grain import (%)*
1921	4,078	27·5	134	0·9	2,534	17·1
1922	11,611	43·5	173	0·6	3,208	12·0
1923	2,415	13·7	796	4·5	3,563	20·2
1924	4,594	18·0	541	2·1	5,556	21·7
1925	20,005	28·6	9,663	13·8	23,405	33·5
1926	22,351	25·3	6,877	7·8	36,017	40·7
1927	19,448	20·6	3,080	3·3	38,540	40·9
1928	19,072	23·5	3,447	4·3	22,850	28·2
1929	49,981	35·0	29,645	20·8	52,287	36·6
1930	33,355	23·5	31,525	22·2	63,351	44·7
1931	14,926	18·9	20,323	25·8	30,244	38·4
1932	4,315	11·8	1,366	3·7	4,413	12·0
1933	3,225	4·1	28,734	36·5	38,321	48·7
1934	3,897	2·5	58,016	37·4	105,264	67·8
1935	3,827	2·2	63,314	37·0	119,436	69·7
1936	4,808	2·9	38,104	23·2	112,111	68·2
1937	4,471	3·0	39,027	25·9	89,867	59·7
1938	4,986	2·5	71,761	36·4	135,612	68·9
1939	5,025	2·5	76,292	37·6	133,134	65·7

Source Tanganyika Annual Trade Reports 1921–39.

a wife or visiting relative brought them from farms in their home areas, rather than depending on market sources. There is no way of knowing just how important this source of supply was but one government official held it to be the most important: '. . . the wages earned by the natives of Dar es Salaam are still largely spent on luxuries. . . . The basic foodstuffs are still produced on his *shamba*',[8] (McCleery 1939:10).

The most outstanding feature of food demand during the 1920s and especially the 1930s which contrasts with the earlier German period was that African labourers were consuming a growing amount of maize rather than rice (see Table 8). There were several reasons for this. While both wetland and highland rice were grown in Tanganyika, maize cultivation was becoming more widespread, displacing millet as the most important staple. Maize was higher yielding, easier to harvest and store and quicker to prepare, although less drought resistant than millet. Employers of 'fed' labour were instrumental in standardising the diet of Tanganyikans. For the sake of expedience and cost, all plantation labourers, regardless of their traditional preferences, were expected to live on a maize-based diet. There is a literature on how to 'wean' banana and rice-eaters to maize. It had been discovered by disconcerted plantation owners that without the gradual introduction of the heavier staple their workers often suffered considerable metabolic upset, which disrupted the work regime (Charron 1944).

Most imported rice came from India and Burma and was subject to customs duty. It was three times more expensive by weight than imported maize coming primarily from Kenya. During the depression real wages drastically declined causing many urban consumers to seek cheaper staple foods (von Freyhold 1977:6–7; Iliffe 1979:352–3). A comparison of the volume of maize and rice imports strikingly illustrates the impact of the depression on grain consumption patterns. In 1930 the volume of maize imports exceeded rice as a proportion of total grain imports for the first time and with the exception of only one subsequent year after that this continued to be the case. When one includes maize meal imports, one sees that total maize imports superseded rice, beginning in the mid-1920s, and was more than twenty-five times greater than that of rice by 1934.

SHIFTING POLITICAL BALANCE: AFRICAN PEASANTS, EUROPEAN PLANTERS AND ASIAN TRADERS

After World War I, with the change from German to British control, the pre-war plantation economy run largely by German settlers was not reinstated. The sisal industry fostered by British and Greek capital was taking shape and peasant commercial agriculture began to emerge, facilitated by the increasing number of Indian traders operating up-country. Under British rule the Indians' legal status improved. They were no longer classified as natives, which gave them considerably more scope for trading (Gillman 1945:17). Africans, on the other hand, were subject to the Credit to Natives (Restrictions) Ordinances of 1923 and 1931[9] which, in combination with official bias against small and itinerant traders, made their entry into trade very difficult (McCarthy 1982:24–49).

The Asian trader had to take more risks in staple food marketing than export crop marketing. Foodstuffs were bulky, spoiled rapidly and were irregular in supply due to the vagaries of annual rainfall variation. The food trader also faced an inconstant demand. Many if not most urban residents depended only partially on the marketed supply of food. If the harvest was good in their home area or on their plot on the perimeter of Dar es Salaam, they could refrain from purchasing in the market. To offset losses, food and export crop produce buying were often combined and the producer prices offered for staple food crops tended to be lower relative to those for export crops. Iliffe notes how peasants specialising in food production, notably in those areas surrounding the sisal plantations of the coast, were less prosperous than those in the coffee-producing areas of Buhaya and Kilimanjaro (Iliffe 1979:314).

Government trade policy became increasingly interventionist over time. In 1923 and 1926 enquiries into district trading practices and requests for trading recommendations were forwarded to provincial and district officers. The District Officer of Dar es Salaam espoused a liberal view, revealing that he did nothing to interfere with barter transactions and permitted bushshops while advocating the establishment of trading centres. The central government effectively allowed local administrators to formulate their own policies. For example, markets outside townships were controlled by district officers without legalised specifications.

The Markets Ordinance of 1928 began to change this, allowing for the establishment and control of markets by Native Authorities. These markets were governed by by-laws regarding the goods to be sold in the market, fees, weights and measures and the fixing of maximum prices. The trading legislation passed in 1932 went considerably further, and laid the foundation for state supervision, if not control, of marketing when it was deemed necessary. Barter was considered undesirable under the new policy. Paddy, which was claimed to be often adulterated by petty traders, was subject to quality control and grading, along with various other crops (TNA SMP 10138, Letter from Director of Agriculture to Chief Secretary, 1.12.30).

The varied sources of Dar es Salaam's food supply by the late 1930s revealed just how elaborate the food trading network had become. The building of the central railway had brought the Dar es Salaam market in touch with many food supply sources. Rice and vegetables from Morogoro, *dagaa* fish and rice from Kigoma, meat from Dodoma, and maize from various points along the line of rail constituted a large share of Dar es Salaam's marketed food supply. But there were other transport lines and hence other sources of supply; a skeletal network of roads brought rice from Rufiji, maize from various outlying points and wheat from the North. Some sorghum and millet continued to be shipped from Lindi by boat.

Between 1907 and 1939, apart from the strife-torn war years, the sources of Dar es Salaam's food supply expanded under the marketing initiative of Asian merchant capital. The city's population growth was moderate, doubling over the period in comparison with the far more rapid growth of the preceding period. Dar es Salaam's food demand was small relative to that of the sisal plantations. Territorial reliance on food imports lessened. World War II, however, was destined to disrupt the territorial and urban food balance.

DAR ES SALAAM 1940–82: METROPOLIS

ACCELERATED GROWTH AND FOOD IMPORT DEPENDENCE

Between 1940 and 1982, Dar es Salaam's population grew at a rate of 7·9% per annum, ranging between 5·4% and 9·9% in different inter-censal periods (see Appendix 1). The first impetus to population growth was the conscription of soldiers during World War II which brought hundreds of men to Dar es Salaam. During the 1950s, migration to Dar es Salaam slowed to a moderate pace. Peasants' terms of trade had improved markedly, engendering a boom in peasant cash-crop production. Between 1951 and 1960 cotton exports quadrupled and those of coffee increased by more than 150%. It was an era of the spontaneous spread of marketing co-operatives, which quickened the political pulse of the countryside in anticipation of national independence. Peasants were experiencing both economic and political gratification to an unprecedented degree and the growth of Dar es Salaam reflected this, being the steady prosperous growth of a city servicing the needs of its hinterland rather than the bloated growth of people in search of escape from the countryside.

The urbanisation process accelerated in the 1960s. After independence there was a rapid expansion of the Civil Service. The 'development' ideology of the post-independence government insisted on investment in industrialisation. Various government-fostered import substitution industries, mostly of luxury consumption articles such as beer, cigarettes, shoes, and so on, were established on the perimeter of the city.

Educated as well as skilled and unskilled labour flocked to Dar es Salaam, while the Asian presence, roughly a quarter of the city's population between 1930 and 1960, was quickly whittled down to ten per cent by 1967. Their economic power as merchant capitalists was being undermined by a highly interventionist African state. The political transfer of power had taken place overnight on 9 December 1961; the economic transfer of power was slower. Over the following decade Asian merchant capital was replaced with a state marketing network in produce buying.

From the mid-1940s onwards, with the exception of 1956–60, Tanzania was a net importer of grain (see Appendix 2). This situation contrasts with the period from 1920 to 1940 when net imports and exports see-sawed. Comparing Appendices 1 and 2, there is a suggestion that periods of high urban population growth roughly coincide with heavy grain importation, although the population data is extrapolated in inter-censal periods, making it difficult to draw any firm conclusions.

Table 9 World War II weekly rations (oz) [a]

Foodstuff	*African*	*Asian*	*European*
Beans	21		
Maize	126–96		
Rice	18	18	8
Wheat			
straightun		28	28
standard		42	42
atta		84	
Sugar	8	16	16
Groundnut	7		
Palm oil	7		
Other oil	7		
Ghee		8	

Source TNA SMP 29549, Essup Dar es Salaam to Chief Secretary, 22.7.44.
Note (a) Applied throughout Tanganyika for Asians and Europeans and applicable to Africans in townships and where 'fed labour' was employed, i.e. plantations.

Their smaller ration suggests that Europeans, with a more varied diet, were less dependent on a supply of cereal staples.

WORLD WAR II: CRISIS AND TURNING POINT

World War II engendered a crisis of food supply which was not of the same horrific dimensions as the crisis of 1916–19 but was a turning point in a way that the earlier crisis never had been. The relationship between town and country was changing.

A drought in 1943 combined with constraints on international shipping space and the more roundabout shipping routes prevalent during the war threatened food security and prompted the Government to establish an array of governmental agencies to control food supplies and distribution (PRO/CO852/428/17600/II). An East African Production and Supply Council was set up to rationalise and co-ordinate food supplies in Kenya, Uganda and Tanganyika. Under Defence Regulations a Produce Controller was appointed in Tanganyika to regulate the internal distribution of food. A rationing system was instituted for the distribution of all grains, beans, sugar and cooking oil (PRO/CO852/428/17630/4; TNA SMP 29549, Essup Dar es Salaam to Chief Secretary, 22.7.44). The rationing system was set up on a racial basis, with the African staple designated primarily as maize, the Asian, rice and the European, wheat (see Table 9).

After the war, rationing continued in the face of territorial grain shortfalls arising from drought and locust attack. In May 1946, the Government actually cut the maize ration from 18 to 16 oz and rice from 12 to 10 oz because of the effects of a prolonged drought. Warnings were made that no further issue of ration coupons would be made without a certificate of permanent employment, and Africans arriving in Dar es Salaam (excepting Civil Servants and the military) would not be issued with coupons (TNA

SMP 31555/1, *Tanganyika Standard*, 2.5.46).

As the rationing dragged on, intense African resentment built up as expressed in an article of the African weekly *Kwetu*.

In Dar es Salaam today . . . the African should feed on the worst machine flour of any kind of corn that is not poisonous to him and the non-native feed on the best foodstuffs procurable. . . . Is this because the whiteman has got the Government in his hands? Or is it because the insides of Africans and non-natives are different from each other[?] . . . (TNA SMP 31555/1, *Kwetu*, 11.7.48).

During and after the war, black markets developed in response to the shortages and widening market margins. Unofficial markets were very pronounced in the environs of Dar es Salaam. High prices led to overselling. Native authorities reacted by restricting the movement of foodstuffs.

The Authority of Uzaramo is very keen to ensure that controlled produce grown in the [area] of its jurisdiction is not poured into the 'bottomless pit' of the Township. Black-market prices are so attractive that there is a strong temptation to oversell, resulting in District food reserves being reduced to a dangerously low level. The Native Authority has therefore published an order forbidding the removal of foodstuffs from the area of its jurisdiction except under permit. (TNA SMP 13044, Letter of District Commissioner Uzaramo to Provincial Commissioner, Eastern Province, 18.10.48).

The ban on the inter-district transport was a source of complaint by Dar es Salaam residents. Many had resorted to self-provisioning, producing food on farms in the environs of the city or relying on produce from farms of up-country relations. Protests were given an airing in the African Press:

. . . their produce [produce of up-country dwellers] should be used by Africans themselves and to take some to their children in the town from the shambas and upcountries (sic.). The people are not to be prevented as it is now, because this act of preventing people from bringing food into the town encouraged station guards to get bribes who threaten to accuse them when they find them with food taking [it] in the town. This action, if not rectified, will cause much more shortage of food because Africans living near the town and in the upcountries, will not cultivate again, but depend on shops sold foodstuffs. (TNA SMP 13044, *Zuhra*, 10.9.48)

Food had become a political issue. African demands for a higher standard of living were fuelled by the enforced austerity of the war years. Long-established colonial race relations were being questioned in the face of blatant discrimination in the city's food distribution and controls. The stage was set for the spread of nationalist sentiment and urban growth, both of which were outcomes of African aspirations for a better life.

MORE MOUTHS TO FEED

Urban growth accelerated after the war, largely due to the transition from an African male migrant-dominated residential pattern in the cities to that of family residence. This process was intimately related to the struggle over African wage levels. Dar es Salaam's working population began taking on the character of fully-fledged urbanites when the Government finally conceded, in 1957, to workers' demands for a minimum wage at a level capable of supporting a wife and children. The sex ratio of the city steadily narrowed. In 1948 the ratio of men to women was 141:100, in 1957, 131:100, in 1967, 123:100 and in 1978, 115:100.

A 'family wage' was, however, only tenuously capable of provisioning the subsistence of a nuclear family, being difficult to guarantee against the incursions of inflation and extended family demands. The impact of the former was particularly acute in lower-income households, as African urban households bifurcated into working class and bureaucratic class strata after independence.

Inflation and extended family demands were interrelated; the size and residential stability of family units responded to the overall state of the national economy. The differential between rural and urban real incomes often determined how the extended family distributed itself locationally. In a period of depressed rural incomes like the 1970s the nuclear family unit based in the urban area received innumerable obligatory requests, if not dictates, from its up-country extended family, which could entail heavy social costs if ignored. Very often these demands entailed the urban household's absorption of up-country relatives who had either come as dependents in need of urban social services, namely schoolchildren and ill or infirm relations, or they had come in search of urban job opportunities and thus required a refuge until they could gain their own economic independence. Others came to render service, since the urban-rural exchange within Tanzanian extended families was by no means one-sided. Young girls or older women from up-country often served as non-waged ayahs looking after the pre-school children of the urban working mother.

Up-country relations swelled the ranks of the well-to-do Dar es Salaam household. For the working class in Dar es Salaam the same demands were made but could be complied with in fewer instances due to limited finance and living space. Interestingly, however, while high-income families had larger memberships than their working-class counterparts, they nonetheless exhibited lower dependency ratios. This enigma can be explained by the fact that the high-income families were often recipient to dual if not triple incomes earned by various educated adult family members. In other words, urban job opportunities were monopolised by educated extended family units, as indicated in the findings of a 1980 survey of 228 Dar es Salaam households stratified by income (see Table 10).

Between 1940 and 1982, the changing size and composition of Dar es Salaam families in combination with inflation expressed itself in a growing proportion of total household expenditure on food in both low and high

Table 10 Dar es Salaam household income, size and dependency ratios, 1980

Income group	*Average monthly household income (TShs.)*	*Average household membership*	*Dependency ratios*[(a)]	*Heads of households with 11 years' education (%)*
I	545	4·8	3·2	1·8
II	1,200	6·5	2·3	15·7
III	2,500	7·0	2·3	53·0
IV	5,170	7·0	1·8	82·7

Source Mgaza and Bantje (eds.) 1980, pp. 22, 29, 86.
Note (a) Defined as working members: non-working members.

income-earning households, particularly after 1965 (see Table 11).

Food demand elasticities calculated from a 1968 Dar es Salaam survey suggest that family size was less influential in the composition of the family's diet than the level of household expenditure (see Table 12).

The expenditure elasticities of all food products with the exception of wheat and maize were of magnitudes exceeding their respective family size elasticities,[10] pointing to the well-known tendency for low-income groups to upgrade their diet with preferred cereals as their income rises. In this case maize became less desired and was replaced by rice and an increasing protein component. This general tendency was, however, counteracted by the rigidities of cultural consumption patterns.

The effects of income and culture in interaction with each other are interesting. A household budget survey in 1969 recorded Africans of both low and high-income earning levels consuming greater amounts of grain than non-Africans. The differences in food consumption patterns between the racially-delineated cultures began to blur only at the very highest echelons of income earning (see Appendix 3). At middle levels of expenditure African consumption bore more in common with the lower levels of African expenditure than with the comparable middle levels of non-African expenditure. Africans with rising incomes had a tendency to hold to a starch-based diet dominated by rice and were not found to be eating as much meat and dairy products as non-Africans. The high consumption of dairy products in the non-African diet can be traced to the predilections of Asian vegetarians and Europeans.

Besides family size and composition, income and culture, other minor factors influenced food demand. Ostby (1968:5) found that educational levels and differences in age had limited impact. There was, however, a factor which undoubtedly came into play more and more after independence, but was difficult to discern in most of the available data, namely the role of women as wage-earners purchasing the family's food. Women increased from four per cent of the Dar es Salaam labour force in 1961 to twelve per cent in 1978, earning nine per cent of the city's wage bill

(Tanganyika 1961, *Statistical Abstract* and Tanzania 1981a, *Survey of Employment and Earnings*).

It was common practice for men to do the family's food shopping because men usually controlled all or most of the household money. In a 1980 survey over fifty per cent of the men in both low and high income households were the sole purchasers of food, but in households where women received earnings this pattern tended to change. There, women were often the sole purchasers or otherwise jointly shared the burden of food purchases with their husbands (see Table 13). Since a strict sexual division of labour prevailed within the household women were always responsible for cooking and it would be likely that as both cook and food purchaser, they would make their food purchases with increasing attention to nutrition and convenience in preparation.

Clearly, the shifting shape of food demand in Dar es Salaam had to do with the size of the purse and whose hands were clutching it. While the evidence from the 1960s suggests that there was a tendency to switch from maize to rice as household income increased, which was, in fact, a return to the original dietary pattern of the city's first immigrants, this tendency could easily be reversed by adverse economic circumstances such as those experienced in the mid-1970s onwards, when inflationary food prices and the sporadic non-availability of rice prevailed.

THE POLITICAL JOSTLE IN RAISING MARKETED PRODUCTION

At first glance, the array of government agricultural policies that unfolded during this period appear as a tangle of contradictory measures aimed at undoing the effects of the policy immediately preceding it. Nonetheless, whether the policies were directed at peasants or European settlers, whether they sought the extension of acreage or the intensification of production through capital investment, whether they entailed coercive penalties, market competition or subsidies, they all had as their ultimate aim the increase of *marketed* food production. But the specific focus and *modus operandi* of any particular policy, i.e. the who, how and where of increasing marketed production, was determined by the political forces of its time.

Throughout this period, grain marketing was plagued by the difficulties posed by poor transport over great distances, small markets and seasonal and annual variations in the volume of produce. Such logistical problems can lead to an uneven spread of traders who may enjoy regional monopolies, or collude at the expense of the producers. Whether or not they did, preventing these tendencies and securing fair prices were the professed aims of state intervention in marketing.

State intervention took two forms: the regulated but decentralised marketing system composed of private traders and/or co-operatives, or

Table 11 *Dar es Salaam household expenditure and proportion spent on food, 1939–80*

	Total household expenditure (TShs./month) and % spent on food according to investigations of household budgets							
	Aug. 1939[a]	*Jan. 1942*[b]	*Aug. 1942*[c]	*Aug. 1950*[d]	*1956–57*[e]	*May 1963*[f]	*May 1965*[g]	*Apr. 1980*[h]
Household membership								
Bachelor			27·50 (37%)	56·30 (59%)		644·99 (21%)	196·02 (45%)	
Married couple	31·54 (52%)	38·43 (51%)	41·47 (44%)					
1·5–3 members				68·74 (64%)				
2 or more members						752·99 (35%)		
3–3·5 members			48·35 (49%)	80·70 (65%)				
All households by income status								
Low income	31·54 (52%)	38·43 (51%)		69·44 (65%)	126·24 (65%)		206·45 (56%)	755·60 (85%)
High income						738·49 (31%)		1,550·47 (40%)

Sources (*a*) Baker's survey, 'Sociological conditions in Dar es Salaam' submitted to the District Commissioner and cited in (*c*) below.

(*b*) Memorandum submitted to the Panel of the Labour Board convened in January 1942 to enquire into grievances of railway employees, and cited in (*c*) below.

(*c*) Tanganyika 1942, 'Report of enquiry into wages and cost of living of low grade African government employees in Dar es Salaam', TNA SMP 30598. An investigation of 2,901 waged government employees earning 60TShs. a month or less.

(*d*) Tanganyika 1951, 'Report of the committee on rising costs', an investigation of 75 Dar es Salaam households with labourers earning 75TShs. a month or less.

(*e*) East African Statistical Department, 'Report on household budget survey of Africans living in Dar es Salaam, 1956–57', a survey of African wage-earners who had an average income of 158TShs., cited in (*f*) below.

(*f*) Tanganyika 1964, 'Family budget survey of middle-grade African Civil Servants', a survey of 50 Dar es Salaam African Civil Servants with salaries of between 670 and 1,670TShs. a month.

(*g*) Tanzania 1967, 'Household budget survey of wage-earners in Dar es Salaam, 1965', a survey of 1,500 Dar es Salaam wage-earners earning between 150 and 300TShs. a month.

(*h*) Mgaza and Bantje (eds.), 1980. A survey of 228 households: 135 low-income earning 1,999TShs. or less per month and 93 high-income earning 2,000TShs. or more per month.

Table 12 Food demand elasticities according to family size and expenditure

Food item	*Family size elasticities*	*Expenditure elasticities*
Wheat & maize	0·52	0·32
Rice	0·44	0·54
Meat & fish	0·28	1·61
Milk & products	−0·15	1·15
Fats & oils		
Sugar & honey	0·48	0·58
Tobacco & beverages	0·23	1·06
Vegetables & pulses	0·05	0·60

Source Ostby 1968. Based on a 1965 survey of 108 African wage-earner households with incomes between 150TShs. and 300TShs., carried out by the Tanzanian Central Statistical Bureau.

Table 13 Household food purchaser patterns by income level, female employment and position in family (%)

Household food purchaser	*Low income household with employed women*	*Low income household with unemployed women*	*High income household with employed women*	*High income household with unemployed women*
Husband	2	56	23	54
Wife	65	21	27	14
Both	33	23	50	32

Source Mganza & Bantje 1980. A survey of 228 households: 135 low-income earning 1,999TShs. or less per month and 93 high-income earning 2,000TShs. or more per month.

alternatively a centralised system consisting of a state marketing agency with exclusive rights of trade.

Four different phases of grain marketing reflecting different socio-political categories of marketing agents can be delineated: first, the colonial state-controlled market (1942–56); secondly, the Asian traders' market (1957–61); the African co-operatives' market (1962–75) and the post-colonial state-controlled market (1976–82). Three different phases of production organisation reflecting the successive dominance of settlers', kulaks'[11] and bureaucrats' interests can be discerned. These are: the subsidy heyday for European settlers (1940–54); the evolution of conducive conditions for 'progressive' peasant farmers (kulaks), (1955–72) and the frontal bureaucratic programme for state-provisioned infrastructure for mass 'villagised' peasant producers (1973–82). Table 14 attempts to show the fairly close correspondence between these four phases and the three phases of grain production relations already outlined. It also indicates, in summarised form, the types of marketing systems and management that will be detailed in the text.

EUROPEAN SETTLERS AND COLONIAL STATE-CONTROLLED MARKETING, 1940–54

During the early 1940s, under the duress of restricted food import supplies engendered by the war, on the one hand, and the food demands of increased numbers of urban dwellers, on the other, the colonial state faced the question of how to effect increased grain production for market sale. Initially coercive measures were introduced to increase peasant production. In May 1942, a Defence Regulation was promulgated which authorised the issue of orders by Native Authorities requiring peasants to produce sufficient amounts of any food or cash crop essential to the prosecution of the war. But a drought struck in 1943, subverting surplus grain extraction from peasant production. Meanwhile, white settler farmers who were very aware of the critical policy juncture at this time, did their utmost to influence decisions in their own favour, and were largely successful. The state turned to non-native food production.

With the enactment of the Increased Production of Crops Ordinance of 1944, non-natives were enlisted to increase production of essential food through the improvement of yields from existing acreages. To do this they were to be awarded minimum returns per acre, guaranteed minimum prices for crops and acreage breaking grants. The considerable bureaucracy involved in such subsidies was to be expedited through the formation of District Production Committees, representative bodies of the non-native farmers (TNA SMP 35061/9). All these measures were used and abused for the rapid expansion of food production in the European settler areas of the North and the Southern Highlands. To protect national supplies, Tanganyikan settlers' demands for further price supports were closely synchronised with those of their Kenyan counterparts (TNA SMP 38804, Memorandum No. 92 for Executive Council, 24.8.49; TNA SMP 38804, Note on Grain Prices to Producers, TNA SMP, MANR Minute, 16.2.51 and TNA SMP 31536, Letter from Director of Grain Storage to Member of Agriculture, 7.6.51).

Capitalisation and mechanisation of the production process were alluring palliatives to the problem of rapidly increasing demands for marketable foodstuffs. Besides boosting settler production the state initiated the Northern Province Wheat Scheme in 1942. Yields achieved on the 8,000-acre state farm were admitted to be low, but were nonetheless seen as positive in light of the savings made on wheat imports (Coulson 1982:50).

Knowing the colonial state's support for capitalised agriculture, settlers tried to press their luck even further. In an agricultural production committee report, they cited Dar es Salaam's food needs as justification for

Table 14 Phases of grain production and marketing, 1940–82

Phase	*Production agents*	*Market agents*	*Type of marketing system*	*Type of marketing management*
Settlers & colonial state controlled marketing (1940–54)	Settlers (1940–54)	State bureaucrats (1942–56)	Centralised & regulated	Bureaucratic accountability
African *Kulaks* & decentralised marketing (1955–72)	*Kulaks* (1955–72)	Asian traders (1957–61)	Decentralised & regulated	Family firm accountability
		Kulaks holding positions in co-operatives (1962–76)	Decentralised & regulated	Localised network of patron-client relations with face-to-face accountability
Peasants & post-colonial state control (1973–82)	Villagised peasants (1973–82)	State bureaucrats (1976–82)	Centralised & regulated	Bureaucracy with network of patron-client relations that engendered a combination of bureaucratic & face-to-face accountability

land alienation, blatantly ignoring the fact that Tanganyika was a League of Nations mandated territory and was bound to specified limitations on the alienation of land for European settlement. '. . . some alienation of land in predominantly food producing areas should be considered to facilitate the production of food by persons sufficiently capitalised to mechanise production to the greatest possible extent in the interests of consumers in large centres such as Dar es Salaam' (TNA SMP 38804, 'Agricultural Production Committee', 1949).

While settlers were experiencing their heyday, the colonial state was tightly supervising Asian grain marketing. Colonial state regulation of grain marketing began with the establishment of the East African Cereals Pool in 1942. The organisation was designed to facilitate the evening out of surplus and deficit areas in Kenya, Uganda and Tanganyika under the duress of war and drought. The establishment of the Pool institutionalised Tanganyika's dependence on Kenyan maize, since Kenya was generally in a position to export grain with its highly-capitalised settler production of grain in the highlands. During the mid-1940s Tanganyika's grain deficit reached an annual average of 30,000 tons (TNA SMP 30626/LV, Extract from Minutes of Standing Finance Committee, 10.12.46). By the end of 1946, Tanganyika's total debit to the East African Cereals Pool was £640,000. Losses on 1947 imports were estimated to be as much as £1 per bag, the basis of the loss arising from the consumer price being below import parity. The colonial government in a self-righteous tone declared: 'These loans amounting in all to over one million pounds [in 1946 and 1947] have been occasioned purely and simply by the necessity to provide staple foodstuffs for Africans at the lowest possible price' (TNA SMP 35085, Circular for Chief Secretary to all Provincial Commissioners, 11.12.46).

Being ever conscious of balancing the accounts, the colonial government promulgated a Food Subsidisation Fund Ordinance aimed at recovering the losses, in 1947 anticipated to be £400,000. The means by which the funds were to be raised were: payment of a cess by employers in the main export industries (sisal, mining, pyrethrum, tea and sugar) which was expected to raise £172,000; a non-native poll-tax amounting to £6,000 and the raising of the native house and poll-tax by ten per cent to generate £77,000. The balance of £145,000 was to be derived from government revenues. Defensive about raising the African poll-tax, the Chief Secretary argued: 'It will be appreciated that Africans have benefitted from [the] subsidisation policy to date infinitely more than any other class and in view of concessions made by other communities as described above it is considered inevitable that Africans should play their part in meeting [the] 1947 bill' (TNA SMP 35085, Circular from Chief Secretary to all Provincial Commissioners, 11.12.46). His statement ignored the fact that not all Africans had benefited from the subsidy. The vast majority of Africans lived in the rural areas and produced their own food. Only the Africans dependent on purchased supplies of food received subsidisation, yet all were to be taxed.

In 1949, the colonial state founded the Grain Storage Department, with the intention of making the country's grain supply strategy Tanganyikan rather than East African based, although the East African Cereals Pool continued to operate as a back-drop. The Grain Storage Department was empowered to prohibit the purchase and sale of produce except at appointed selling places and by those holding a valid permit. In effect, monopsony conditions were instituted with the requirement that all produce be sold to the Department through authorised traders (TNA SMP 31536, Memorandum No. 1 for the Grain Storage Committee, n.d.).

Maize accounted for ninety-five per cent of the storage and trading of the Department. In the first six years of its operation, the Grain Storage Department was faced with an overall deficit of 107,316 tons of maize and

Table 15 Grain Storage Department annual trading results of maize/mtama (tons)

Years	*Deficit*	*Surplus*	*Import*	*Export*
1949–50	95,219	—	94,739	—
1950–51	—	11,416	—	—
1951–52	—	25,029	—	7,679
1952–53	34,285	—	23,601	—
1953–54	38,833	—	48,457	—
1954–55	—	24,576	2,644	9,133
1955–56	—	109,902	—	124,178
1956–57	—	1,363	276	25,158
Total	168,337	172,286	171,871	174,538
Net		3,949		2,667

Source Tanganyika Grain Storage Department 1957, Appendix V.
Mtama= Sorghum.

sorghum. The exceptionally good harvests of 1955–6 and 1956–7 changed this and the Grain Storage Department found itself with a glut of grain which had to be exported at such uneconomic prices that the decision to fold up the agency was made. Grain self-sufficiency had been achieved, but at a financial cost that could not be sustained by a government agency. It was clear that the spatial and temporal variation of grain supply in a country the size of Tanganyika was difficult to reconcile with the economic viability and internal organisation of a government agency. The Grain Storage Department was disbanded in 1957 (TNA SMP 31536, Memorandum No. 1 for the Grain Storage Committee, Grain Storage Department, n.d.; Tanganyika Grain Storage Department 1957:1) (see Table 15).

AFRICAN KULAK FARMERS, 1957–72

In the 1950s colonial officials began to voice reservations about the capitalisation of agriculture.

> With regard to mechanisation I think we must beware of letting this word become a shiboleth or panacea. It is nothing of the sort and some of the most eminent agricultural Economists (sic) of our day have expressed doubts of the true economic value of mechanisation with its heavy load of fixed capitalisation and the complexities of maintenance particularly in a country like this which lacks a mechanically educated labour force. (TNA SMP Secretariat Minute by PAS (Agriculture and Natural Resources (ANR)), 16.2.51).

As with rationing, Africans voiced bitter resentment over the favoured position of settlers in procuring productive inputs. Due to government price control, the increased prices of agricultural commodities brought about during the war had not been immediately felt by peasant producers. But after the War, when producer prices began to approximate more closely world market conditions, peasants were responsive. Officialdom began to appreciate the meaning of this. 'The days of "increased production" by means of the stick are over and we must rely on some more reasonable incentive. The easiest to hand is the price incentive which, as we have seen recently is working . . .' (TNA SMP 30626, Secretariat Minute by PAS (ANR), 16.2.51).

It was, however, not until 1954 that the legislation giving Europeans planting bonuses was lifted (TNA SMP 31886/II, Memorandum No. 92 for Executive Council, 29.4.54). Colonial agricultural policy in the 1950s was imbued with a liberal developmental approach that to that point had no parallel in Tanganyikan history. The Department of Agriculture was bolstered with personnel and funds which boosted extension work and the planning and execution of projects. Native Authority tractor-ploughing schemes were subsidised. Settlement schemes employing improved technology were launched. A stratum of wealthy 'progressive' African farmers was encouraged. Interestingly these *kulaks* were most successful in capitalised food production, notably in the mechanised cultivation of maize in frontier areas like Ismani and the plains surrounding Mount Kilimanjaro, as well as wheat in Mbulu.

Meanwhile, settler production, while not receiving the more overt official attention it had previously enjoyed, nonetheless prospered. In 1950 the Government parcelled out the land of the former Northern Province Wheat Scheme to four settlers, and two years later, large thousand-acre farms in the forest land of West Kilimanjaro were awarded to eight British war veterans for wheat farming. The rich volcanic soils gave two harvests yielding twelve to sixteen bags per acre annually. Northern Province wheat production was steadily increasing to feed the growing numbers of urban bread eaters. Between 1950 and 1960 the Province's officially marketed wheat rose from 7,475 to 11,397 tons and then almost tripled in the following six years (Raikes 1970:33).

Along with the shift from reliance on white settlers' grain production came the liberalisation of trading policies. In the years following the disbandment of the Grain Storage Department, and until independence, grain was purchased and sold on the open market. Between 1957 and 1960 harvests were good. Grain trade was largely in the hands of Asian traders. Although there was considerable African resentment against them, their profit-making tended to be on the slow-moving items like tinned foods rather than grain. Traders still faced the perennial problems of transport and annual fluctuation of marketed food output, but the market was changing on the demand side. By the late 1950s, in consonance with the economic prosperity of the times, a substantial staple food consumer market existed. Every trader stocked grain as a basic item. Competition was intense since everyone was well aware of the quality and price of such standard lines; the traders' margins were low in the retail sale of grain. In fact the retail margin in grain was identified in a marketing survey in 1961 as 'probably the most competitive in the whole distribution system' (Economist Intelligence Unit 1962:14). The small margins of Asian traders were attributed to the low overheads that resulted from using family labour in the business, keeping paperwork to a minimum and operating from very modest premises (Economist Intelligence Unit 1962:171).

Unlike the previous system, the Asian trade combined wholesale and retail functions at all levels. Produce buyers in the regional centres often combined produce trade with grain milling and retail trade in a variety of food and other consumer items. They developed an extensive interregional transport of grain which kept Tanganyika almost entirely self-sufficient in foodstuffs during the late 1950s. Below the regional level of produce buying, the village trader also combined produce buying and retail distribution.

> The practice enables the retailer cum produce buyer to sell goods on credit to growers against future delivery of crops. This in itself is not necessarily undesirable but the retailer normally takes advantage of his position to obtain very favourable terms for himself. In some areas buyers carry on a system of barter, paying for the produce with consumer goods. This again usually leads to abuses. Furthermore, the fact that the trader is both buying produce and retailing gives him more room to manoeuvre and to indulge in sharp practices. He can give the appearance of making a generous offer on one half of the deal, thus capturing his customer while making a very large profit out of him on the other half. (Economist Intelligence Unit 1962:123).

The post-colonial state, fuelled by rural suspicion of Asian traders, moved quickly after independence to edge Asians out of rural trade through the expansion of the co-operative movement. Registered co-operative societies numbering 172 in 1952 proliferated, rising to 857 at independence in 1961 and 1,714 in 1969. The National Agricultural Production Board (NAPB), a state marketing agency established in 1963, served as the umbrella for the co-operatives' grain trading. Co-operative unions were appointed as the NAPB's agents such that by 1966 almost all purchases of maize acquired by the NAPB came through the co-operative movement. Both Temu (1975:109) and Kreisel recognised the tendency for marketing costs to increase, especially at the lowest level of co-operative activity, the society.

> Expenditures per ton of product handled by both the societies and the union tended to increase in the short life of the single-channel marketing and NAPB operations. In part, this apparently reflected increases in some cost items but to a large degree, particularly at the society level, it resulted from an escalation in the allowances for *posho*[12] to local farmers servicing their society. (Kreisel 1970:28)

Generally kulaks held the official positions in the co-operatives at the society and union levels, benefiting at the expense of less prosperous peasants (van

Velzen 1973, Cliffe *et al.* 1975, Migot-Adholla 1976; von Freyhold 1979). Aware of the many problems in the co-operative movement, the Government appointed a committee of enquiry in 1966 which put sixteen of the thirty-three unions in the country under direct government control. In 1968, under the Co-operative Societies Act, all unions became subject to periodic government inspection. Direct state intervention in co-operative affairs became more pronounced over time. The Village Act of 1975 vested villages with the function of being multi-purpose co-operative societies, which rendered the co-operative societies redundant. Finally in May 1976 co-operative unions were disbanded and their functions were handed over to the parastatal crop authorities.

PEASANTS AND BUREAUCRATS, 1973–82

In the early 1970s, the developmental concerns and financial needs of the central Government led to a number of forceful state measures that rocked the specialised grain production of kulaks and settlers (Bryceson 1982, 1983). In 1973, the Government took steps to nationalise the settler holdings in various parts of the country. The large wheat farms of the North became state farms. More importantly, a mass villagisation programme was launched in 1973 which aimed at nucleating peasant settlement for the easier provisioning of social services and productive inputs. Prior to 1973 only the more remote areas of the country, those facing climatic hazards or those relatively unintegrated in commodity production had been villagised. In 1973 and 1974, according to official estimates, between six and seven million peasants were involved in Operation Sogeza, the nation-wide villagisation campaign. Follow-up campaigns resulted in the aggregated relocation of another four million peasants, bringing the estimated villagised population to ninety per cent of the total rural population, approximately thirteen million peasants residing in 8,000 villages (Tanzania 1975, 1977).[13] In operations of such magnitude it was inevitable that blanket bureaucratic orders prevailed. Government officials with little time or expertise for checking the suitability of the soils and access to water tended to designate the location of the new settlements with regard to their proximity to the road.

Both poor and prosperous peasants were relocated. Although there have been no in-depth case studies of the effects of villagisation on village stratification, general observation at the time of the campaigns indicated that despite the fact that rich peasants had the ear of local and government officials, when the militia came in to carry out the relocation exercise, as it did in a number of areas, kulaks' claims over land were ignored as much as those of poor peasants. They, too, had to leave their homes and live in hastily constructed shelters near the road. It is highly likely that one of the effects of the relocation process between 1973 and 1975 was a decrease in grain production for the market by kulaks. The main thrust was toward small farmer production.

Village communal production, although encouraged, was never made mandatory at the level of national policy. However at the village level, zealous party and government officials in many areas were known to make production in a village communal farm obligatory. Nevertheless, total farm acreage devoted to communal production remained fairly small. In a 1979 study of twenty-six villages in Iringa, Mbeya and Ruvuma, only four of the villages had a mean communal area per adult equal to or above 0·3 acres. The overall mean of all the villages was 0·024 acres (Tibaijuka 1980:31) and the most common crop grown on these communal farms was maize.

Peasant production on village 'block farms' was more the norm. The block farms involved peasants producing on private plots which were contiguous to one another, thus affording economies of scale with regard to tractorisation, insecticide and fertiliser application.

The villagisation policy was aimed at creating nucleated settlements for the easier provisioning of productive inputs and services by the state bureaucracy. In the sphere of grain production this involved the National Maize Programme, instituted in 1975. Under this programme, input packages of fertilisers and hybrid seeds were introduced into the ten most important maize-growing areas of the country.[14] Inputs were to be subsidised by the Government initially, with gradual removal of subsidisation upon recommendations arising from annual project review. An evaluation of the National Maize Programme's first year of operation revealed that there were numerous constraints besetting the project: management problems, poor extension, lack of or late delivery of the inputs and certified seed and finally, the peasants' discretionary purchase and use of the inputs (Fortmann 1976:27–8).

The amounts of inputs and seeds recommended by the state extension services and the input usage did not necessarily coincide with the peasants' economic calculation of labour time and anticipated returns. Peasants discovered that their yields could increase while they themselves fell into financial debt. Throughout the late 1970s and into the 1980s, efforts to increase national maize production were riddled with the charges and counter-charges of debtor and creditor. The peasants complained that the inputs were not delivered on time nor in the specified amounts and were too expensive. The Tanzania Rural Development Bank, the parastatal executing the programme, on the other hand lamented that peasants continually defaulted on their loan repayments, causing the bank itself to face severe financial distress. The problems were openly discussed in the national English daily; the following headlines are examples: 17.3.78, 'TRDB loan terms are too severe', 27.12.78, 'They work more, get very little'; 20.1.79,

'Peasants "don't want" fertilizer'; 7.8.80, 'TRDB seeks help over credit repayments'; 5.1.81, 'TRDB loan recovery: legal organ proposed'; 20.11.81, 'TRDB: non-payment crippling bank', 25.1.82, 'Mara villages refused loans'; 7.2.82, 'Deliver loans fast – Magani'. It was difficult to ascertain whether or not the programme had generally effected higher yields, but what was exceedingly clear was that financial chaos reigned.

Meanwhile, the full circuit of grain marketing came under centralised bureaucratic control after the disbandment of the co-operatives in 1976. The National Milling Corporation (NMC) parastatal was vested with the onerous task of being the sole authorised agency handling market transactions of grain, ranging from produce-buying to ultimate consumer sale throughout the country. With such an overly-centralised system of marketing, in addition to transport difficulties and storage constraints, market margins tended to increase over that prevailing previously when co-operatives were charged with produce-buying (Bryceson 1985a). Furthermore, subsidised consumer prices were set by a parliamentary sub-committee with little regard for the NMC's actual marketing costs. As a result the NMC faced staggering financial debt.

The NMC's management problem was an amalgam of clientage practices and inefficiencies on the part of NMC personnel in conjunction with pricing, transport and procurement difficulties. The inefficiencies of state marketing personnel did not seem to be alleviated by bureaucratic reorganisation. The problem was rooted in the motivations and actions of the state marketing personnel themselves rather than any fault in the bureaucratic chain of command. Almost all the personnel were sons and daughters of peasants. Their earnings had to be stretched to not only maintain their immediate families but, very often, had also to meet expenses incurred by rural kin during the rapid inflation of the 1970s and 1980s (Bryceson 1985b:514).

Unlike the Asian trader, who strived to maintain the profitability of his family's business because it was the sole source of his family's welfare, the bureaucratic agent's monthly salary did not directly depend on the economic viability of the agency he worked for. He collected his salary even when national distribution of grain became increasingly paralysed with inefficiencies. But the purchasing power of his wage was being eroded at an alarming rate. As a result, some sought pecuniary gain on the job (e.g. *Daily News* 23.12.78, 'NMC man on theft charges'; 10.1.80, 'Causes for shortages explained'; 5.8.81; 'Morogoro NMC clerks found stealing from NMC').

The NMC's management problem was further exacerbated by the ambiguity of its status as a parastatal. It had been placed in the position of having to be financially accountable like any other parastatal, while having to function largely as a government welfare agency offering subsidised consumer prices. The consumer price of staple grains, especially *sembe* maize meal, was heavily subsidised during the late 1970s (Bryceson 1985a). This was done as a concession to working-class demands in the face of the fact that the minimum wage was being held constant for a number of years despite rapid inflation. Minimum wages, however, were finally raised in 1980 and in 1981 the price of *sembe* doubled (Kaberuka 1983).

In 1982, the NMC's financial debts, a worry not only to the NMC management but also to national economic planners, were one of the main catalysts for the passage of legislation to reinstate the co-operatives. The NMC would no longer have to shoulder the expensive costs of getting staff and transport to village buying posts.

One very salient aspect of the high market margins reigning during the NMC's centralised marketing system that contrasted with the decentralised co-operative system of the 1960s, and that will perhaps reappear as co-operatives are reinstated, was the location of the 'sponge', i.e. bloated marketing costs. In the 1960s the 'sponge' was at the very lowest level of the system, the village co-operative societies, where village officialdom benefited most. That situation, detrimental as it may have been for poorer, less influential peasants, was nevertheless far healthier for the economic dynamics of the countryside than later, when the 'sponge' lodged itself at the NMC headquarters in Dar es Salaam. At least in the earlier situation some of the peasant producers, notably kulaks, had incentives to produce. Centralised state marketing, on the other hand, was an active disincentive for all peasants to produce grain for the official market.

FOOD CRISES COMPARED

As mentioned in the introduction, from 1974 Dar es Salaam experienced food shortages which eased between 1976 and 1978, then intensified thereafter. It is useful to compare and contrast this most recent crisis with the two previous crises in 1916–19 and 1943–50. All resulted in part from the impact of drought: the droughts of 1919, 1943 and 1973–4 were nation-wide in their incidence. In all three cases political and economic factors of an international dimension figured prominently. War affected the food supply directly in all cases; the world wars of 1914–18 and 1940–45 and the Ugandan War in 1979. In the 1970s, however, the international economic constraints were more important than military shocks, although the latter came at a particularly inopportune moment. Many lorries and motorised vehicles which would have otherwise been used for food crop transport were requisitioned for the war effort soon after the dramatic rise in oil prices. Tanzania's terms of trade were on the decline save for a temporary recovery during 1976 and until 1978 (World Bank 1981:174). The need for massive food imports coincided with very high world grain prices on the open market and increased import shipping rates (Bryceson 1982:117).

All three crises were met with state intervention in trade. During the 1970s the National Milling Corporation parastatal was vested with sole control over grain distribution. An official rationing system was not initiated,[13] although many places of work contracted grain supplies from the National Milling Corporation to sell in rationed amounts to their employees because of the widespread shortages in retail outlets. In all three crises, recourse to food importation was very pronounced.

The dissimilarities between the three are evident, less in the forms that the crises took and the immediate responses made to them, than in the substratum of causative factors leading to the crises and then what followed in the aftermath. In the 1916–19 crisis there was a very quick recovery indicated by a huge net export of grain in 1921, just two years after the severe drought. Interestingly, the volume of net exports of grain achieved in 1921 was not surpassed until 1956 (see Appendix 2). In view of the horrendous devastation suffered by producers in Tanganyika during World War I this is remarkable.

On the eve of the war, in 1913, German East Africa was a prospering colonial economy, newly provisioned with a cross-country railroad. After the war the capitalised sector of the economy, namely the plantations and settler farms, were in a state of disarray, having been taken out of German hands, and disease and mortality had taken a heavy toll on the peasantry. It was, however, the peasant sector which provided the bulwark of productive dynamism in the recovery.

The crisis of the 1940s was different. There was no quick recovery. Dar es Salaam had experienced a rapid increase in population connected with the stationing of conscripted troops. In the post-war period the population of the city continued to increase (see Appendix 1). Locust attacks, which inflicted loss on grain crops, combined with an international shortage of grain and shipping space, gave the state the rationale for maintaining control over the grain trade in the form of a Grain Storage Department. Recovery came in the 1950s as peasants' terms of trade took an encouraging upturn.

The crisis of the 1970s has been prolonged and was still continuing in 1984. Structural conditions have shifted and it is difficult to see an easy resolution in the absence of a drastic improvement in terms of trade, both of the peasants and internationally, and the performance of state and market agents involved in the country's marketing and input delivery infrastructure.

In 1981 Tanzania was reported as having only two months' supply of grain in the face of an eight-month wait before the next harvest (*The Economist* 31.10.81, 6.11.81; the *Guardian* 28.10.81; *The Times* 29.10.81). Aid agencies, however, responded with alacrity and food import deliveries came before the two months had elapsed. In actual fact, even more pressing circumstances had been known to occur in the past. In 1949, 'food in Dar es Salaam was, on several occasions reduced to less than a week's supply' (TNA SMP 35181, Press Communiqué issued to the Tanganyika News Service, 10.8.50).

How much had changed over the thirty years? The volume of imports had increased eightfold, but then the city's population had multiplied almost twelve times (see Appendix 1). As a rough indicator, the importation of maize for Dar es Salaam residents was estimated at 151 kg *per capita* in 1951 and had gone down to 103 kg in 1981. But even if this represents an improvement, such levels of grain importation were problematic in a primarily agricultural country (Tanganyika 1951 and Marketing Development Bureau figures).

The state's immediate response in all food crises has been to escalate food imports and, secondarily, to intervene in marketing. Dar es Salaam consumers, on the other hand, have had their own instinctive responses under food stress, namely to resort to unofficial markets and to intensify home production of food.

BRIDGING THE GAP: UNOFFICIAL MARKETS

State control of the market can give rise to three kinds of unofficial 'black' markets as identified by Temu (1975). The first type arises when the state agency fails to offer purchasing services to producers and black-market prices are lower than those officially set. The second type arises from wide margins between state-controlled producer and consumer prices leading black-market prices for both producer and consumer goods to be somewhere within that margin, in other words operating on smaller margins. The third type arises from a shortage of the commodity supplied by the state marketing agency, which raises the black-market producer and consumer prices above those officially set. A variant of the first type of unofficial market arises when peasants, who are distant from the official purchasing point, sell their produce to traders *in situ* rather than taking their produce to market, thereby fetching a price lower than what is officially offered.

During the 1960s, as marketing margins widened under co-operative trading, the second type of black market prevailed in the major maize supply areas. Farmers refused to sell their maize to the co-operative because the producer price was too low (Temu 1975:149,157). In the late 1970s and early 1980s, under the NMC parastatal marketing, this tendency was very pronounced with the free market ex-farm price of maize over twice the official price (Keeler *et al.* 1982:98).

Dar es Salaam's role in the unofficial market trade was less pronounced than in the towns closer to the food surplus areas. Dar es Salaam was primarily reliant on food imports channelled through the NMC, with unofficial markets serving as a supplementary source of supply, as opposed to the reverse situation in most other urban centres (Keeler *et al.* 1982:83–7; Moore 1981:20).

Government reaction to unofficial markets where retail prices were over those officially set was most vocal. The Press frequently carried reports of retailers found to have been hoarding essential commodities. In 1980 it was charged that there were 1,000 bogus businessmen with trading licences but without premises, who were assumed to be involved in serious malpractices (*Daily News* 15.3.80, 'Kaduma clarifies new trade rules'). In the nation as a whole between June 1979 and March 1980 the Price Commission fined 1,850 traders a total of 700,000 T*Shs*. for overcharging their customers (*Daily News* 18.7.80, 'RTCs get cash boost').

The existence of the type of unofficial market in which producer prices were lower than those officially set was also recognised, especially when the NMC started buying peasants' crops on credit promising to pay them eventually in cash. Exhortation on the part of high-ranking party and Government officials called for the NMC to resume buying only on a cash basis (*Daily News* 6.6.81, 'Pay peasants promptly', 10.3.81, 'Pay now NMC told').

It was also sometimes publicised in the Press that party and Government officials themselves were engaged in the unofficial grain market. The Dar es Salaam Regional Party Secretary charged that: 'Dishonesty among some workers in the institutions responsible for the distribution of essential commodities and unscrupulous businessmen are the main cause of shortages being experienced in Dar es Salaam at the moment (*Daily News* 10.1.80), 'Causes for shortages explained').

FIRST AND LAST RESORTS: NON-MARKET SUPPLY

Outside official and unofficial markets, Dar es Salaam residents were, as in previous decades, deriving a portion of their food needs directly from subsistence production. With the urban population expanding, all of the fertile valley areas where rice flourished were being cultivated and more and more of the higher land was put under maize cultivation. Just as maize supplanted rice in purchased supply, it was edging forward in the sphere of non-marketed supply as well (TNA SMP 19533, Letter from Provincial Commissioner, Eastern Province to Chief Secretary, 19.1.40).

In the 1950 Survey of African Labourers in Dar es Salaam, fourteen per cent of those interviewed had farms on the perimeter of the town, the majority of which were devoted to subsistence crops, mainly rice (Tanganyika 1951:63), as opposed to a 1968 survey of the Kinondoni area of Dar es Salaam which did not find the residents engaged in farming, a reflection perhaps of the more prosperous economic environment of the 1960s (Hoad

1968). In contrast, in a 1980 survey, thirty-three per cent of the high-income and forty-four per cent of the low-income earners owned a farm either somewhere around Dar es Salaam or in their home areas (Mganza & Bantje 1980:89). Often wives or other unemployed women in the household returned to their upcountry homes for a period encompassing planting, cultivating and harvesting. A whole range of exchange relationships between rural and urban kin evolved over time such that rural-based members of the extended family were often supplying the grain requirements of the urban family in exchange for cash or goods and services. The grain was frequently transported by members of the family travelling between the upcountry home and Dar es Salaam for various business and social reasons.

During the food shortages of the 1980s, although district border checks were reinstated, the Government remained tolerant of the transport of small amounts of food. '. . . Ndugu Mnzavas [a judge] cautioned the police to act sensibly when looking for smugglers, particularly those carrying food crops to avoid harassing innocent citizens carrying small food quantities for domestic use' (*Daily News*, 24.10.81, 'Judge warns law organs').

During the 1974–5 food crisis the Government instituted an agricultural production campaign, *Kilimo cha Kufa na Kupona* (Agriculture for Life or Death). At that time government offices, factories and other places of work were issued with land outside the city for cultivation by their employees. Problems of transport, time taken from normal working hours for cultivation, and the inexperience and lack of co-ordination evidenced in the production effort limited the campaign's usefulness in alleviating the city's food shortfall. Nevertheless, it did heighten people's awareness of the food deficit (Bryceson 1982:117). In the 1980 food crisis the campaign was not re-invoked, but the Prime Minister issued a directive to urban councils to allocate farming areas to town dwellers (*Daily News*, 27.3.80, 'Teach land conservation, Nyerere'). On the other hand, repeated directives against cultivation within the city limits due to health regulations and the unsightliness of maize fields were also issued (*Daily News*, 11.4.79, 5.3.81, 5.4.81).

With the extension of the Dar es Salaam city limits, one retired Civil Servant living and working on a farm a short distance outside the city expressed his concern in a letter to the editor of the newspaper:

> The creeping city of Dar es Salaam is going to dispossess the people of their valuable land. . . . I retired in 1976. To keep going with my family, I bought a few cashewnut trees on a 5-acre piece in Mbezi. I have improved the place with bananas, pineapples, cassava; and each year I plant seasonal crops like maize and beans. . . . Now when the city takes over my land, what shall I do? . . . I ask the party and Government to think again over this matter. Retired people like me decided to farm and alleviate Dar es Salaam's problems of food. (*Daily News*, 21.2.81, 'Expanding Dar City')

But the further expansion of Dar es Salaam seemed inevitable and its food deficit was unlikely to be resolved through suburban agriculture. The balance between rural supply and urban demand required effective action on the part of the state and market as well as the household.

CONCLUSION

Over the century Dar es Salaam has witnessed many changes. The social system and productive order upon which the original food supply of Dar es Salaam was rooted, that of master and slave, has completely disappeared. As a capital city, modern port and the residence of over a million people, Dar es Salaam has expanded its influence and compounded its food requirements. The oscillation between periods of crisis and periods of relatively balanced urban population growth and food supply demonstrate tremendous dynamism.

The problem posed by the fluctuating supplies of the city's staple foods and their transport over huge distances has generated different institutional solutions over the century. Some marketing and production arrangements appear to have been more successful than others, notably those prevailing in the late 1950s and the 1960s. However, one must exercise caution in stating the superiority of one type of marketing and production arrangement over another. The causal relationship between food supply adequacy and trade and production policies is unclear. Do specific policies generate the adequacy of food supply, or does the adequacy of supply generate the policies? In a country like Tanzania where the productive base exerts so little control over the natural environment, the latter is more likely. But the acknowledgement of this predicament should prompt more painstaking policy formulation, not fatalism.

Tanzania has yet to become industrialised, although urbanisation, the social form of an industrial economy, is proceeding at a very rapid pace. While few industrialising countries over the past century have experienced closely-synchronised technological and social change, there is an abysmal gulf between the two in Tanzania, along with many other countries in sub-Saharan Africa recording historically unprecedented rates of urban growth.

Under these circumstances, Dar es Salaam's food deficit and reliance on food imports are neither desirable nor surprising. Many countries in the world have resorted to heavy reliance on food imports as they have become urbanised. Food importation is an economic expedient, but the food deficit is not a strictly economic problem. De-agrarianisation and urbanisation are societal processes with social, cultural, political and economic dimensions. They involve the material aspirations of vast numbers of people with diverse and contradictory objectives arising from the clash of town and country values. The food deficit problem which arises from these two processes is many-sided. If the solution to the problem is seen solely as one of balancing Tanzania's external trade and finance and lifting government controls on trade, it is over-simplified. Multi-faceted policies which aim to restrain urban migration within feasible limits, yet fire the initiative of the trader and the producer and imbue the bureaucrat with professionalism, are at the crux of achieving an enhanced productive capacity in the countryside and bringing Dar es Salaam food demand in balance with domestic production.

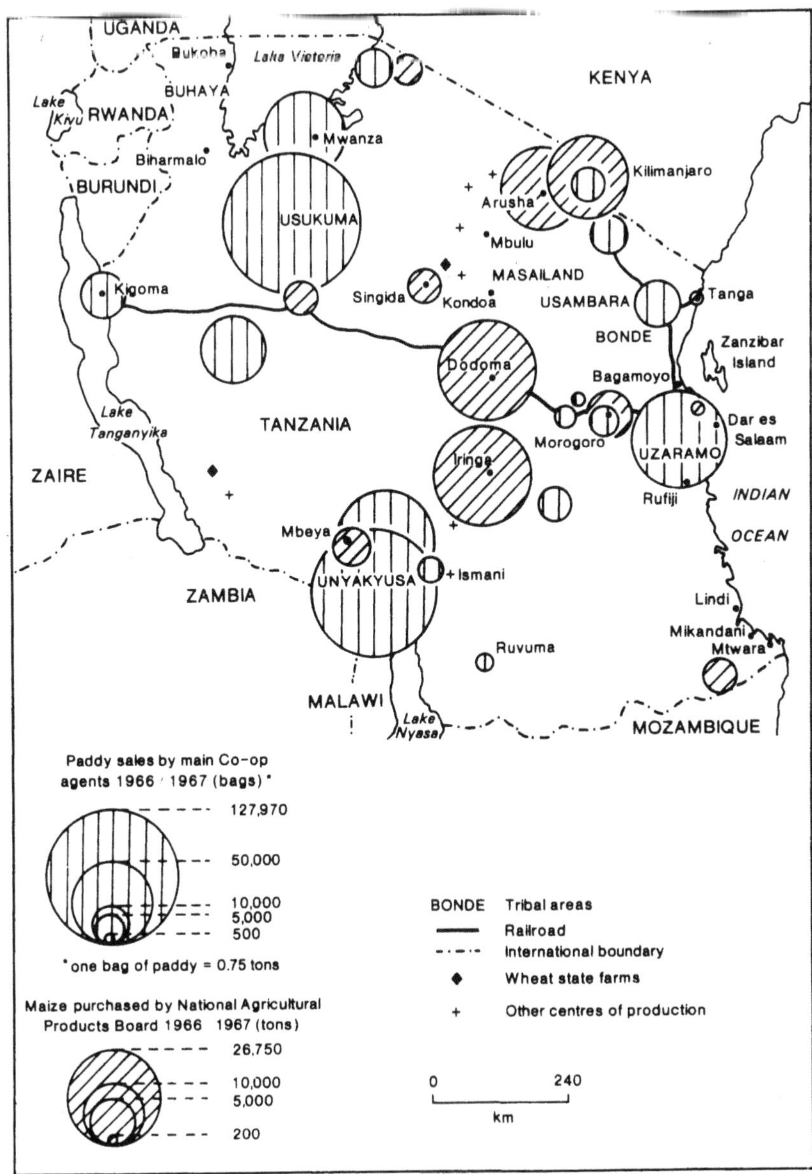

Figure 12 Officially marketed maize, rice, wheat and other grains, Tanzania, 1966/7
Source Berry 1971:59.
Tribal areas, foreign countries and oceans in capital letters.

APPENDIX 1

The population of Dar es Salaam

Year	*Total population*	*Population growth*[a] *rate (%)*	*Population by race*					
			Africans		*Asians*		*Europeans*	
			No.	%	*No.*	%	*No.*	%
1867	900							
		7·7						
1886	3–5,000							
		14·0						
1894	10,000		4,000	90	620	6	400	4
		12·2						
1900	20,000		18,000	90	1,480	8	360	2
		0·9						
1913	22,500		19,000	84	2,500	11	1,000	4
		1·1						
1921	24,600		20,000	81	4,000	16	600	2
		3·4						
1931	34,300		24,000	70	9,000	26	1,330	4
		2·3						
1943	45,100		33,000	73	11,000	24	1,100	2
		9·0						
1948	69,277		50,765	73	16,270	24	1,726	3
		9·4						
1951	99,140		72,300	73	22,547	23	3,603	4
		5·4						
1957	128,742		93,363	73	29,986	23	4,479	4
		7·8						
1967	272,515			84		11		4
		9·9						
1978	769,445		n.a.		n.a.		n.a.	
1982	1,122,276 (est.)							

Note (*a*) Population growth rates for the periods delineated in this paper are 1866–1906: 8·2% p.a.; 1907–39: 2·1% p.a.; 1940–82: 7·9% p.a.
Sources 1867–1967: figures as listed in Sutton 1970:19; 1978: Tanzania 1981b, 1978 Population Census, Vol II, p. 762.

APPENDIX 2

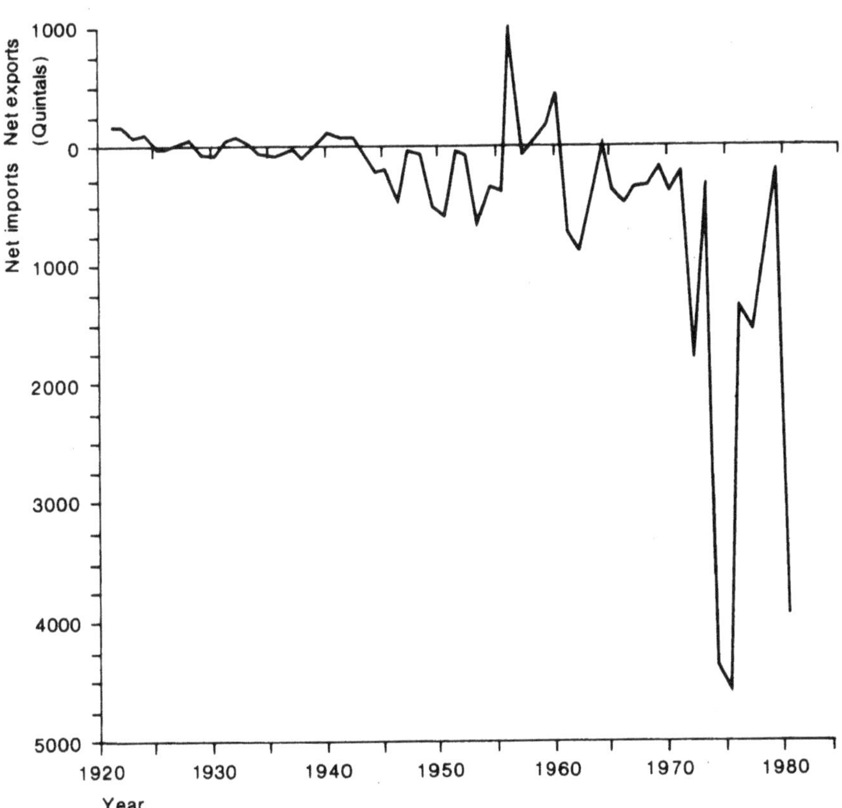

Appendix 2 Tanganyika/Tanzania physical net grain imports or exports, 1921–80
Note Includes wheat, maize, rice, millet, barley, oats, rye, other unmilled grain, wheat meal and flour, maize meal and flour, other meal and flour, groats, semolina and cereals either flaked, pearled or prepared in a manner not otherwise specified, as well as unspecified grain.
Sources *Tanganyika Blue Books*, 1920–45; *Tanganyika Trade Reports*, 1946–8; *East African Trade Reports*, 1949–76; *Tanzania Trade Reports*, 1977–80.

APPENDIX 3

Dar es Salaam household food expenditure

A. African low-income households – % expenditure on specific food items out of total food expenditure [a]

Food item	*1950*	*1956–7*	*1965*	*1969*[a]		
Total annual expenditure (TShs.)	—	—	—	*0–999*	*1,000–1,999*	*2,000–3,999*
Staple grains & roots	43	45	45	47	44	39
Maize meal	(21)			(24)	(17)	(13)
Rice	(8)			(23)	(16)	(13)
Bread	(9)				(7)	(9)
Cassava & sweet potato	(5)			(1)	(4)	(4)
Beans	2			16	6	4
Meat & fish	30	21	20	7	14	17
Milk & dairy products	n.a.	3	5	—	3	6
Sugar	3	9	7	8	6	5
Food expenditure as % of total expenditure	65	65	56	48	52	48

Note (*a*) Figures are for Dar es Salaam excluding centre, where the African population is preponderant.

Sources 1950: Tanganyika 1951, 'Report of the Committee on Rising Costs'; 1956–7: East African Statistical Department. 'Report on Household Budget Survey of Africans living in Dar es Salaam, 1956–57'; 1965: Tanzania 1967, 'Household Budget Survey of Wage earners in Dar es Salaam, 1965'; 1969: Tanzania 1972, 1969 Household Budget Survey: Income and Consumption, Vol. I.

B. African high-income households – % expenditure on specific food items out of total food expenditure

Food item	*1964*	*1969*[(a)]				
Total annual expenditure (TShs.)		*4,000–5,999*	*6,000–7,999*	*8,000–9,999*	*10,000–24,999*	*24,999+*
Staple grains & roots		37	29	35	28	27
Maize meal		(11)	(8)	(9)	(7)	(6)
Rice		(14)	(11)	(13)	(11)	(10)
Bread	25	(9)	(8)	(11)	(8)	(9)
Cassava & sweet potato		(3)	(2)	(2)	(2)	(2)
Beans		4	4	3	3	4
Meat & fish	23	17	15	14	17	19
Milk & dairy products	12	6	8	7	7	8
Sugar	4	5	5	6	6	7
Food expenditure as % of total expenditure	32	37	36	31	25	24

Note (a) Figures are for 'Dar es Salaam excluding centre', where the African population is preponderant.
Sources 1964: Tanganyika 1964. 'Family Budget Survey of Middle-Grade African Civil Servants'; 1969: Tanzania 1972, 1969 Household Budget Survey: Income and Consumption, Vol. I.

C. Non-African households – % expenditure of specific food items out of total food expenditure[a]

1969 total annual expenditure	*4000–5999*	*6000–7999*	*8000–9999*	*10000–24999*	*Over 24999*
Staple grains & roots	18	22	24	24	23
Maize meal	—	—	—	(1)	(1)
Rice	(7)	(7)	(10)	(9)	(7)
Bread	(9)	(13)	(13)	(11)	(12)
Cassava & sweet potato	(2)	(2)	(1)	(3)	(3)
Beans	5	—	2	1	1
Meat & fish	18	21	16	11	14
Milk & dairy products	19	22	14	14	13
Sugar	3	5	3	5	4
Food expenditure as % of total expenditure	52	78	44	34	17

Note (a) Figures are for 'Dar es Salaam centre', where the non-African population is preponderant.
Source Tanzania 1972. 1969 Household Budget Survey: Income and Consumption, Vol. I.

NOTES

1 This is an expanded version of an article entitled, 'Food and urban purchasing power: the case of Dar es Salaam, Tanzania', *African Affairs*, 84 (337), 1985. I am indebted to Jane Guyer, John Iliffe, Richard Palmer-Jones, Abdul Sheriff, Nick Westcott and Gavin Williams for their advice and criticism.

2 In the mid-1970s the Government announced the intention of building a new capital at Dodoma, a town in central Tanzania. Although construction on the new capital has been going on for several years and many ministries have moved personnel there, nonetheless, at the time of writing (1984), most government business is still carried out in Dar es Salaam.

3 Sorghum and millet still play an important role, forming the basis of nutritious brews in up-country areas, but the brewing of traditional beer receives official discouragement in Dar es Salaam for fear that it cannot be controlled and, maybe more importantly, it cannot be taxed. In any case, bottled beer lends its drinker status and is part of the sophisticated urban identity a working-class man would like to project when his monthly finances allow.

4 A *jumbe* was a native official authorised by the German Government.

5 In 1907 when the railway reached Morogoro, its impact was immediate. Morogoro peasants started cultivating fields two to three times bigger than before to produce a marketable surplus (German East Africa 1907/08).

6 During the first two years of the East African campaign the railway was in the hands of the Germans. But by 1916 when the British began their occupation of Dar es Salaam, the railway had slipped from German control. Thus the Germans did not reap the benefits of their momentous railway investment for very long.

7 The 1927 Labour Department Annual Report estimated the total territorial labour force at 135,537: 18,837 contract labourers, 72,000 migrant workers, 10,000 occasional workers (estimate in terms of full-time workers), 21,000 domestic servants, 13,000 workers in mines, ports and minor work, and 700 porters (full-time porters calculated from the figure of 32,678 porters working an average of 5·8 days, with the assumption that 270 days constitutes an average work year). The territorial total excludes those employed in government departments. An overall estimate of the total labour force is not available for 1931, but based on what figures exist for the total number of contract labourers between 1928 and 1930, it appears that the level of the labour force remained fairly stationary, while the total numbers fluctuated from year to year.

8 *Shamba* is the Kiswahili word for farm plot.

9 These Ordinances restricted Africans' access to credit as a paternalistic measure aimed at pre-empting the development of a landless peasantry.

10 This would probably pertain to wheat as well if it was separated from maize.

11 *Kulak* refers to a well-to-do, innovative peasant farmer who employs non-familial labour.

12 *Posho* is a Kiswahili term that originally referred to the maize meal that formed the bulk of the plantation wage labourer's diet, and is more recently used as slang for the means by which one survives, one's 'daily bread'.

13 Some commentators feel that the official villagisation figures are gross overestimates and that the actual population moved was closer to fifty per cent of the rural total rather than ninety per cent.

14 Arusha, Dodoma, Kilimanjaro, Mbeya, Morogoro, Rukwa, Ruvuma, Tabora, Iringa and Tanga.

15 In 1983 rationing did take place.

REFERENCES

Baker, E. C. 1931, 'History and Social Conditions of Dar es Salaam during the Early Days'. Rhodes House Library, Oxford: unpublished ms.

Berry, L. (ed.), 1971. *Tanzania in Maps*. University of London Press Ltd.

Bryceson, D. F. 1982. 'Tanzanian grain supply: peasant production and state policies', *Food Policy*, May: 113–24.

—— 1983. *Second Thoughts on Marketing Cooperatives in Tanzania: background to their reinstatement*. Plunkett Foundation for Cooperative Studies.

——1985a. 'The organisation of Tanzanian grain marketing: switching roles of the co-operative and parastatal', in Arhin, K., P. Hesp & L. van der Laan (eds.), *Marketing Boards in Tropical Africa*. London: KPI Ltd.

—— 1985b. 'Food and urban purchasing power in Tanzania', *African Affairs*, 84 (337): 499–522.

Charron, K. C., 1944. *The Welfare of the African Labourer in Tanganyika*. Dar es Salaam: Government Printer.

Cliffe, L. *et al.* (eds.) 1975. *Rural Cooperation in Tanzania*. Dar es Salaam: Tanzania Publishing House.

Coulson, A. 1982. *Tanzania: a political economy*. Oxford: Clarendon Press.

East African Trade Reports 1949–76. Nairobi: Customs & Excise Dept.

Economist Intelligence Unit. 1962. *A Survey of Wholesale and Retail Trade in Tanganyika*. London.

Fortmann, L. 1976. 'An Evaluation of the Progress of the National Maize Project at the End of One Cropping Season in Morogoro and Arusha Regions', USAID/ Tanzania.

von Freyhold, M. 1977. 'On Colonial Modes of Production'. Seminar paper, Department of History, University of Dar es Salaam.

—— 1979. *Ujamaa Villages in Tanzania*. London: Heinemann Educational Books.

German East Africa. 1901/02, 1906/07, and 1907/08 (trans. A. Sheriff). *Annual Report about Development in German East Africa*. University of Dar es Salaam.

Gillman, C. 1945. 'Dar es Salaam, 1860 to 1940: a story of growth and change', *Tanzania Notes and Records*, 20.

Henderson, W. O. 1965. 'German East Africa 1884–1918', in Harlow & Chilver (eds.), *History of East Africa*, Vol. II, pp. 123–62. Oxford University Press.

Hoad, P. 1968. 'Report on a Socio-Economic Survey of Kinondoni'. University College, Dar es Salaam: Institute of Public Administration, Physical Training Course.

Iliffe, J. 1979. *A Modern History of Tanganyika*. Cambridge University Press.

Kaberuka, D., 1983. 'Evaluating the Performance of Food Marketing Parastatals (FMPs)'. Paper presented at the Marketing Boards in Tropical Africa Seminar, Leiden, 19–23 September.

Keeler, A., G. M. Scobie, M. A. Renkow & D. L. Franklin. 1982. 'The Consumption Effects of Agricultural Policies in Tanzania'. Sigma One Corporation, prepared for USAID.

Kreisel, H. C. *et al.* 1970. *Agricultural Marketing in Tanzania: background research and policy proposals*. East Lansing: Michigan State University.

McCarthy, D. M. P. 1982. *Colonial Bureaucracy and Creating Underdevelopment: Tanganyika, 1919–1940*. Iowa State University Press.

McCleery, H. H. 1939. 'Extent and Conditions under which Natives are Occupying Land in the Outskirts of Dar es Salaam'. Rhodes House Library, Oxford: unpublished ms.

Mganza, D. & H. Bantje. 1980. *Infant Feeding in Dar es Salaam*. Dar es Salaam:

Tanzania Food and Nutrition Centre and the Bureau of Resource Assessment and Land Use Planning.
Migot-Adholla, S. E. 1976. 'Power differentiation and resource allocation: the Cooperative Tractor Project in Maswa District', in Hyden, G. (ed.), *Cooperatives in Tanzania*, pp. 39–57. Dar es Salaam: Tanzania Publishing House.
Moore, M. P. 1981. 'Smallholder Food Production in Tanzania'. A Report to the Swedish International Development Authority and the Government of Tanzania.
Orde-Browne, G. St. J. 1926. *Labour in the Tanganyika Territory*. London: HMSO.
Ostby, I. 1968. 'An Econometric Study of Demand Patterns in Dar es Salaam: Preliminary Review'. University of Dar es Salaam: Economics Research Paper 68.5.
Public Records Office (PRO). Assorted files of the British Colonial Office.
Raikes, P. 1970. 'The Historical Development of Wheat Production in Northern Mbulu Distrct'. University of Dar es Salaam: Economics Research Bureau Paper 70.11.
Raum, O. F. 1965. 'German East Africa: changes in African life under German administration 1892–1914', in Harlow & Chilver (eds.), *History of East Africa*, Vol. II, pp. 163–207. Oxford University Press.
Seward, G. E. 1866. 'Letter from the Acting Political Agent and H.M. Consul, Zanzibar to the Chief Secretary to Gov., Political Depart., Bombay. Dated, Zanzibar, Nov. 10th, 1866', reprinted in *Tanzania Notes and Records*, 71:201–2.
Stainburn, J. M. 1982. 'Production Costs of Major Agricultural Commodities in Tanzania'. Dar es Salaam: Marketing Development Bureau, October.
Sutton, J. E. G. 1970. 'Dar es Salaam: a sketch of a hundred years', *Tanzania Notes and Records* 71: 1–19.
Tanganyika Territory. 1921–39. 'Annual Trade Reports', *Blue Books*. 1920–45. *Tanganyika Blue Books*. Dar es Salaam: Government Printer. 1927–30. *Labour Department Annual Reports* Dar es Salaam: Government Printer.
—— 1933 & 1938. *Provincial Commissioner's Annual Report Eastern Province*.
—— 1942. 'Report of Enquiry into Wages and Cost of Living of Low Grade African Government Employees in Dar es Salaam'. TNA EMP 30598.
—— 1946–8. *Tanganyika Trade Reports*. Dar es Salaam: Government Printer.
—— 1951. 'Report of the Committee on Rising Costs'. Dar es Salaam: Government Printer.
Tanganyika Grain Storage Department. 1957. *Annual Report of the Grain Storage Department*. Dar es Salaam.
Tanganyika. 1961. *Statistical Abstract*. Dar es Salaam: Government Printer.
—— 1964. 'Family Budget Survey of Middle-Grade African Civil Servants'. Central Statistical Bureau.
Tanzania. 1967. 'Household Budget Survey of Wage Earners in Dar es Salaam, 1965'. Dar es Salaam: Central Statistical Bureau.
—— 1972. *1969 Household Budget Survey: income and consumption*, Vol. I. Dar es Salaam: Bureau of Statistics.
—— 1975. *Maendeleo ya Vijiji*. Dodoma.
—— 1977. *Kujenga Ujamaa Tanzania*. Dodoma.
—— 1977–80. *Tanzanian Trade Reports*. Dar es Salaam: Department of Commerce.
—— 1981a. *Survey of Employment and Earnings 1977–78*. Bureau of Statistics.
—— 1981b. *1978 Population Census*, Vol. II. Bureau of Statistics.
Tanzania National Archives (TNA). Assorted files.
Temu, P. 1975. 'Marketing Board Pricing and Storage Policy with Particular Reference to Maize in Tanzania'. Stanford University, unpublished PhD thesis.
Tibaijuka, A. K. 1980. 'An Economic Survey of Village Projects in Iringa, Mbeya

and Ruvuma Regions 1979; Analysis of Product Mix, Size, Initiation, Planning and Financial Conditions of Communal Farms'. Economics Research Bureau Seminar Paper, November.

van Velzen, H. U., E. Thoden. 1973. 'Staff, kulaks and peasants: a study of a political field', in L. Cliffe & J. Saul (eds.), *Socialism in Tanzania*, Vol. II, pp. 153–79. Dar es Salaam: East African Publishing House.

World Bank. 1981. *Accelerated Development in Sub-Saharan Africa*. Washington, DC.

Wright, M. & T. J. Butler. 1979. 'Port and external trade statistics – an introduction to the German Period in Tanzania', Institute of African Studies. New York: Columbia University, June.

Newspapers and journals

Daily News (Dar es Salaam English daily)

The Economist

The Guardian

The Times

5 *Paul Mosley*

THE DEVELOPMENT OF FOOD SUPPLIES TO SALISBURY (HARARE)

1. BACKGROUND

Unlike other cities discussed in this book, Salisbury (Harare)[1] did not exist before the end of the nineteenth century. It was not a traditional African settlement; it was founded in September 1890, by the Pioneer Column of white colonists and their escort of policemen from the British South Africa Company. It quickly became not only the capital of the colony of Southern Rhodesia, but also a centre of distribution, services and light industry; thus the population has grown rapidly by both natural increase and rural-urban migration, as set out in Table 16.

The division between white and non-white races set out in Table 16 has both a geographical and an income-distributional dimension, and both are relevant to the analysis of food supply. The former can be seen by examining Figure 13, which illustrates the patterns of land use prevailing in 1930 and 1972. From the first, commercial development took place on a grid

Table 16 Population of Salisbury, 1910–81

Year	*White*	*Non-white*	*Total*
1910			3,000
1931	11,000	24,000	35,000
1941	19,700	37,000	56,000
1951	45,900	105,000	150,900
1961	94,500	215,810	310,310
1971	105,900	280,100	386,000
1981	95,000	535,000	630,000

Sources Before 1951, *Yearbooks of the Colony of Southern Rhodesia*, various; 1951 and after, Kay & Smout 1977. There was no proper census of the African population before 1961 and hence before this date all estimates of total population should be treated as rough guesses.

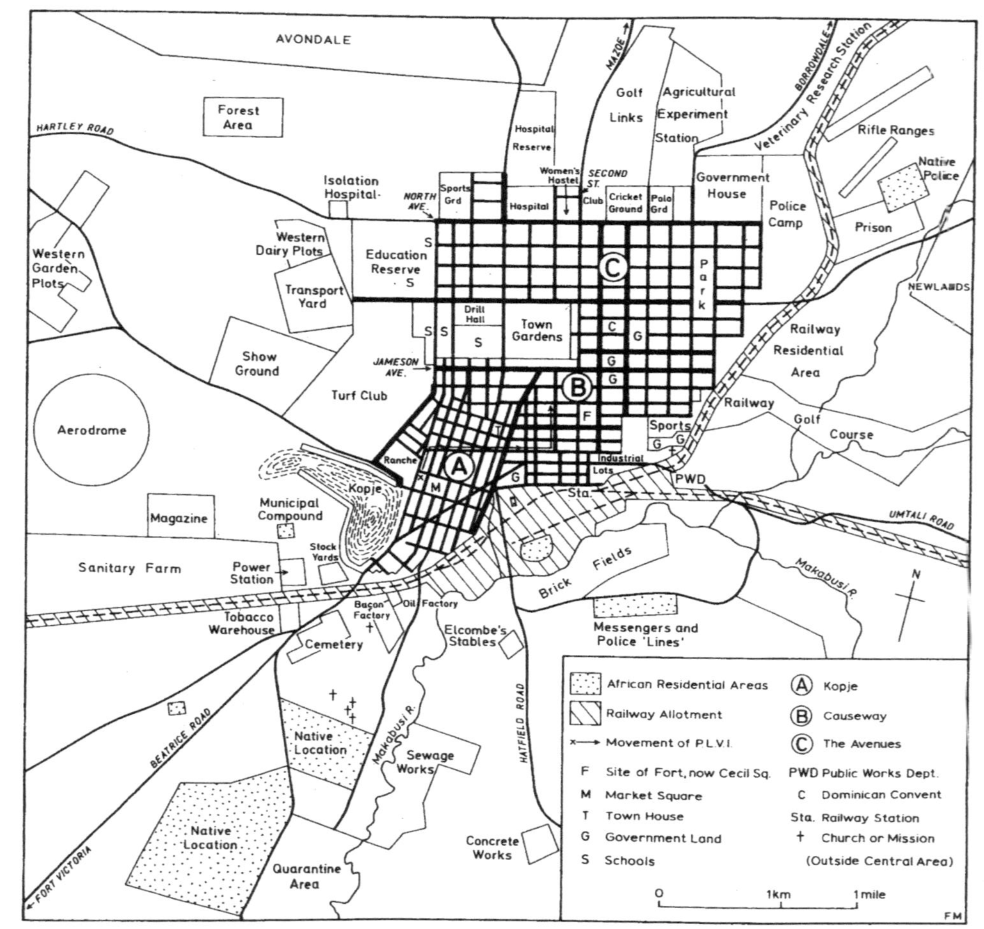

Figure 13a (left)
Land use in Salisbury, 1930
Figure 13b (below)
Land use in Salisbury, 1972
Source Kay & Smout 1977.

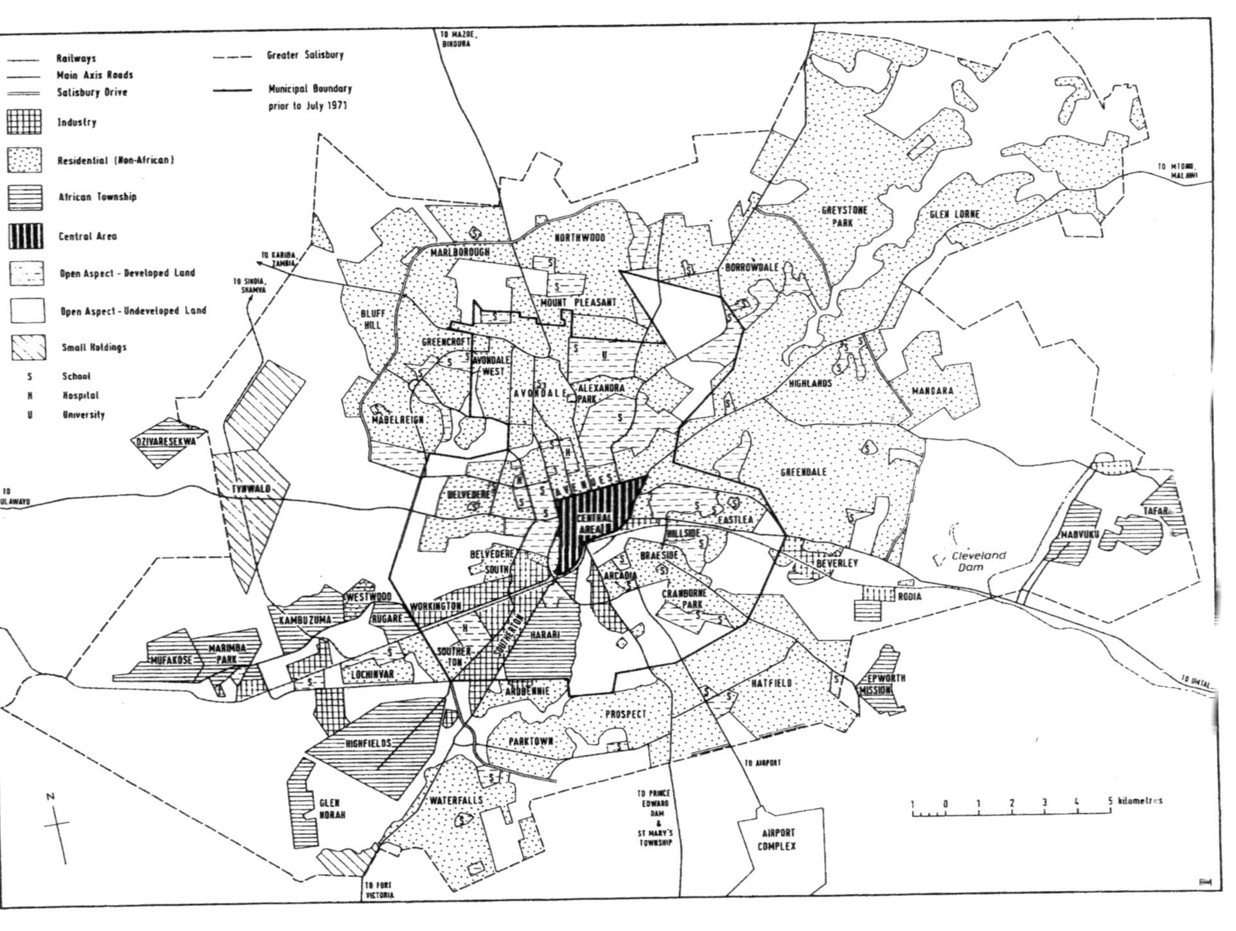
Railways
Main Axis Roads
Salisbury Drive
Industry
Residential (Non-African)
African Township
Central Area
Open Aspect - Developed Land
Open Aspect - Undeveloped Land
Small Holdings
S School
H Hospital
U University
Greater Salisbury
Municipal Boundary prior to July 1971
TO MAZOE, BINDURA
TO KARIBA, ZAMBIA
TO SINOIA, SHAMVA
TO BULAWAYO
TO FORT VICTORIA
TO PRINCE EDWARD DAM & ST MARY'S TOWNSHIP
TO AIRPORT
TO UMTALI
GREYSTONE PARK
GLEN LORNE
NORTHWOOD
MARLBOROUGH
BORROWDALE
MOUNT PLEASANT
BLUFF HILL
GREENCROFT
AVONDALE WEST
AVONDALE
ALEXANDRA PARK
HIGHLANDS
MANDARA
MABELREIGN
DZIVARESEKWA
TYNWALD
BELVEDERE
AVENUES
CENTRAL AREA
EASTLEA
HILLSIDE
GREENDALE
MABVUKU
TAFARA
Cleveland Dam
BELVEDERE SOUTH
BRAESIDE
ARCADIA
BEVERLEY
RODIA
CRANBORNE PARK
WESTWOOD
WORKINGTON
KAMBUZUMA
RUGARE
SOUTHERTON
HARARI
MUFAKOSE
MARIMBA PARK
LOCHINVAR
ARDBENNIE
HATFIELD
EPWORTH MISSION
PROSPECT
PARKTOWN
HIGHFIELDS
GLEN NORAH
WATERFALLS
AIRPORT COMPLEX
N
1 0 1 2 3 4 5 kilometres

pattern to the north of the railway station; Europeans built their houses to the north and east of this central business district. Africans who were working as domestic servants to Europeans were usually accommodated in huts on European premises, but larger employers of African labour such as the railways and the municipality built their own African housing estates in the classic position 'across the railway tracks' in Highfields and Harare. This racial distribution of population was congealed by the Land Apportionment Act of 1930, which remained in force under various guises until 1978. This Act established areas of separate European and African tenure in both urban and rural areas, and made it legally impossible for members of one race to own land in the territory of the other. Thus Salisbury, more than any other African city outside South Africa, has its 'black' and 'white' areas. In the African areas population densities average between 100 and 300 persons per hectare, or about ten times the densities prevailing in the European areas,[2] but even at these high densities many Africans manage to cultivate their own vegetable gardens. Until recently most land in the African areas both for residential and for commercial purposes was rented from the municipality on short and insecure leases.[3]

By coincidence, it also happens that the differences between average European and African incomes in Salisbury are of a similar order. As the educational system has developed and the informal colour bar has loosened,[4] more and more Africans have percolated upwards into the administrative and professional segments of the job market. But as late as 1980 it was estimated that within the city of Salisbury the incomes from employment of Africans averaged $236 against average earnings of $1,753 for other races.[5] In general, the earnings distribution has always been more unequal in Southern Rhodesia than in other African countries, as demonstrated by Figure 14. This has implications for the pattern of food consumption, for the extreme inequality of income between the races has led to a bifurcation in diet and in expenditure patterns more generally.

Europeans, on average (see Table 17) spend twenty per cent of their income on food of which a large proportion consists of imported luxury goods such as wines and tinned food from overseas; Africans spend over half of their incomes on food, nearly all of which is home-produced.

The data in Table 17 suggest that grains (particularly maize) are the most important item in the African diet, and in particular dominate meat; the European diet is more diversified, but meat is the single most important category of food and expenditure. In the historical review and assessment which follow, we shall confine ourselves to a study of the main food staples. These are: beef (consumed by both Europeans and Africans); maize (consumed largely by Africans); groundnuts (consumed largely by Africans) and dairy products, fruit and vegetables (consumed by both races).

Table 17 Salisbury Africans and Europeans: allocation of household expenditure between different food categories, 1971

Categories	% of total expenditure spent on category by: Europeans	Africans
Beverages	0·7	1·2
Bread & cereals	2·4	21·0
Fats & oils	1·0	2·9
Fish	6·4	0·8
Fruit & vegetables	3·2	5·2
Meat	6·2	12·7
Dairy products & eggs	3·6	3·8
Other foodstuffs	4·0	6·4
Total food	21·5	54·9
Total expenditure	100·0	100·0

Source Rhodesia, *Urban African Budget Survey 1971; European Household Budget Survey 1971*. Government Printer, Salisbury, 1972.

The major argument in what follows will be that the efficiency of food supply to Salisbury has suffered from a situation in which the interests of food *producers* have dominated the interests of food *consumers* to a greater degree than is normal even in Third World countries.

2. HISTORICAL REVIEW

In the first twenty years of Salisbury's existence there were very few European food producers: the land which was sold or given away in such vast quantities by the colonial administration was, as a rule, held as a speculative proposition and/or mined for gold rather than being farmed.[6] As a consequence, almost the only food supplies available to sustain the considerable growth of Salisbury in the early years had to be bought from African farmers. An early settler relates that

> . . . the policy of the Chartered Company in those days was to encourage the mining of the country, and not to worry about the farming, in spite of the fact that they were paying over £2 per bag[7] to traders for native maize and rupoko (finger millet). Butter was 5/- per pound, eggs £1 per dozen, bully beef 5/- per tin, and potatoes when procurable at all cost 2/- per pound, with all foodstuffs proportionately exorbitant in price. This was partly accounted for by the Railways not having been completed yet from the South to the East, which made transport very difficult, except at a high price.[8]

In those days the population of Salisbury was supplied with food from within the narrow catchment shown in Figure 15. The ox-wagon owners (who were rumoured to be involved in a price ring through the first decade of the century, until their power was broken by the coming of the railway)[9] bought grain, poultry, and farm animals from both African and the very few

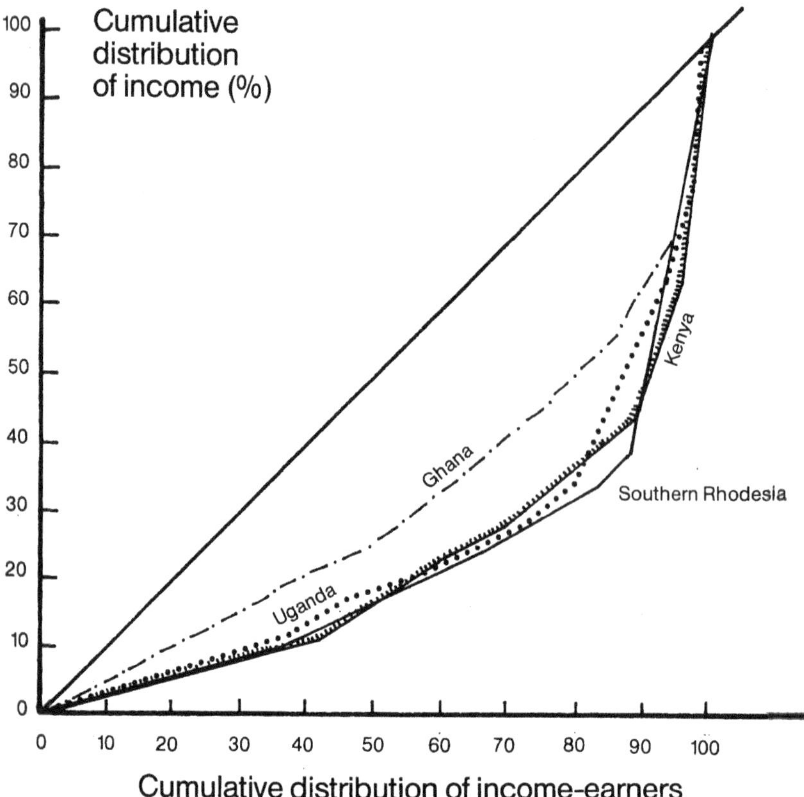

Figure 14 Southern Rhodesia and other African countries: Lorenz curve estimate of distribution of incomes from employment, 1960
Source Mosley 1983: 231.
Cumulative distribution of income (%)
Cumulative distribution of income-earners

European suppliers, applied elementary processing such as drying grain in the sun, and sold their produce to a Salisbury wholesaler. In the case of grain the trade was entirely free from government interference, and the advent of rail transport, together with an increase in production and competition amongst European farmers, had by 1921 driven the price of a 200 lb bag of maize down to 10*s*,[10] thus incidentally helping to puncture a boom which had brought a measure of prosperity to many African farmers. In the case of meat, particularly beef, freedom of trade was restricted by the policy measures which the Government adopted against animal disease. Cattle

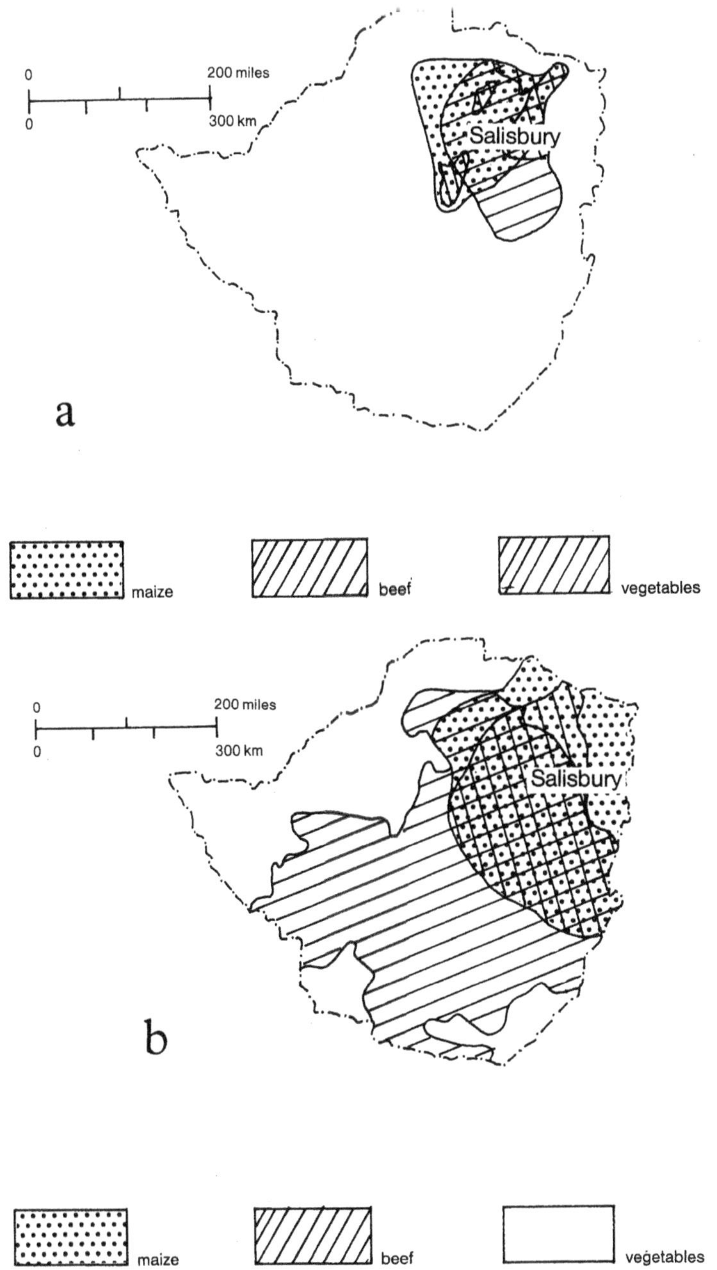

Figure 15a Food supply area for Salisbury, 1900
Figure 15b Food supply area for Salisbury, 1960
Note Excludes occasional imports of maize.

were subject to pleuro-pneumonia, rinderpest, foot-and-mouth and East Coast fever, and the only defence against the last three of these, bearing in mind the very small number of dip tanks which existed in African areas, was thought to be quarantine of entire African reserves, often for years at a time.[11] This artificially restricted the amount of African stock coming on to the market and helped to keep the consumer price of meat high. This, in turn, helped to discourage European employers in Salisbury from providing their African employees with a meat ration.

It is now time to consider the African diet. There are two basic elements in a Zimbabwean African meal, *sadza* (grain meal porridge) and a relish (*usavi*) which can be prepared in literally hundreds of different ways, and which commonly includes meat, fish, vegetables, pumpkins, roots, beans, spices, etc. Over the twentieth century there has been a tendency for maize flour to supplant millet flour in making *sadza*, and for bakers' bread to supplant *sadza* itself. But the basic balance between grain and 'other foods' remains unaltered. The basic ration given by European employers to their African employees was, until long after World War II, 2 lb of maize meal a day – i.e. the *sadza* element only – in addition to cash wages. But some employers – probably a minority in the years before 1945 – gave more than this. In 1907 the Wankie Colliery Company gave its African employees:

2½ lb. maize meal or 1¼ lb. per diem
3½ oz. salt per week
1 lb. meat per week
2 lbs. vegetables per week
plus *one* of: 20 oz. of lard, 20 oz. of monkey-nuts, kaffir beer.[12]

This was a foreign-owned firm employed in heavy industry. Locally-owned firms engaged in trade, services or light industry (which description fitted a majority of employers in Salisbury) tended to give a less generous ration, both in quantity and in quality. Often they provided maize only, and maize is almost entirely carbohydrate. This supplied energy and satisfied hunger, but being deficient in protein, could contribute little towards growth or the replacement of lost tissue after illness or injury. The low consumption of fresh milk by Africans exacerbated the problem.[13] Professional medical opinion in Southern Rhodesia was well aware of this problem from the early days, and adjured employers to feed their African workers on a diet containing more protein (for example by switching from maize to cassava as basic foodstuff) and more vitamins (for example by adding bananas and sweet potatoes to the ration).[14] But few of them paid any attention, and the low level of cash wages was to preclude the majority of African workers, right through until the 1960s, from making up these deficiencies by purchases of supplementary foods on the open market.

The decade of the 1920s was one of gradual development of European farming, with a tendency at this stage towards concentration of production on maize in wetter areas and beef ranching in drier ones, and away from 'riskier' crops such as cotton, tobacco and citrus fruit. During this period a division of labour developed: European farmers shared the urban market for maize, beef and vegetables with Africans, whereas Africans continued to supply rural mines, plantations and farms at a fraction of the cost.[15] In some crops, such as wheat, there was official discouragement of African production;[16] but as long as most European farmers could sell at a price in excess of the cost of production, there was little interference with a free market in foodstuffs.

In the depression of the 1930s all this changed. By 1930 European farmers were selling both maize and beef in local and export markets below their cost of production, and this state of affairs was widely perceived to be critical for the survival of the entire European settler community, as maize growing and stock raising were among the few activities which were accessible to the small under-capitalised settler rather than the large multinational company. There was strong pressure from European producers, who were a powerful interest-group on the all-white legislature, to resolve the problem by exporting a large proportion of total output, thereby pushing up the price in the local market above the cost of production, and then somehow giving the European producers a larger share of the local market. This was a tricky political enterprise, as it involved not only discrimination against Africans whose power to fight back was limited, but also against local consumers of maize and beef as a whole. One such consumer did argue that the long-term prosperity of Rhodesia was based 'on maize grown at 4s. a bag – not by the European, but by the native producer'[17] and that 'if we are to make a success of our export trade we want every beast that a native can produce'.[18] But to speak with the voice of economic rationality was not, in Rhodesia during an economic depression, to win the argument. The objective of preserving the white agricultural community was judged more important than the objective of minimising the cost of food, and by the Maize Control Act (1931) and the Beef Bounty and Export Levy Act (1935) African local transactions were taxed in order to finance exports. This aroused considerable resentment among Africans,[19] but had the desired effect, from the European farmers' point of view, of depressing African supply and raising local prices a little, as illustrated by Table 18. This supply response we may note in passing, is entirely 'orthodox' but conflicts with experience in western Kenya, Uganda and many West African countries during this period, where African marketed production of both cash and food crops rose rapidly during the period of falling prices from 1929 to 1934.[20] The wholesale trade in both maize and beef was transferred from private individuals into the hands of a statutory authority – the Maize Control Board and the Cold Storage Commission respectively – with the power to fix producer and consumer prices. When the level of export prices

Table 18 Southern Rhodesia: maize sales and prices, 1930–61

	Prices paid per 200 lb bag on local market			Quantities delivered to marketing board (200 lb bags) ('000)				
	(1)	(2)	(3)	(4)	(5)	(6)	(7)	(8)
Crop year	To European producer[a]	To Africans at store	On export market	European	African	Exports (200 lb bags) ('000)	Imports (200 lb bags) ('000)	Import cost per 200 lb bag
	s d	s d	s d					s d
1930/31	6'6	—	5 2			701	0	0
1931/32	5 3¼	—	5 1	1,183	317	1,302	0	0
1932/33	8 5	—	6 10	831	107	255	0	0
1933/34	7 7¾	—	6 4	1,150	222	609	0	0
1934/35	8 6½	—	5 11	805	204	396	0	0
1935/36	8 3¾	—	7 8	1,409	442	1,065	0	0
1936/37	7 11¼	—	7 0	1,491	591	1,303	0	0
1937/38	9 3¼	5 0–7 1	7 8	952	309	275	0	0
1938/39	9 7½	5 0–9 4	7 9	740	325	48	0	0
1939/40	8 11½	—	6 11	1,059	389	552	50	9 10
1940/41	11 3½	—	—	682	136	0	0	0
1941/42	12 3	—	—	686	208	0	495	12 6
1942/43	13 6	—	14 0	906	320	104	374	19 8
1943/44	15 6	—	16 0	960	448	267	0	0
1944/45	16 6	—	—	866	469	0	0	0
1945/46	18 6	—	—	795	302	0	24	20 6
1946/47	25 0	—	—	394	203	0	20	22 0
1947/48	30 0	19 3	—	1,970	655	0	1,766	42 11
1948/49	30 0[b]	18 5–23 9	—	705	370	0	117	42 11
1949/50	35 0	23 9	—	988	855	0	436	40 1
1950/51	37 6	24 3	—	465	200	0	81	40 0
1951/52	45 0	28 0	—	1,402	662	0	1,577	70 6
1952/53	41 6	27 0	—	1,364	909	0	91	74 1
1953/54	40 6	25 6	—	1,735	890	0	167	49 1

1954/55	40 6	25 0	—	1,780	706	0	13	49 [illegible]
1955/56	41 6	25 7	—	2,419	1,395	940	0	0
1956/57	40 0	23 9½	26 4	2,708	831	2,396	0	0
1957/58	41 6	22 10	34 3	2,432	536	2,313	0	0
1958/59	36 3½	22 2	34 3	2,653	728	2,360	0	0
1959/60	24 8	24 8	34 10	1,866	513	2,624	0	0
1960/61	31 6	20 0	33 2	4,169	1,186	1,765	0	0

Notes Dashes denote data not available.

(*a*) Payout figures for European producers are average, and do not indicate what individual producers received because of varying quotas of different classes of producers in the local pool. These producer prices include government subsidies and good farming bonuses.

(*b*) The government producer price was guaranteed from the 1948/9 crop year onwards. The level of guaranteed prices was announced in May of each year.

Sources Cols. (1) and (3) to (8) – Federation of Rhodesia and Nyasaland 1963a(B2); Col. (2), 1937/8 and 1938/9 – NAR: S 1215/1090/172, Maize Control Board minutes 1938; 1947/8 to 1960/1 – Guaranteed minimum price; from *Annual Report of the Chief Native Commissioner 1961*: 'Report of the Under-Secretary, Native Economics and Markets Division'.

sagged once again, in 1937/8 (see Table 18) there was further panic among European farmers, and a suggestion that the right to market crops, like the right to own land, should be partitioned between the races, with Africans being given a monopoly of the sale of sorghum, millets and groundnuts, and Europeans being given a monopoly of the sale of wheat, potatoes, onions, citrus fruit and apples in addition to cash crops such as tobacco, 'otherwise', the Secretary of Agriculture concluded, 'the extinction of the European farmer through native competiton must be merely a question of time'.[21] But the growth of demand in wartime was such as to make such drastic discriminatory legislation unnecessary. It was important under such circumstances to boost food supplies from all possible sources.

World War II, in fact, was to lead to a transformation of the entire food-supply position in Southern Rhodesia. The interruption of imports from outside Africa created favourable conditions for import substitution in the manufacture of cotton, steel and processed foods, and in Salisbury effective demand was further swelled by a scheme for training British air-force pilots in Southern Rhodesia, and by the arrival of 5,000 (mostly Italian) internees. The country as a whole moved from having a large exportable surplus of maize, beef and other foodstuffs, to a position of needing to import large quantities of food from South Africa: the position in relation to maize is set out in Table 18. But even imports were not enough to prevent a situation of serious food shortage amongst the African population of Salisbury, which had been much augmented by the industrial boom. Two surveys of the city's population were made during the period; the first of these, taken between August 1942 and June 1943, demonstrated that sixteen per cent of Salisbury Africans were earning less than 20*s* per month, and fifty-one per cent were earning less than 30*s* per month, against an estimated 'minimum requirement' of 95*s* for a family with two children simply to buy the necessities of food, clothing and shelter.[22] The majority of the African population were, therefore, only able to survive in the city by 'informal' and sometimes illegal activities: employment of children, prostitution, liquor sales. Even with the help of such additional income, most Africans in Salisbury were forced, according to shopkeepers, to reduce their purchases of food towards the end of the month.[23] Some writers have blamed this food shortage exclusively on low African purchasing power, and in particular on low wages.[24] But the problem also lay with inefficiency of the distribution system, which made food so expensive for the urban African to buy. As a witness to the 1944 Native Production and Trade Commission reported,

> (the Africans') complaint is not so much what they can sell maize at, but the great differences when they sell and buy. That is what they do not understand. If they got 6/- and it cost only 6/6 to buy a bag of meal it would be all right, but they do not understand why they have to pay 22/-. . . . for a bag of mealie meal.[25]

This had become a particularly serious issue because so many Africans had become dependent on the purchase of grain for cash. So long as they had their own subsistence plot in the reserve, and their employer provided them with free maize as part of the wage, their exposure to the injustices of the marketing of crops was limited. But the rapid growth of population in the reserves during the 1920s and 1930s,[26] coupled with widespread land erosion, created a position where many urban Africans were no longer able to grow a significant part of their grain requirements. At the same time, many urban employers began to pay wages in cash rather than in kind. In such a position, the African employee had few means of defence against fluctuations in food prices.

The end of the war provided an opportunity for a freeing of the marketing system in all essential foodstuffs, but in fact the opposite occurred. The Maize Control Board's monopoly over the wholesaling of grain, millets and groundnuts was now supplemented by setting the elements of cost intervening between the African producer's price and the final consumer price at fixed levels, as illustrated in Table 19.

Meanwhile the wartime system of requisitioning African cattle at fixed prices proved too attractive for the Cold Storage Commission to abandon. This provoked violent African resentment,[27] and when this eventually gave way in 1961 to a system in which African cattle were bought at free auctions in the reserves, it became clear that the Cold Storage Commission had been buying the lower grades of cattle – most of which were produced by Africans – well below the free-market price.[28] A factor which added insult to injury was the fact that communications within the African reserves were so poor as frequently to preclude producers from getting their surplus to market.[29]

Towards the end of the 1950s, when the export loss problems appeared once again for both maize and beef producers, it seemed briefly that the system of state-controlled marketing might be relaxed. Cattle auctions were instituted in the African reserves, as already described, and the difficulty resulting from an exportable surplus of maize was met in 1959 by allowing the price to fall, rather than by attempting to segregate the home from the export markets as in the 1930s. But after UDI the system was in fact extended, with the powers of individual marketing boards being strengthened, and with their activities being co-ordinated through the Agricultural Marketing Authority established in 1967. In 1965 only an estimated thirty-five per cent of total agricultural sales were handled by statutory agencies, but by 1973 they handled over seventy per cent.[30] In short the system of food marketing handed over in 1980 to the independent government of Zimbabwe reflects, more than anything else, the needs of distressed white producers during the depression of fifty years previously. It remains to be seen whether that Government will now move towards a policy which

Table 19 *Structure of maize prices, 1940–57 (s d per 200 lb bag)*

	1940		*1948*		*1957*
Basic price to African producer	variable (probable range 5s–6s)		19s 3d		23s 9½d
Trader's handling margin	variable	standardised 1946	2s	made flexible in 1955	3s 1[illegible]d (max.)
Cost of bag	1s 6d (average)	standardised 1948	2s 9d		3s 2½d
Transport to railway	variable	standardised 1948	3s		5s 2d
'Rake-off'	variable (min. 1s 6d max. 5s)	abolished 1948			
To Native Development Fund	—	instituted 1948	3s		3s 11d
Maize Control Board's buying price at railhead (i.e. effective price to European producer)	10s 6¾d (local pool) 6s 10d (export pool)		30s		40s

Note After 1947 maize prices to African producers varied between regions on account of variations in transport charges, and, subsequently, variations in district council cases.
Sources Johnson 1964, Table 13, p. 199; Southern Rhodesia, Maize Control Board, *Annual Report* 1940/1.

favours consumers a little more or whether it will, like its Kenyan counterpart, preserve the colonial system in the interests of the new generation of African commercial farmers.

3. ASSESSMENT

There are many criteria by which one may assess a food-supply system, but the most obvious one to apply is whether it manages to satisfy the nutritional needs of the people for whom it caters. On this criterion, the Salisbury food-supply system still does not satisfy the nutritional needs of the lowest quintile of the population in respect of a number of basic foods, including their staple of maize meal, as Table 20 demonstrates.

Table 20 Consumption of lowest income quintile in relation to nutritional needs, Salisbury Africans, 1969

Food	*Monthly consumption of lowest quintile by income*	*Minimum dietary requirement for moderately active man*	*Difference*
Bread	5·4	3·4	+2
Maize	9·7	10·6	−0·9
Meat	2·1	1·7	+0·4
Potatoes	0·1	1·7	−1·6
Fresh vegetables	2·3	5·1	−2·8
Fruit	0·2	0·9	−0·7
Milk	1·3	0·9	+0·4
Sugar	2·1	0·4	+1·7
Margarine	0·1	0·4	−0·3
Groundnuts	0·1	0·4	−0·3
Tea	0·1	0·4	−0·3

Source V. S. Cubitt & R. C. Riddell, *The Urban Poverty Datum Line in Rhodesia*. Faculty of Social Studies, University of Rhodesia, 1974.

Of course, as we have recently been reminded by Sen (1981), food shortage is not simply a question of inadequate supply but of the relationship between supply and demand; and one of the main causes of nutritional deficiency in Zimbabwe has always, historically, been the low purchasing power of the African unskilled worker. However, there is some evidence that in Zimbabwe the nature of the food-supply system may have contributed to the overall difficulties of feeding the population. For the imperative of minimising the cost of food was dominated, from the 1930s onwards, by the rival imperative of ensuring a living for even the most inefficient European producers of maize, beef and dairy products in particular. As a consequence, the producer price of food was pushed up unnecessarily: but beyond this, the centralisation of purchasing and wholesaling in the hands of one state monopoly organisation caused mark-ups on many foods, and thus consumer prices, to exceed those prevailing in countries where the marketing system was freer.

Let us consider in more detail the case of maize. In the 1962–3 crop year (chosen because there was a detailed enquiry into the marketing system in that year, but the essentials of the system have not changed since World War II) the price was as shown in Table 21.

Table 21 Southern Rhodesia: price structure for maize (s d), crop year 1962/3

		s d	*s d*
1	Guaranteed price to African producer selling to trader in reserve	—	12 0
2	Transport levy	7 0	—
3	Trader's handling margin (maximum permissible)	3 0	—
4	=(1+2+3) Guaranteed price to African producer delivering direct to Grain Marketing Board	—	22 0
5	African Development Fund levy	3 0	—
6	(=4+5) Guaranteed price to European producer	—	25 0
7	Grain Marketing Board handling margin	16 9	—
8	(=6+7) Price of a bag of grain to miller	—	41 9
9	Miller's permissible margin	5 10	—
10	(=8+9) Price of a bag of maize meal to retailer	—	47 7
11	Retailer's permissible margin	2 9	—
12	(=10+11) Gross retail price of a bag of maize meal	—	50 4
13	Subsidy on retail price	4 0	—
14	(=12−13) Retail price of a bag of maize meal	—	46 4

Source Federation of Rhodesia and Nyasaland (1963).

Three things are notable about this structure, which remains unaltered today except for the fact that the African Development Fund levy was removed in 1979, and retail margins are now flexible.[31] The first is that the levying of a flat transport charge tends to cancel out the competitive advantage that would otherwise be enjoyed by producers living close to their market: thus Salisbury tended to be supplied rather more by distant maize producers than would have occurred in a free market. The second is that the price to the small African producer was only twenty-four per cent or forty-three per cent of the final consumer price of a bag of maize meal depending on whether he delivered to the marketing board direct, whereas in Ibadan at the same time the producer price was sixty-eight per cent of the final consumer price,[32] *even though* the Southern Rhodesian system is 'simpler' than the Nigerian in the sense that the grain passes through fewer hands, on average, between farmer and ultimate consumer.[33] The third is that the Grain Marketing Board's maximum buying price for a 200 lb bag of maize was 25*s*, whereas its selling price *at the same point* was 41*s* 9*d*: a piece of monopoly profit-taking that has at all times given rise to a lively black market, and also encouraged legal attempts by Africans to grow maize, however low their productivity, for their own families working in town rather than buy it from the most efficient farmers. These same characteristics – the standardised transport fee, the high differential between producer and consumer price and the high level of profits made by the statutory authority – have also been a feature of the marketing of beef since the middle 1930s, except that since the beginning of free cattle auctions in 1956 the profits of the Cold Storage Commission have been much reduced.

State-buttressed monopoly systems, of course, are nothing unusual in Africa, nor are critiques of them anything new. In 1955 the East Africa Royal Commission, criticising a slightly less racially discriminatory set of food-marketing systems than those prevailing in Rhodesia, wrote:

> In their anxiety to achieve security in the matter of food supplies (the East African Governments) have tended to regard the ordinary mechanism of the market as an obstacle to the solution of their difficulties rather than as a solvent of the problem. Instead of encouraging specialisation and the free sale of surplus production of food and other agricultural products in suitable areas in order to even out shortages in other areas by the use of the normal machinery of the market, government policy has frequently looked on the normal functioning of the market with suspicion.[34]

More recently the World Bank, in its report on *Accelerated Development in Sub-Saharan Africa*, has attacked the price-control policies adopted by governments all over Africa, and argues for a general freeing of the market, noting that the cities of Lagos and Ibadan, both with well over a million inhabitants, are supplied almost exclusively by private trade.[35] In general in Africa, the Bank notes, the motive for price-control policies has been twofold: 'to provide adequate incentives for increasing food production, and to protect the interests of consumers at the same time'.[36] This statement is generally accurate, and indeed applies to much of Latin America as well. In more developing countries the primary political worry has been urban unrest and the most common response, as Bates argues, 'to appease those interests . . . not by offering higher money wages but by advocating policies aimed at reducing the cost of living and in particular the cost of food. Agricultural policy thus becomes a by-product of political relations between government and their urban constituents'.[37]

Southern Rhodesia provides an exception to this pattern. It provides an exception because the centre of gravity of politics lay away from urban wage-workers, most of whom, until 1980, were black and disfranchised, and unable to mount violent protest of a type which unsettled the white ruling group. Rather, it lay with large farmers: throughout the colonial period, most white professional people and businessmen also owned farms, likewise their representatives in the Legislative Assembly, who cast their vote, in the event of any conflict of interest, not as urban consumers but rather as farmers. The consequence was a structure of agricultural prices in which the price paid to farmers generally exceeded the export price, instead of falling short of it by a large margin,[38] and of subsidies paid not to consumers but to producers. These subsidies have been continued and indeed expanded by the Mugabe government.[39] Few more striking exceptions to the hypothesis of 'urban bias', propounded initially by Lipton (1977) and more recently by Bates and the World Bank, could be imagined.[40]

There are recent signs of movement in Salisbury's food supply system. Retail margins in distribution, which used to be strictly controlled (cf. Table 21) are now almost entirely untouched by government intervention. Agricultural subsidies, which used almost entirely to be concentrated on rural producers, have more recently been introduced on the consumer price of some processed foods, for example beef, milk and cooking oil.[41] This began as an everyday device by the Smith regime to restrain inflation, but has been widely extended by his successors. However, the network of wholesale trade remains firmly in government hands. The analysis of this chapter suggests that the way the Southern Rhodesian government has managed this monopoly of food supply in the past has been in part responsible for the high cost of food in Salisbury, and hence for the defective nutritional standards of the Salisbury African as revealed by Table 20. There are, to repeat, other reasons for the defects there revealed, including in particular what may be cultural rather than financial limits on the consumption of certain foods.[42] But in the last analysis the food supply system to Salisbury must be seen as dictated by political rather than economic imperatives; and for this the urban African has paid dearly.

NOTES

1 The city of Salisbury changed its name to Harare after Zimbabwe became independent in 1980. We shall use the name Salisbury throughout this chapter, both as the name by which the city was known during most of the historical period discussed here and because Harare has always been, in addition, the name for one of the major African suburbs (see Figures 13a and 13b), thus creating the possibility of confusion.

2 Kay & Smout 1977, p. 49.

3 This testimony to the Native Production and Trade Commission of 1944 gives an idea of the implications of this for food distribution within the African areas: *Chairman* What do you intend trading?

Charles Mzengle (Native Labour Party) As a grocer.
Chairman Have you learned that trade somewhere?
C.M. I was doing it some time ago.
Chm. Trading on your own?
C.M. Yes.
Chm. Why did you stop?
C.M. I had some trouble and financial difficulty in 1941 and I lost the place I was renting. In Salisbury when we trade we have to hire our own buildings from the Indian people. I was paying £5 and somebody went behind my back and offered £6.10s.
Chm. You did not have enough capital?
C.M. I could not afford to pay rent. That was the trouble with the business, there was too much competition.
Chm. They did not give you a lease?
C.M. No, they know what it would mean, and they preferred to make a gentleman's agreement.
Chm. Who took it from you?
C.M. Another African.
Chm. Is he still there?
C.M. No, they don't last there. They kick out one after another.

4 There has never been a formal colour bar in the South African sense in Zimbabwe. But educational opportunities for Africans have until recently been extremely limited (as of 1950, there was only one school offering secondary education for Africans); and restrictive legislation has until recently made it difficult for Africans to compete for skilled jobs by accepting lower wages than those agreed for European employees by European trade unions. Hence most administrative and professional jobs were until recently held by Europeans, and most unskilled jobs have always been carried out by Africans.

5 Riddell 1981, para. 269.

6 By 1920, twenty-one million acres (i.e. half the land area of England) had been alienated, but only 237,000 were being farmed: Wilson Fox 1913, p. 21.

7 This price was not reached again until 1951: see Table 18.

8 Southey, p. 7.

9 *Ibid.*, p. 17.

10 Public Record Office: CO 417/619, report in *Rhodesia Herald*, 8 March 1921.

11 For detail on quarantine policy see Mosley 1983, pp. 41–3.

12 National Archives of Zimbabwe: A 3/18/30/42. 'Conditions of services applying to natives engaged . . . at the Wankie Coal Mine', 16 December 1907.

13 E. Baker Jones, 1942, pp. 324–39.

14 For an early example see Swynnerton, 1904, pp. 70–1.

15 A Rhodesian rancher wrote that in the 1920s, 'by trading locally (i.e. with Africans) I could buy for about five or six shillings a sack; the railhead price would have been more than double for inferior stuff, plus the time and wages cost of long wagon transport through the bush'. Robertson 1935, p. 41.

16 'Some years back the Prime Minister issued a circular in which he used the words that the native was to be discouraged from growing wheat': National Archives of Zimbabwe: ZBJ 1/1/3, Evidence to the Native Production and Trade Commission 1944, p. 1439, evidence of A. J. Cripwell, Native Commissioner Gutu.

17 Gilchrist, Southern Rhodesia Legislative Assembly Debates, 28 April 1931, 1221. The cost of production of European maize was estimated at 8*s* a bag at the time.

18 National Archives of Zimbabwe: ZAH 1/1/3, evidence of R. D. Gilchrist to 1925 Land Commission, para. 5508.

19 The Native Commissioner, Darwin, put the matter as follows in relation to maize:

> The natives are frankly not enthusiastic (about control). The trouble is that prior to the introduction of this year's Amendment Act consumers were only too keen to buy any maize offered by natives at anything up to 7/6 a bag . . . whereas trader-producers buying grain for resale have more or less been told that they are not to pay more than 4/- a bag. One trader has told me that the most he can pay to make anything is 3/6. Natives having in mind last year's price are not too keen on this.

(National Archives of Zimbabwe: S 1542/M2, N. C. Darwin to C.N.C., 7 July 1934).

20 Mosley 1983, Table 3.2; van Zwanenberg & King, 1975, pp. 150–55.

21 National Archives of Zimbabwe: S 1215/1090/103, Secretary of Agriculture to Minister of Agriculture, 31 May 1938.

22 Ibbotson 1943. This figure excludes any provision for tax, education, travel, or any items of luxury consumption.

23 *Ibid.*, no. 18.

24 e.g. Gray 1960.

25 National Archives of Zimbabwe: ZBJ 1/1/1, evidence to Native Production and Trade Commission 1944, p. 214, evidence of C. J. Bisselt.

26 It is estimated to have proceeded as an average of 2·4% during these decades, so that the population of the reserves swelled from 700,000 to 1·2 million during this period: see Mosley 1983, Table 3.1 and Appendix 2.

27 From 1942 African cattle were bought at so-called 'weight and grade' sales at which, quite often, there were no scales and the African seller had no appeal from an arbitrary judgement of the weight and grade of the animal he was selling from an (invariably) European grader. This led a representative of the Bantu Congress to complain that 'there is an African price, and there is a separate European price', National Archives of Zimbabwe: ZBJ 1/1/1, p. 591.

28 In 1961/2 'inferior' grade cattle sold at auction for 96*s* 7*d* against an average Cold Storage realisation of 64*s*; i.e. the Cold Storage Commission was buying that grade of cattle from Africans at a discount of about fifty per cent on market price. Federation of Rhodesia and Nyasaland 1963b, p. 35.

29 A trader testified as follows to the 1944 Native Production and Trade Commission:

> If the Government want to increase Native production they have got it in their own hands. All they want to do is to give the existing traders some roads to take the grain on to the main roads. At the present time all our roads are worse than river beds. Why, we often cannot buy (the African's) grain because we cannot transport it. Often the transporters will not come down over our roads. . . . I could double, yes treble, my own output of grain if I had decent roads.

(National Archives of Zimbabwe: ZBJ 1/1/1, Evidence to Native Production and Trade Commission, p. 1490).

30 Tickner 1979, p. 27.

31 *Ibid.*, p. 26; Riddell 1981, pp. 65–7.

32 Jones *et al.* 1972, p. 225.

33 For maize, there were on average, in 1966, 3·4 transactions between producer and consumer, by comparison with 2·6 in Southern Rhodesia. *Ibid.*, p. 215.

34 Great Britain 1955, p. 66.
35 World Bank 1981, p. 64.
36 *Ibid.*, p. 16.
37 Bates 1981, p. 33.
38 For the relationship between local and export prices of grain in Zimbabwe for the 1930s to the 1950s see Table 18; this relationship continues (for example, in the 1984 crop year the Grain Marketing Board price to farmers was $130 per ton, and the average export price $115). For data on the same relationship in other African countries see Bates 1981, Appendix B, pp. 136–45.
39 These subsidies grew from $121 million in 1981 to $250 million (6 per cent of GDP and about twenty per cent of government revenue) in 1984. For a detailed account of subsidy policy see Callear (1981a, 1981b).
40 Bates does refer to the fact that in the Ivory Coast and Kenya, as in Zimbabwe, 'planters, large farmers and agribusiness have secured public policies that are highly favourable by comparison with those in other nations'. (1981, p. 98)
41 See Callear 1981a, p. 269.
42 E.g., 'They have a saying "the vegetable cuts the knees" and say that green vegetables make them vomit': Howman 1942, p. 18.

REFERENCES

Baker Jones, E. 1942. 'The food of the Rhodesian native from the dietetic point of view', *NADA* (Southern Rhodesia Native Affairs Department Annual), 19: 34–8.

Bates, Robert H. 1981. *Markets and States in Tropical Africa. The Political Basis of Agriculture Policies*. Berkeley: University of California Press.

Callear, D. 1981a. 'Resettlement: Zimbabwe's first step', *Food Policy*, November: 266–70.

—— 1981b. 'Food Subsidies in Zimbabwe'. Paper presented to the Zimbabwe Economic Society Conference on Rural Development, Harare, June.

Federation of Rhodesia and Nyasaland. 1963a. *Report of the Commission of Enquiry into the Maize and Small Grains Industry of Southern Rhodesia*. Salisbury: Government Printer.

—— 1963b. *Report on the Commission of Enquiry into the Beef Cattle Industry of Northern and Southern Rhodesia*. Salisbury: Government Printer.

Gelfand, M. 1973. 'The dietary habits of the African and European, with particular reference to the Shona-speaking peoples', *South African Medical Journal*, 47. (August): 1501–03.

Gray, Richard. 1960. *The Two Nations*. Oxford University Press.

Great Britain. 1955. *Report of the East Africa Royal Commission 1953–1955*. London: HMSO.

Howman, R. 1942. 'The native labourer and his food', *NADA* 19: 3–25.

Ibbotson, P. 1943. *Report on a Survey of Urban African Conditions in Southern Rhodesia*. Bulawayo.

Johnson, R. W. M. 1964. 'African agricultural development in Southern Rhodesia 1945–1960', *Food Research Institute Studies*, 4: 165–223.

Jones, William O. & associates. 1972. *Marketing Staple Foods in Tropical Africa*. Ithaca: Cornell University Press.

Kay, G. & M. A. H. Smout. 1977. *Salisbury: a geographical study of the capital of Rhodesia*. London: Hodder & Stoughton.

Lipton, M. 1977. *Why Poor People Stay Poor*. London: Maurice Temple Smith.

Mosley, P. 1983. *The Settler Economies: studies in the economic history of Kenya and Southern Rhodesia 1900–1963*. Cambridge University Press.

Riddell, R. 1981. Chairman, *Report to the President of Zimbabwe on Incomes, Prices and Conditions of Service*. Salisbury: Government Printer.
—— and V. S. Cubitt. 1974. *The Urban Poverty Datum Line in Rhodesia*. Faculty of Social Studies, University of Zimbabwe.
Robertson, W. 1935. *Rhodesian Rancher*. London: Blackie.
Sen, A. K. 1981. *Poverty and Famines*. London: Oxford University Press.
Southern Rhodesia. 1971a. *Urban African Household Budget Survey*. Salisbury: Government Printer.
—— 1971b. *European Household Budget Survey*. Salisbury: Government Printer.
Southey, C. W. R. 1943. 'Memories of an Early Settler in Rhodesia'. Rhodes House Library, Oxford: unpublished MS. Mss. Afr. s. 875.
Swynnerton, C. F. M. 1904. 'Native food', *Rhodesian Agricultural Journal*, 1: 70–1.
Tickner, V. 1979. *The Food Problem* (*From Rhodesia to Zimbabwe*: 8). London: Catholic Institute of International Relations.
Wilson Fox, G. 1913. *Memorandum Upon Land Settlement in Rhodesia*. London: privately printed for Board of British South Africa Company (Royal Commonwealth Society Library, London).
World Bank. 1981. *Accelerated Development in Sub-Saharan Africa: an agenda for action*. Washington: International Bank for Reconstruction and Development.
van Zwanenberg, R. M. A. & A. King. 1975. *An Economic History of Kenya and Uganda, 1800–1970*. London: Macmillan.

6 *Jane I. Guyer*

COMPARATIVE EPILOGUE

The agenda set out in the Introduction was to explore the historical connections amongst three aspects of regional food supply systems: the income/price relationship for producers and consumers, organisational forms in production and trade, and the broader social dynamic resulting from the interface between regional social organisation and colonial and post-colonial policies. The case studies address particular situations in all their richness and individuality. It remains to speculate as to whether there are common patterns in the growth of urban food markets in Africa which would suggest further directions for analysis: issues to focus on, strategies to follow, and conceptual inadequacies demanding attention.

The results of these studies do not lend themselves to the precision of mechanistic comparison. This is due not only to the paucity of sound data and to a level of empirical complexity demanding that an unacceptably wide range of factors would have to be held artificially constant to allow tight comparisons to be made. It is also due to the approach itself. Centring on a three-way interrelationship between welfare levels, organisational forms and political dynamics rules out the possibility of establishing a two-way causal connection between, for example, sociological variables such as state policy and peasant behaviour, or a two-stage historical connection made between the 'roots' and the full florescence of the present 'crisis'. The following discussion is therefore in the nature of inference and argument; it is hoped that the case studies are detailed enough to allow other interpretations.

The idea of 'growth', now accompanied with its obverse – decline – underlies the whole endeavour of understanding modern Africa: the growth of markets, urban centres, the state and so on. 'Growth', however, is an ambiguous organic metaphor, implying as it does both incremental development and metamorphosis. The two major intellectual traditions in African economic studies, neo-classical and neo-Marxist paradigms, place differential emphases on these two qualities. As exemplified in the work of W. O. Jones, the former approach implies that the growth of the market is fundamentally a cumulative process involving the increase in demand and supply. As exemplified in many of the neo-Marxist critiques, the growth of the market is more fundamentally a process of commoditisation which characteristically develops through qualitatively different stages, crossing identifiable structural watersheds. Both, however, share an assumption of directionality, also encoded in the concept of growth. Although basic assumptions are rarely invoked directly in empirical work, they do inform interpretation and judgement. My own interpretation of the case studies differs from both the cumulative and the watershed approaches in ways which will be outlined in more detail below. To the extent, however, that my reservations arise from my own viewpoint as well as inference from the data, let me make the former more explicit.

The disconcerting sense that both interpretations apply and that both have their limits stems, I believe, from the assumption of directionality; too great a burden is placed on seeing cases as examples of, or stages in, the development of a universal convergence. With this assumption the characteristics of every individual case automatically become defined into one of two categories; they are either examples of the general or idiosyncracies of the particular. The elucidation of the former then becomes the domain of the analytical disciplines, and of the latter, the domain of description or ethnography. Apart from the awkward theoretical implications of such a dichotomy, the assumption itself is implausible for modern Africa; the direction of change is not a clear example of a universal case. These are systems literally in the process of construction, shaped on the one hand by powerful forces from the international economy to bring income and consumption for urbanites into consonance with international price and labour conditions, and on the other by powerful interests, cultural standards and production practices originating in indigenous social organisation. In this situation, the course of change itself has to be seen as problematic: the sequences and timing of innovations, the processes by which new occupations and living standards become accepted or struggled over, and the terms of coexistence between 'planned' and 'unplanned' organisations and institutions.

With this perspective, a 'retreat' to the particularism of case studies is not an a-theoretical endeavour, but the essential basis for searching out and identifying configurations in the development of standards of living, occupational categories and differentiated power structures. The assumption is made that such configurations may be identifiable, that a level of comparative analysis between the highly general and the highly particular needs to be addressed, and that attention to the parameters for that level of comparison in African economic studies is one of urgency on the research agenda. Guiding questions include whether there are identifiable kinds and frequency of crisis, and whether crises have challenged or entrenched the organisations responsible for the food supply. The central concern is whether an interpretation of underlying dynamics can be made without falling into the closed and circular arguments associated with holistic approaches and static typologies.

Other reservations on the 'growth' approaches are based on inferences drawn from the available data. The interpretation I explore on the basis of the case studies is that the three aspects of urban supply – price/income levels, trade organisation and political dynamics – show certain consonances with one another. Over time, and in spite of a whole variety of differing circumstances, Kano and Salisbury show high and quite violently fluctuating food prices relative to incomes for the poor, a constancy in the form of organisation at the dominant level of the food trade, and finally, powerfully institutionalised social differentiation. By contrast, Yaoundé and Dar es Salaam show relatively low and more stable food prices, and periodic dramatic shifts in personnel in the food trade, related to a narrower, less defined and less closed scale of differentiation.

These observations may seem a simple empirical restatement of the different implications of monopolistic versus competitive markets. I want to avoid these terms, however, because they lose all accuracy when applied to dynamic patterns. Both Dar es Salaam and Yaoundé have been served by monopolistic trade organisations, and the great merchants who dominate the Kano grain supply have experienced periods of acute competition with traders serving other centres. The important point is the relative fluidity of organisational form in the market, not at a particular moment but over long stretches of time. Both 'monopoly' and 'competition' are produced by a variety of social dynamics in modern Africa: they perpetuate themselves in a variety of ways, may succeed one another over relatively short time-periods, may coexist in the same system in different niches or on different levels, and cross-cut the classic policy division between the public and the private sector. Substituting alternative words for inexact and overcommitted analytical terms is a deliberate strategy for this stage of exploration: sequential fluidity and recurrent constancy rather than competition and monopoly with respect to organisational form, differentiation rather than class with respect to race and income scales, and relative vulnerability and security with respect to the income/price relationship.

Using these provisional terms, the following sections (a) discuss the shortcomings of both cumulative and watershed approaches to interpreting directions of change, (b) elaborate the suggestion that there may be different kinds of configurations, and (c) advocate the study of organisational forms in the food system, over time and in coexistence with one another, as a way of linking material and political dynamics to one another.

1. EVOLUTION AND WATERSHEDS

An admittedly highly stylised formal model of market growth implies a development of (a) level of demand, (b) capitalisation of trade, (c) expansion of the hinterland boundaries and (d) intensification and specialisation of production. Although in a general way all the cases could fit this rubric, the process has been far from even or uniform. While the level of demand has continued to grow throughout this century, neither the timing nor the direction of change corresponds neatly with urban growth. The inconsistencies are clearest for the location of boundaries and the kinds of staples supplying urban markets.

In Kano, the grain catchment area had to be considerably extended in the early decades of the century, not because the urban population was growing particularly quickly, but because the Hausa hinterland became a groundnut-producing region. Unlike the Yaoundé region, where cocoa cultivation for export by men did not directly undermine food production by women, in the Hausa rural areas, groundnuts and grain competed with one another in the cultivation cycle in male farmers' work schedules. Around the same period, Hausa peasantries in southern Niger became a poor source of grain for the great northern Nigerian cities because of heavy in-kind taxation imposed by the French. Incursions further south were successfully made for some years, until competition developed between Kano grain merchants and the Jos mine employers. By this point, the Niger sources opened up again, presumably partly as a result of tax payment in cash in the French-ruled areas. Whereas the opening up of the southern forest markets to trade took place early in the century for luxuries such as kola, it was the influx of southern ethnic groups into Kano, particularly after independence, which accounts for the staple food trade extending beyond the grain belt. The hinterland was therefore a fluctuating one, responding more directly to regional conditions than to the growth of urban demand *per se*. Unlike Dar es Salaam and Salisbury, however, which had recourse to imports from abroad at certain moments, Kano did rely more or less exclusively on its own geographical hinterland for staple foods throughout most of this century; the urban and rural food economies had to be directly responsive to one another.

For the Dar es Salaam case, the hinterland also grew in ways not directly reflective of demographic expansion and concomitant growth in demand. Obviously, the completion of the central railway influenced supply sources. But so also did the shifts in urban diet from sorghum and millet to rice in the early years of this century and then from rice to maize in the early 1930s, and the subsidy of white plantation production in the 1940s. These were all developments associated with the changing ethnic/racial composition of the urban population and with shifting political influences in the economy as a whole. These shifts took place at a time of very slow urban growth. Dar es Salaam was a primate city, but due to the importance of white settler plantations, it was not to the same extent a prime site where the conditions of food production and distribution were set; the shape of the hinterland and the type of staple changed decisively during a time of slow change in conditions of urban demand.

Conversely, it appears that the Yaoundé hinterland actually contracted during a period of rapid urban population growth in the early 1970s. The growth of other urban areas within Cameroon and beyond its borders set up competition for the rural product throughout the south. Different ethnic categories in the food trade operated within different, and only partially overlapping, geographical spheres. As conditions changed within their own operating spheres, repercussions were necessarily felt in the Yaoundé market, thereby significantly reducing the capacity of Yaoundé to dominate its own hinterland.

As would be expected, the means and cost of transport were of decisive importance. In the early years of this century, Kano was the only city to cement relations with fairly distant producers, due to the use of animal transport. Although headloading goods for long distances and several days' march continued well into the middle of the century, the decline of slavery made it uneconomic as a method of provisioning cities; it may be that sources of goods for ports such as Dar es Salaam shrank as slavery was phased out. In the era of rail and road transport, hinterlands have expanded and contracted with transport taxes and subsidies. When the Provident Societies were dismantled in Cameroon, distant places which had been sources of specialist supplies – Nango Eboko for rice, Meiganga for milk products – were simply left high and dry. Conversely, Mosley argues that the flat transport levy for maize farmers in Rhodesia resulted in a diminished competitive advantage for producers close to the market and retention of distant farmers in the effective urban food supply system at equivalent returns. On the other hand, distant African beef producers were also retained in the market, but by virtue of extremely low producer prices justified by the poor transport conditions on the reserves. It is clear from the Salisbury case that hinterland boundaries cannot be explained by, or reduced to, a function of price structures in isolation from the political context in which the price conditions were set.

The indeterminacy of boundaries is related to two conditions: firstly, the expected 'distortions' due to the fact that conditions of production and trade for cities were competing with other centres of economic activity – mines, plantations, other regional centres, and export production within immediate hinterlands; and secondly, to the importance of state policy and ethnic and other social factors in the construction of prices, production and transport conditions. For ecological and socio-political reasons, shifts in catchment boundaries often entailed shifts in the kinds of staples coming onto the market. For example, particular African ethnic groups tend to specialise in, and promote wider consumption of, the crops of their home area. By contrast, when settlers have become dominant in the market, they have promoted home consumption of crops which also have an international market for the sale of surpluses.

Through the link between particular geographical regions and particular social categories, the hinterland question is related to the more difficult question of the emergence of specialised and capitalised food traders. Again, in so far as it can be accurately documented, the development of a trading sector seems to follow a discontinuous course. In fact, one could argue that large operators in both production and trade were significant in the early years of the century, followed by some fragmentation in the mid-years, and a possible increase in large-scale operations again in the 1970s. Even a small urban population can provide a lucrative market if access is controlled and cheap labour is available. Kano was served by slave plantations and merchant 'princes' in the late nineteenth and early twentieth centuries, Dar es Salaam by slaves and, in the 1940s, by large settler farms, and Yaoundé by indigenous chiefs. The Yaoundé chiefs earned substantial incomes and undertook significant agricultural experiments on the basis of privileged access to forced or client labour, and to the institutional buyers and open market in the capital. As soon as the various buttresses built in their support by the colonial government were pulled out, the effective hinterland was opened up and it became absolutely uneconomic to operate as a specialised, large-scale agricultural producer or trader. Except in Rhodesia, large-scale food producers lost their positions in the period of liberalisation in labour control and political mobilisation some time between 1945 and the mid 1960s. Even in Salisbury, African producers were considerably more active in the food market in 1965 than at early periods; only one-third of total agricultural sales were handled by the statutory agencies at that time, by contrast with earlier and later monopolies. In the context of rapid urban growth small-scale trade had expanded, not just absolutely, but probably as a proportion of the total market.

The data to support this assessment, however, are elusive; their credibility depends on a more exhaustive knowledge of the relative proportions of the market served by the various operators than presently exists for any urban area. Only for the Yaoundé case, and even there only in basic descriptive terms, have we integrated the question of how the urban market is served with the crucial question of how the army and other important institutional buyers are served. Indeed, we have not been able in our own studies to go much further than a regrettably impoverished literature in illuminating the actual distribution channels for imported grain and food aid. Perhaps as a result of a too literal adherence to the idea of markets, the place of large-scale capital in the current African food supply remains to be explored, and therefore informed judgment about its increasing or decreasing importance remains to be made.

Decline in self-provisioning is another predicted outcome of urbanisation. While the sheer numbers involved in urban growth necessarily imply a growth in demand, it is less clear that self-provisioning has been undermined consistently or uniformly. It seems rather to be an option jealously maintained where possible, and resorted to intermittently by all sectors of the urban population except those totally deprived of access to land. Self-provisioning is particularly mentioned for Dar es Salaam in the 1920s and 1930s; urbanites either kept their own farms or were brought substantial contributions from up-country kin. All careful urban income studies note contributions in kind from the rural areas, although any sense of their fluctuating value over time remains impressionistic. Recent shortages in Dar es Salaam have resulted in a premium on home farming, even by the middle class. In fact, the greater involvement of the middle class in farming was actively advocated in Nigeria, Cameroon and Tanzania during the 1970s through such policies as 'Operation Feed the Nation' and the *Ceinture Verte*. This kind of phenomenon, along with a host of smaller scale activities, is misleadingly dealt with under the simple rubric of 'self-provisioning', with its implication of continuity from the past. It now often depends on the market as the means through which land, credit, inputs and sometimes labour are acquired, and may develop into primarily market-oriented production. On the other hand, and to anticipate the following paragraphs, the continuing importance, but shifting terms, of self-provisioning resist neo-Marxist conceptualisation as the 'deepening' of commodity relations.

The case of self-provisioning illustrates a general conclusion, namely that shifts in boundaries, size of enterprise, staple food-types and so on, do not represent straightforward progressions. Nor can particular cases be interpreted as following a hesitant, back-and-forth movement along a single path. What may seem a 'return' to self-provisioning, small-scale trade, or clientage networks always involves new contextual and instrumental elements even though the rubrics under which they are justified appear 'traditional'. The fact that one gets trapped in the awkwardness of the evolutionary metaphors suggests that there is a limit to their utility in the study of what is manifestly a modern, non-teleological process. There are inevitably cumulative aspects of urban food supply growth in the past hundred years; it is hardly possible that one or the other of the predicted processes fail to take place. But concentrating exclusively on these draws attention away from the uneven course of the path itself. Concentrating on the shape of fluctuations and discontinuities, rather than the starting point and the destination, demands a change of focus. In the above summary of particular courses of growth in market relations – in their empirically documentable dimensions of hinterland size, type of staple in relation to regional production patterns, level of specialisation and capitalisation – the question of who the major actors were, and what interests they were able to pursue, continually forces itself to the fore and thereby commands more central attention.

The assumption underlying a structural, watershed model of change is the capacity of external power to alter definitively, even if only partially, the dynamics of local systems. In the Introduction and in our own cases, the imposition of colonial rule, the Great Depression, World War II and the unstable economic conditions of the 1970s are examined as critical phases in the development of food supply systems, as they are in more general arguments about African economic and political change. It is striking, however, that the changes wrought under these general pressures were more fundamental in some urban economies than others. Such variability in the impact of externally generated crises is perhaps more predictable in rural economies than in the somewhat more formal and managed sectors of urban economies; it is primarily urban-based institutions which interact most directly with external conditions.

Effects of the Great Depression show the greatest variation. Mosley argues that the Depression was the context in which embattled white commercial farmers set up a kind of co-operative collusion with the Government which they were able to protect and extend for the next fifty years, through the crisis of World War II, and which was reinforced during the 1970s after UDI. The effects of World War II on the food economy appear, in the long run, more as a test of the power of the white farmers than a transformational change. Import-substituting industrial development and concomitant rapid growth in the African wage labour force exceeded the capacities of white agriculture, but without forcing a change in the structures governing production and marketing within the country. African opposition was defeated, although in the longer run, into the mid-1960s, white predominance in agriculture and marketing was very slowly eroded. In the 1970s, the politics of UDI turned this tide back, thereby producing an effect quite contrary to the increasing role of the 'informal sector' – legal and illegal – elsewhere at the same time.

Nowhere else were the effects of the Depression and war so profound. In fact, these crises appear more as the test-by-fire in which colonial governments realised the limits of their control over economic dynamics. In Kano, the Depression resulted in an expanded range of operators in the agricultural market, as Levantine businessmen took advantage of the moment to insert themselves into the trade networks. Farmers were also severely subjected to the consequences of indebtedness, a fact of economic life, however, which predates the crisis. During the war, attempts at price control by the Government were almost wholly ineffective, ignored by the big merchants, and unenforced by the authorities. The overall result, it is argued, was less a series of structural changes than a gradual intensification of processes already present, and a test of the resilience of those organisations already managing the market. They apparently survived, possibly consolidating and extending their range of options and raising to new levels of sophistication their means of shifting risks. In the 1970s this same category of operators, or people from the same social stratum, have entered the grain import business and become involved in large production projects.

In Dar es Salaam, one of the most important effects of the Depression was a definitive shift in the staple food base from rice to maize. This was not initially a response to settler maize producers, but a result of the sudden increase in the cost of rice imported from Asia to cover intermittent shortfalls. The change in staple did, however, initiate a period of expansion for settler farmers, who then used wartime conditions to press their advantage, and put in place, for the first time as a comprehensive policy, the management of food supply fluctuations by the state. State control resulted directly in the redefinition of certain kinds of trade as black market, and provided incentives for such parallel markets to develop. The configuration of state control and parallel markets has been a recurrent motif in the history of food supply to Dar es Salaam since the war, even though the particular organisational forms it has taken have changed several times.

Yaoundé's history seems less structurally affected by such crises than any of the others, possibly due in part to the solid and constant productivity of the food cultivation systems on which it relies. The Depression initiated the long, slow decline of chiefly power, which the post-war liberalisation definitively terminated. But, in the long run, these appear more as phases in a succession of organisational forms and types of government intervention than as turning points in the structural relations linking producers and consumers.

Without trying artificially to define the kinds of shifts produced by externally provoked crises in the different cases, it seems nevertheless clear that the stresses were felt, sustained and managed in different ways: in some cases policy and organisation had to be reformulated, in others established relationships and processes were further intensified, while in others new conditions were set up which became the locus of powerful interests which were then able to dominate food supply for decades.

If structural change is defined in terms of the kind and degree of commoditisation, particularly of labour – i.e. the production of specialist consumers in both rural and urban areas – then only the Rhodesian case shows a clear watershed pattern in the twentieth century. The rapid shifts in the other cases have been limited to one or other level of the system: government policy, the ethnic or other bases for trade organisation, the sheer numbers involved as either producers or consumers. In order to develop a more discriminating comparative framework one is forced to think about the possibility of defining 'stages' of 'articulation' with the external system, or alternatively, to retain the focus on the home market in a more theoretically eclectic framework which opens questions about dynamics rather than trying to impose schema. As mentioned earlier, I am reluctant to define such responses into 'stages', because their interpretation depends on analysis over the much longer time frame, in which the whole notion of the watershed becomes problematic. Again, the problem of directionality intervenes crucially in the effort to determine the relative significance of the various turning points which might be thought of as watersheds. Rather than focus on the possibility that there is a common, recapitulated sequence of change, whether of the evolutionary or watershed kind, one can look at whether there are persistent or recurrent situations within each case and whether there are common features from one case to the other.

2. PATTERNS OF CHANGE

For most of this century, most African cities and certainly all the cases discussed here, have been fed from their own hinterlands. Consumers living from the fixed incomes determined by wage contracts and national budgets, and from fluctuating incomes in self-employment, have had to cope with ecologically and politically provoked variation in regional food supply conditions. The relationship between urban incomes and food prices over time indicates how the stresses and adjustments have been distributed in different urban systems. In this respect Dar es Salaam and Yaoundé show a quite different distribution to that of Kano and Salisbury, and this seems to be associated with broader characteristics of the food trade and the wider political and economic structure structure of which it is a part. In the following discussion the three themes of (a) the income/price relationship, (b) organisation of the food trade, and (c) forms of differentiation will be examined in turn, followed by a discussion of the role of state policy.

A. THE INCOME/PRICE RELATIONSHIP

For Dar es Salaam and Yaoundé, food prices have never gone beyond the capacity of urban consumers to provision themselves from the market. Since the inflation and unstable conditions of the 1970s set in, prices have crept up relative to incomes, resulting in a gradual erosion of the standard of living for the lower-income groups. But for the earlier part of the century, the income/price relationship rarely resulted in the mean food costs for families studied in budget surveys exceeding sixty per cent of income; even since 1970, it is only among the lowest groups that the proportion has gone as high as eighty-five per cent. Apart from the blockade period during World War I, food has been obtainable by the consumer population of Dar es Salaam at manageable prices. According to Bryceson's figures, the actual proportions of family (non-bachelor) incomes spent on food since 1939 have fluctuated between thirty-five per cent and an all-time high – in a category by itself – of eighty-five per cent for poor households recorded in 1980. For substantial periods, she argues that consumers were doing adequately. From the 1920s onwards, intermittent absolute shortfalls were met through imports, and when the cost of living rose and the efficiency of retail distribution declined in the late 1970s, the populace turned to self-provisioning, parallel markets and vocal complaint, and the Government turned to consumer subsidies.

Yaoundé has a similar, although considerably more dependable, history for the wage-price relationship. There has never been a profound enough shortage to drive the price up beyond levels allowing an urban life-style, with budget allocations for rent, transport, school fees and other expenses. Prices were managed by the Government until 1960, with the express purpose of keeping the wages of the Civil Servants, who dominate the urban labour force, within acceptable and predictable limits. The level of one-third to one-half of income spent on food appears remarkably stable from the inter-war years into the 1960s, although the post-war figures are for a family rather than an individual. In 1964–5, thirty-two per cent of household expenditure went on food and drink; only twenty-five per cent on food taken alone. Even the 'unemployed' spent only forty-six per cent of their income on food. Such low levels of food expenditure are not accounted for by poor nutrition or by high levels of self-provisioning. Unlike the population of many other small cities, the Yaoundé population in the 1960s gained relatively little from farming or from rural kin, and the National Nutrition Survey of 1977 revealed high levels of dietary adequacy.

The figures for Kano and Harare, I would argue, reveal a quite different pattern. In both cases, food prices appear to have been chronically high relative to capacity to pay, and also liable to move out of the wage-earner's range altogether. In Kano in 1914 the wage was only half enough to purchase daily grain needs, and the situation worsened yet further until a worker needed employment for eight days to earn enough to buy a single day's worth of grain. Such pressures predate the colonial period but were dealt with through the Emir's grain stores from tithe. They continued intermittently during the first half of the century without centralised redistribution. Until the era of imports in the 1970s, strategies for managing included a resort to clientage ties, migration and, presumably, hunger. It is particularly striking, by contrast with Yaoundé and Dar es Salaam, that until the 1970s there was relatively little apparent political agitation, to the extent that the colonial authorities might have no sense of the gravity of the situation.

Salisbury's consumer crises were apparently less frequent, but Mosley argues that the cost of food has been chronically high relative to income (54·9% for Africans in 1971, by comparison with a White rate of twenty per cent), and has also fluctuated out of reach altogether. In 1943, fifty-one per cent of Africans were earning less than 30*s* per month, while the cost of the necessities of food, shelter and clothing for a family with two children was as high as 95*s* per month. Again, people resorted to a range of personal strategies to make ends meet, but collective political pressures apparently brought no concessions and the Maize Control Board's monopoly continued in force. Like the Kano case, the poor on both sides of the urban–rural border suffered under conditions of high consumer prices, low producer prices and/or absolute shortage for subsistence and sale.

It is worth noting that a fluctuating pattern in urban and rural welfare is characteristic of cities which have little in common on some other relevant grounds: government was highly interventionist in one and relatively *laissez-faire* in the other, drought was a serious aggravating factor in one and not the other, formally organised international trade was a major recourse in one and not the other. Correspondingly, the more secure situations also contrast with one another on ecological and policy lines: government monopolies were broken up in the one at exactly the historical moment when they were strengthened in the other; the one draws on a predictable farming base while the other manages drought. The one possible important dimension which aligns more exactly with the vulnerable versus secure pattern in income/price relations is the division of labour in small-scale farming and trade; women's work is more significant in the entire food supply chain in Southern Cameroon and Tanzania. Any expanded comparison would have to look carefully at whether there have been markedly different dynamics according to the division of labour. Assessing the veracity of such an association should be part of the larger endeavour of tracing the regional pressures and capacities which may account for patterns over time. In this context, it must suffice to concentrate on the broader approach within which such a question could be addressed, namely the historical pattern in income/price relationships in relation to the social organisation of trade over time.

B. ORGANISATION IN THE FOOD TRADE

The implications of risk for the organisation of trade are some of the most interesting to trace. From the present cases, it seems that the longevity of any organisation in the food trade depends on its ability to cushion against sudden fluctuations in conditions of supply and demand. The only long-term successful operators have been able to pursue at least two of three strategies: shift the cost to another category in the food chain, diversify their activities into other commodities, or depend on protection and subsidy from the public sector. Kano and Salisbury provide examples of cities in which risks and costs could be moved onto the small producers and urban consumers, hence the fluctuating welfare pattern described above. In the Kano case, merchants were also able to diversify; in Salisbury, the public sector picked up some of the risks and costs. As a result, in each city there was a dominant organisational form in the food market, able to protect itself over periods of crisis. By contrast, in Dar es Salaam and Yaoundé, risks were not passed on through the same lines, and instead of welfare levels fluctuating, the intermittent crises of growth destroyed the viability of existing market organisations. In both places there were periodic changes about every ten to fifteen years throughout the twentieth century.

Considerable variation in strategy underlies the overall pattern. In Kano before the oil boom, diversification was one of the main strategies of the great Hausa merchants. Few, if any, of the controllers of large capital in the clientage networks depended on the grain trade alone for their income. As soon as conditions became difficult and margins squeezed, they could move part of their capital into other economic sectors, thus ensuring the survival of the organisation itself and its eventual return to momentarily abandoned commodities. It is the ability to diversify activities while drawing on the same relationships of clientship which allows a complex system such as the Hausa grain trade to seem to collapse and reconstitute itself so quickly. Indigenous African commercial organisations often show a remarkable ability to survive famine and war as well as lesser disturbances, precisely because they can go in and out of particular businesses. From a government perspective, this recurrent constancy in the distributive system has the advantage of institutionalisation; routines, the norms of business behaviour and integration with the producers are all enforced with minimal monitoring and sanction at the public expense. On the other hand, there are both clear limits to government control and potential political repercussions of the welfare situation of the consumers. As long as it is politically feasible to allow the poor to suffer through crises there is limited incentive for government intervention. Reluctance to intervene was reinforced in Kano during the colonial period by the transport problem of being too far from a port to mobilise outside supplies within budget possibilities.

Where the state has provided institutional supports, as it did in Southern Rhodesia, the large farmers and traders have been protected from the highly exigent necessity of maintaining an actually or potentially diversified set of economic activities. Again, the organisations themselves have survived crises and have become deeply institutionalised, in the sense that the whole apparatus of trade became consonant with farmers' production strategies, patterns of urban living, and with the structure of politics and administration. The Salisbury case shows a combination of cost and risk-shifting to the poor and heavy subsidy from the state, with apparently limited investment of the major operators in maintaining diversified economic activities.

In the Yaoundé and Dar es Salaam cases, the possibility of shifting the costs of fluctuations to producers and consumers has been far more limited. Both urban populations have included important numbers of Civil Service employees. Simply allowing a whole series of differently diversified organisations to take care of their private interest in the hope that public good would emerge, has not historically seemed a plausible approach for governments to take. (Parenthetically, I would suggest that the difference between Bryceson and Watts on the regulatory capacities of the colonial state are actually empirical differences between Nigeria and Tanganyika; in the latter case, there was greater political pressure to protect urban standards of living, and the city was better placed geographically to solve the problem through imports.) Mistrustful of diversified private trade, and unable to force the wage/price relationship into negative balance, even for a short period, both governments have intervened in various ways as themselves operators in the food trade. In organisational terms, however, government-constituted trade has been fragile. Specialised trade in goods whose supply fluctuates is both expensive and dangerous. The economic, and therefore budgetary, costs have been pointed out for both cases: the subsidy of transport for the Provident Society and the substantial state and foreign aid support for MIDEVIV in Yaoundé, the inability of the Tanzanian Grain Storage Department to sustain the economics of glut conditions in the late 1950s. But there are also political costs. In situations where the rubrics for differentiation have little public legitimacy, whether sustained by cultural or violent means, the high visibility of an organisation attracts opposition. Neither the government Provident Society in Yaoundé nor the private Asian traders in Dar es Salaam depressed welfare levels more, and arguably considerably less, than other trade systems. But they were highly visible during a period when basic structures and norms were brought into question by the struggle for independence. Both Yaoundé and Dar es Salaam are a litany of 'successful failures': forms of organisation which worked for a limited time within the framework of a planned policy, only to run up against rigidities in the face of fluctuations and shifts, either in food supply itself, or in the broader political context.

The question arises whether the longevity of some forms and the fluidity of others is more a function of their internal organisation or the sociopolitical context. Ethnic, religious and familial bases for trade organisation are universal, and certain groups within Africa have more highly developed modes of capitalising, diversifying and reconstituting through social ties than others. However, from the urban vantage point, all these cities could be served by such groups; they exist within the urban hinterland. For example, the economic strategies of Asian traders in Tanzania over the post-war period, when they were the primary grain traders, bears comparison with the Hausa merchants. As Bryceson points out, food was only one of their commodities, so that the conditions in the grain trade reflect their broader economic strategies. At one time, for example, she argues that they were willing to accept very low commercial margins on grain because compensating gains were made on the consumer items which the producers bought with their income. In the Yaoundé area, the Bamileke are particularly known for their business networks. Like private traders in all ranks of society and in every instance, they keep options open in case sudden changes in conditions force a retreat to other income-earning activities or commodities other than food.

The reasons for attempting to bypass or limit the activities of ethnic or religious organisations in the urban food trade can be traced to the social and political context: to avoid food supply crises being paid for by the consumers, and to contain the traders' potential access to, and claims on, the government. There are political costs to the strategies needed to keep profit-making businesses in the food trade, and once government has accepted responsibility for the consumers they are forced to manoeuvre around, co-operate with and otherwise accept the conditions of the currently organised private traders or try to create alternative networks. In other words, whether particular organisations have this feature of recurrent constancy depends at least as much on the place they occupy in the wider social and political process as on the kind of internal structure.

C. DIFFERENTIATION

A major difference between the two sets of cases is related to patterns of differentiation. On the one hand there are the stratified systems of Kano and Harare; powerful pressures have been exerted on the standard of living of the poor, the political voice of the consumers and poorer producers has been muted, and the intermediaries and larger operators in the system have weathered the crises through adroit political and economic strategies. On the other hand, we have the cases of Dar es Salaam and Yaoundé, where different categories rise and fall in the differentiation system over time, giving them the character, not of egalitarian systems, but of systems in which achievement of economic and political power depended, over the long term, on a political dynamic amongst interest groups. The consumers tended to be wealthier, because of the relative absence of a proletariat; they were vocal enough to avoid conditions of food supply incompatible with an adequate level of living, and consequently a large measure of the inevitable risk fell on the intermediaries, whoever they happened to be, private or public. Hence, I would argue, a historical association between security in the wage/price relationship and sequential fluidity in the organisational form of the market, and between vulnerability in the wage/price relationship and recurrent constancy in the form of the market. For much of their history in the twentieth century, these urban food supply systems have been stable in their organisation or in the income/price relationship, but not in both, and this is related to the structure of differentiation.

The question then arises of how, in social orders which are in the course of construction, certain positions, activities and levels of living become legitimised and sanctioned, and therefore why the struggles in a particular sector have the character and the terms which they do. It is a remarkable cultural and political 'achievement' to alter both absolute and relative standards of living and persuade people that they are culturally acceptable and pragmatically livable. These are changes of the most intimate and immediately exigent kind: the diurnal and seasonal routines of consumption; reconsideration of the diet in relation to the pragmatics of such things as water and fuel supply; changing consumption according to the division of labour in purchasing and preparation; adjusting the ideal standards in the light of cultural imperatives of religion and commensality; the mutual adjustment of other budgetary demands such as housing, education, clothing, transport and so on, to dietary standards. Unlike the case in industrialised economies where macro-economic variables depend on consumer behaviour, in Africa there is no constant barrage of cultural commentary on the proportions of income which should be devoted to the various functions of life, and no one site outside the labour unions formalising a counteracting model. As was asked in the Introduction, why should food be an issue rather than housing, why have some consumer populations been so vocal while others apparently cope and suffer, if not in silence, then without effecting redistributive change? In comparative terms, it is striking how apparently effectively the various participants in the food system of Yaoundé and Dar es Salaam have responded to relatively limited inroads into their welfare, often through the pressure of non-compliance, rather than the confrontation of protest. By contrast, the profound cultural legitimation of Hausa status differentiation is reflected in very limited confrontation, even in severe conditions. The almost total lack of such legitimation in the Salisbury case was associated with recurrent suppression of protest, as happened with respect to discriminatory beef purchase in the 1940s.

At this stage, the patterns cannot be exaggerated. With no independent measure of degrees or kinds of legitimacy, and no clear way of assessing the institutionalisation of living standards, one is in danger of inferring these crucial dimensions of the social order from the data on resistance, and then engaging in entirely circular arguments. Local, intermittent and apparently short-lived protest about the whole range of market conditions, from prices to traders' taxes, is poorly documented by comparison with the great struggles of modern political history. They must, however, be drawn out of obscurity, not just as events in themselves and examples of 'struggle', but as potentially highly formative influences on the development of new standards of living and of the institutions which deliver, ensure and enforce them. As the means and the moments of resistance become better recorded, the outside analyst drawing on largely documentary sources necessarily loses some confidence in presenting any neat picture. But with the sources presently available, it does seem that focused removal of particular policies or organisation comes about in the multi-ethnic, weakly stratified systems, whatever the formal nature of state or city government, while the terms of confrontation in the deeply stratified systems reflect the framework within which the differentials are justified to the people who have to live with them.

The real issue with government policy is not, therefore, the extent or type of government intervention and management of urban food supply, but rather the interests represented at government level and the facility with which the policy apparatus responded politically and administratively to pressures. Mosley criticises the generality of urban bias on these grounds, that the farmers and not the consumers called the tune. But neither is it a question of replacing urban bias with rural bias. The oppositions between rural and urban, formal and informal, the public and the private sectors hardly capture the way in which interests have been institutionalised and positions challenged. The case studies show that the categories and coalitions are more numerous and their successive forms less amenable to stereotyping. The term 'private sector' can encompass the Kano merchants, the Rhodesian farmers, and the female traders and farmers of Yaoundé; by virtue of their employment structures and formal legal status, Rhodesian farms undoubtedly qualify as 'formal sector' by contrast with the clientage networks of Kano merchants, but the latters' import businesses and agricultural projects depend on state support and intervention. The important questions relate to who is operating in the food system, for how long, from what power basis, and in what relation to government policies. Looking from the inside, at how policies have *intersected* with the development of food supply organisation, takes the burden off a state-centred approach with its central concern of control.

D. STRATEGIES: A FOCUS ON ORGANISATION

If, as I have argued, there have been characteristic configurations over time, then the study of organisations loses its descriptive 'ethnographic background' qualities with respect to the analysis and interpretation of change. The way in which the organisations operating in the food trade coexist, succeed one another over time, and manage to shift the risks of a risky sector of the economy, may be consonant with the wider political and economic dynamic, and may therefore be a key area of enquiry in the current situation where the prices, the forces of differentiation, the productivity levels, and the modes of political pressure are all difficult to study directly.

So far, I have drawn most heavily on the material for the period before price inflation and rapid urban growth set in in the early 1970s. Given the relatively narrow range of operators in the food systems up to that point, it has been sufficient to dwell on *patterns of succession* in the organisation of urban food supply; possible *patterns of coexistence* of different organisational forms has been dealt with mainly in terms of the politics of dominance of one over the other. The present situation is certainly constructed on the basis of the past, but the degree to which the same pattern continues and the specific ways in which the dynamic has changed are still difficult to specify. In spite of the expansion of the literature on food supply, the sources are still too incomplete on, for example, the volumes traded and the geographical networks developed by the parallel market in East and Southern Africa and the degree to which imports and food aid are distributed along older channels. Watts mentions the profits made through rice imports in Nigeria, thereby undermining any facile assumption that imports were organisationally a new element, simply responding to new conditions such as a shortfall in local production of urban protest. Many of the forms appearing in the market, from black markets to government price control and extensive recourse to imports, have been seen intermittently throughout urban history and therefore have organisational rubrics already worked out and available. The difficult and crucial sociological question for the past decade or so is how they relate to one another: whether certain hierarchies of size or function are developing, whether ethnicity is a principle in the division of labour in the market, whether certain forms are encroaching steadily on older ones, or whether new activities are being assimilated into the old structures.

Limited indications from Kano and Salisbury cases suggest that the former interests have retained some of their power. The Kano merchants now operate in the import business, and in Harare 'the network of trade remains firmly in government hands'. Both have become, however, more complex systems, accommodating new policies and food sources which may well represent or provoke quite new sets of interests. All evidence from

Yaoundé and Dar es Salaam suggests a major surge in small and mid-scale trade, in the first case with ineffective and perhaps unconvinced opposition from parastatals and in the second with a more vigorous attempt to retain control. The much greater importance of international interests, agendas and conditions in the grain trade means that the field of study also has to be opened up considerably beyond the limited arenas we have covered in this volume.

Nevertheless, these much more intrusive interests do meet an established system in place with certain characteristic dilemmas, constraints and manoeuvres. Organisational analysis of how these have coexisted and succeeded one another in the past allows directions of change to emerge more clearly than either implicitly directional models or the synchronic oppositions posed between the peasant and the state, the public and the private sectors.

The purpose of this collection, and in particular of the Epilogue, has not been to develop a new and rigid typology; the cases are too few, their complexity and under-documentation too great. It has rather been to focus attention on the critical need to conceive of the food market in a broader sociological and historical context, and to provoke awareness of the conceptual challenges of describing dynamics in a theoretically useful manner. In substantive terms, the cases serve to illustrate the resilience of the African construction of material life, not as a static quality, but as a product of regional political processes, achieved over a period of extraordinary instability and structural change.

Index

GOVERNMENT SCHEMES, LEGISLATION AND PARASTATAL ORGANISATIONS

Lightning Source UK Ltd.
Milton Keynes UK
UKHW020630140521
383717UK00006B/249

9 780367 000455